BRITAIN'S STRATEGIC NUCLEAR DETERRENT

BRITAIN'S STRATEGIC NUCLEAR DETERRENT

From before the V-Bomber to beyond Trident

ROBERT H. PATERSON

FRANK CASS & CO. LTD
LONDON • PORTLAND, OR

First Published in 1997 in Great Britain by
FRANK CASS & CO. LTD.
Newbury House, 900 Eastern Avenue
London, IG2 7HH

and in the United States of America by
FRANK CASS
c/o ISBS, 5804 N.E. Hassalo Street
Portland, Oregon, 97213-3644

British Library Cataloguing in Publication Data

Paterson, Robert H.
  Britain's strategic nuclear deterrent : from before the
  V-Bomber to beyond Trident
    1. Nuclear Weapons – Great Britain – History   2. Deterrence
  (Strategy)   3. Great Britain – Strategic aspects   4. Great
  Britain – Military policy
  I. Title
  355.8'2'5119'0941

ISBN 0 7146 4740 3 (cloth)
ISBN 0 7146 4297 5 (paper)

Library of Congress Cataloging-in-Publication Data

Paterson, Robert H.
  Britain's strategic nuclear deterrent: from before the V-bomber
  to beyond Trident
      p.   cm.
  Includes bibliographical references (p.   ) and index.
    ISBN 0-7146-4740-3 (cloth). — ISBN 0-7146-4297-5 (pbk.)
    1. Nuclear weapons—Government policy—Great Britain.
  2. Deterrence (Strategy)   3. Fleet ballistic missile weapons
  systems—Great Britain.   I. Title
  UA647.P29   1997
  355.02'17'0941—dc21   96-37620
                                                          CIP

Typeset by Regent Typesetting, London
Printed in Great Britain by
Bookcraft (Bath) Ltd, Midsomer Norton, Avon

For Andrew and Sandy

Contents

Abbreviations   viii

Preface   xi

Introduction   1

1 The Historical Background to Britain's Deterrent 1938-1956:
   From Nuclear Fission to the V-Bomber   3

2 The Development of Nuclear Strategy   12

3 The Decision to Deploy a British Nuclear Deterrent   29

4 The Decision to Replace Polaris   61

5 Arms Control: Problems, Progress and Proliferation   95

6 British Political Decision Making, CND and Public Opinion   116

7 The French Experience: A Comparison   135

8 Tomorrow's World: The Post-Cold War Arena   151

9 The Past as Prologue: From the V-Bomber to Beyond Trident?   166

   Chronology   179

   Select Bibliography   187

   Index   192

Abbreviations

ABM	Anti Ballistic Missile
ALCM	Air Launched Cruise Missile
ASBM	Air to Surface Ballistic Missile
ASMP	*Air-sol moyenne portée*
ASW	Anti Submarine Warfare
BAOR	British Army of the Rhine
CENTO	Central Treaty Organisation
CEP	Circular Error of Probability
C3I	Command Control Communications and Intelligence
CIS	Commonwealth of Independent States
CND	Campaign for Nuclear Disarmament
CSCE	Conference on Security and Co-operation in Europe
CTBT	Comprehensive Test Ban Treaty
DAC	Direct Action Committee Against Nuclear War
EC	European Community
ECM	Electronic Counter Measures
EMF	European Monetary Fund
EMT	Equivalent Megatonage
EU	European Union
GDP	Gross Domestic Product
GLCM	Ground Launched Cruise Missile
GPALS	Global Protection Against Limited Strikes
IAEA	Independent Atomic Energy Agency
ICBM	Inter-Continental Ballistic Missile
IFOR	UN Peace Implementation Force in Bosnia
INF	Intermediate Nuclear Forces
IRBM	Intermediate Range Ballistic Missile
JSTPS	Joint Strategic Target Planning Staff
kt	Kiloton
MAD	Mutual Assured Destruction
MARV	Manoeuvrable Re-entry Vehicle
MAUD	Military Application of Uranium Detonation
MIRV	Multiple Independently-Targetable Re-Entry Vehicle

MLF	Multilateral Force
MRV	Multiple Re-Entry Vehicle
mt	Megaton
NACC	North Atlantic Co-operation Council
NATO	North Atlantic Treaty Organisation
NCANWT	National Council for the Abolition of Nuclear Weapons Tests
NPT	Nuclear Non-Proliferation Treaty
NSC	National Security Council
PFP	Partnership for Peace
R&D	Research and Development
SAC	Strategic Air Command
SACEUR	Supreme Allied Commander Europe
SALT	Strategic Arms Limitation Talks
SAM	Surface to Air Missile
SEATO	South East Asia Treaty Organisation
SIOP	Single Integrated Operational Plan
SLBM	Submarine Launched Ballistic Missile
SLCM	Submarine Launched Cruise Missle
SRAM	Short Range Attack Missile
SSBN	Nuclear Powered Ballistic Missile Submarine
SSCN	Nuclear Powered Cruise Missile Submarine
SSN	Nuclear Powered Submarine
TERCOM	Terrain Contour Matching
TSR	Tactical Strike and Reconnaissance (Aircraft)
USAF	United States Air Force
USN	United States Navy
WEU	Western European Union

Acknowledgements

T HE AUTHOR IS grateful to the Controller of HMSO for permission to reproduce Crown copyright material and to Oxford University Press for permission to reproduce material from Navias M.S. 'Nuclear Weapons and British Strategic Planning 1955–58', Clarendon Press, Oxford, 1991.

Preface

T HIS BOOK IS about Britain's strategic security policy in the second half of the twentieth century. I have had a professional interest in this subject for much of my life and I was able to complement that experience during a period of postgraduate research in the early 1990s. I hope that I have been able to combine these two perspectives to maximum effect while writing this book.

A primary duty of all states is to ensure their continuing survival as independent entities. When the state's security is threatened it requires its citizens to contribute directly to its survival. Twice during the first half of this century British citizens responded magnificently to the call to protect Britain's vital national interests, albeit with very considerable loss of life. Sadly our record regarding the development of rational strategic security policies has been rather different. The armed forces make a unique, but by no means exclusive, contribution to the nation's security policy. Indeed the move from reactive defence to proactive deterrence requires policies to be perceived as credible, both at home and abroad. This, in turn, requires the contribution of informed politicians, officials, academic analysts and, increasingly, a spectrum of citizens. Without the contribution of the latter the legitimacy, and therefore the credibility, of national security policies will remain open to question. This book seeks to help a wider public acquire a greater understanding of Britain's strategic security requirements. More specifically it should be of interest to those who wish to understand why Britain chose to procure and deploy a succession of strategic nuclear deterrents and what the implications of that policy have been.

The period that this text covers corresponds to my life span. I was born a few months after the theory of nuclear fission was first published. The bombing of Hiroshima and Nagasaki took place a month before I started school. By the time I had left school the V-bombers were operational, Britain had conducted her first H-bomb test and had adopted the doctrine of massive retaliation. In the summer of 1961, when the Berlin Wall was erected, I was a platoon commander in an infantry battalion in West Germany. When American and Soviet tanks faced each other at Checkpoint Charlie we were placed on operational stand-by to drive up the Helmstedt corridor to Berlin. Happily the international tension dissipated and we were not deployed but I can still remember the adrenaline pumping and my imagination running riot! During the early 1960s I led a number of operational patrols along the Inner German Border. Throughout that period the minefields and other obstacles just to the east of the border were continually being improved to stem the flow of men and women to the West. The opportunity to witness these events on a day-to-day basis, literally on the border between East and West, made a profound impact on my understanding of the division of Europe. By the mid-1960s I was in Cyprus where the V-bombers, based at RAF Akrotiri and capable of reaching targets in the Crimea, were being phased out, leaving Britain without a viable strategic nuclear deterrent. During the early 1970s, by which time the Polaris fleet was operational, I contributed to the planning, conduct and evaluation of the WINTEX series of exercises – NATO's biennial command post exercises that rehearsed procedures for the transition to war and operational procedures up to, and including, selective nuclear release. By the late 1980s I was working in a British Embassy in Western Europe. At the start of my tour of duty Britain was maintaining pressure on her allies to deploy land-based cruise missiles in response to the earlier deployment of Soviet SS-20 missiles in Eastern Europe. By the time I left both the intelligence community and informed open sources were reporting massive and startling changes within the Warsaw Pact's force structure. The Berlin Wall was breached in 1989 and a year later Germany was reunified. Half my military service had been spent in Western Europe and the division of Germany had been the focus of my professional life for three decades. The Moscow coup took place in August 1991 and three years later the first Trident boat sailed from the Clyde on an operational patrol. These were momentous events that heralded major changes in Britain's security requirements.

I have dedicated this book to my sons Andrew and Sandy both of whom aspire to have a professional interest in strategic studies. Their generation will have to manage Britain's future security needs and the task will not be an easy one. Ostensibly Western Europe is a much safer place today than it has ever been before but recent events have resulted in many old strategic truths being changed overnight. The one thing that it seems safe to predict is that the new Europe will be more dynamic than the one in which I grew up. It is my hope that this work, by providing an analysis of the past, will make some small contribution to an understanding of Britain's future security needs. We have arrived at a strategic crossroads that presents choices. Whether we grasp this opportunity or simply sail with the tide remains to be seen.

I must record my thanks to one group of people and to two individuals. This text draws heavily on a large number of earlier works and I am greatly indebted to many eminent authors who have written on this subject in the past. The bibliography and notes at the the end of chapters bear testament to their number and to the breadth and vision of their work. I am particularly grateful

PREFACE

to James H. Wyllie, Lecturer in International Relations at the University of Aberdeen, who guided my period of postgraduate research on this subject with an admirable balance of wisdom and encouragement. I have plagiarised his mastery of the subject, but the opinions expressed, and any errors in the text, are entirely my responsibility. Finally I wish to thank my wife, Maggie, for her stoical forbearance during the preparation of this manuscript. She had reason to believe that I had deserted her for a word processor. That, however, was but a momentary lapse on my part and, with the publication of this book, I am looking forward to restoring the *status quo ante bellum*.

Robert H. Paterson
North Queensferry, 1996

Introduction

On 15 July 1980 the Government published the texts of letters exchanged between the Prime Minister and President Carter providing for the United Kingdom to buy from the United States the Trident weapon system, comprising Trident I ballistic missiles and supporting components for a force of British missile-launching submarines to replace the present Polaris equipped force.[1]

DESPITE THE ENORMITY of that decision, which indicated that Britain would retain a strategic nuclear capability until at least the second decade of the twenty-first century, it provoked little serious debate either within Parliament or throughout the country.[2] This could, and perhaps still can, be construed as an indication of consensus rather than indifference. Nevertheless was it the 'right' decision when it was made? If it was the 'right' decision at the time, was it made for the 'right' reasons? Is it still the 'right' decision? What, if any, are the indicators for the future?

Sometime early in the next century a decision will have to be made on whether Britain should embark upon the quest for a fourth generation of strategic nuclear weapons. Will that decision also 'go through on the nod'? Is Britain so obsessed with domestic socio-economic issues that its politicians and public have neither time for, nor interest in, decisions that enable the country to wreak a level of destruction that is colossal compared with the bombing of Hiroshima and Nagasaki.[3] At the time when a replacement decision has to be taken will the prospects for geopolitical stability be as predictable as they were when the Trident decision was made or might they be fundamentally different? Will the British government wish to replace Trident? If it does, will that decision remain essentially British, or will we want to, or indeed have to, take such a decision jointly with other states?

This analysis seeks to address these questions through a rigorous assessment of the factors that influenced Britain's decision to acquire and maintain a strategic nuclear deterrent. The scene for this assessment is set by a description of the historical background and a *résumé* of the development of nuclear strategy. This is followed by a detailed examination of the political, operational and economic perspectives surrounding the decision to procure and deploy Polaris and subsequently to replace it with Trident. Two chapters follow, the

I

first of which examines the British political decision-making process regarding the nuclear weapons programme and the impact of the Campaign for Nuclear Disarmament and public opinion while the second describes developments in arms control and assesses their impact. Following this assessment a comparison is made with France's experience of a strategic nuclear force. Finally the post-Cold War strategic scene is summarised to provide a setting for the concluding chapter. The conclusion draws out the principal themes of the study and seeks to provide a framework for prescribing possible options for the future of Britain's strategic nuclear capability.

While the theme underlying this work is the relative influence of a strategic nuclear capability as a determinant of political power, the text seeks to provide answers to specific questions. Is Britain's possession of a strategic nuclear deterrent justified? Has Britain procured the right deterrent to meet its perceived needs? What are the indicators for the future of Britain's strategic nuclear deterrent?

NOTES

1. Pym F., *Britain's Strategic Nuclear Force: The Choice of a System to Succeed Polaris*, Defence Open Document 80/23 (London: Ministry of Defence, July 1980) p.1.
2. See Freedman L., *Britain and Nuclear Weapons* (London: Macmillan, 1980) p.63 and p.68. Freedman records that the Conservative Defence Secretary's announcement that the Government was to seek a successor to Polaris met with a muted response from Labour who were more concerned with the overall cost of the programme than the morality of the issue, or its impact on the arms race. Freedman also notes that there was much less public debate on the matter than had been anticipated.
3. The bomb dropped on Hiroshima on 6 August 1945 had a 13 kiloton yield and is estimated to have killed around 130,000 people while each Polaris A-3 missile carries three warheads giving a combined yield of 600 kilotons. Furthermore Trident represents a very considerable increase over Polaris in destructive capacity.

CHAPTER ONE

The Historical Background to Britain's Deterrent 1938–56: From Nuclear Fission to the V-Bomber

The year 1939 produced one of the most extraordinary coincidences of all history: the discovery of the result of splitting an atom of uranium (a material hitherto considered pretty worthless) and the outbreak of the Second World War.[1]

THAT BRITAIN PLAYED a seminal role in defending Western liberal democracy between 1939 and 1945 is well understood and widely acknowledged. That it simultaneously played a critical role in developing the potential, and recognising the significance, of nuclear fission is comparatively unknown. Britain was a key actor in the conception of nuclear weapons and its technical expertise and political acumen were to have a profound effect upon the development of its nuclear policies.

The first step in the process towards the understanding of nuclear fission occurred in 1896 with Henri Becquerel's discovery of radioactivity. Until then the atom had been regarded as indivisible. The next two crucial discoveries were attributable to teams of British research physicists led by the New Zealander, Ernest Rutherford who, in the two decades before the Second World War, held the post of Professor of Physics, initially at Manchester University and thereafter at Cambridge. In 1911 Rutherford published a paper announcing the discovery of the nucleus of the atom and identifying its positive electrical charge. In 1920 he demonstrated that the nucleus, like the atom, was also divisible, and he coined the term 'proton' for the basic building block. In 1932 James Chadwick, a Cambridge researcher, discovered the neutron. This provided a powerful new research tool for bombarding the atom to probe its structure. It rapidly became obvious that nuclei eagerly swallowed neutrons that came sufficiently close and, as a consequence, produced new kinds of nuclei, or even atoms, some of them hitherto unknown. Enrico Fermi, an Italian, led this area of research and one of the nuclei with which he and others experimented was that of uranium. Initially the results were baffling;

however the puzzle was solved in December 1938 when two German chemists, Otto Hahn and Fritz Strassman discovered that a uranium nucleus, after swallowing a neutron, could split into two smaller nuclei of roughly equal size and that, in the process, some of the nuclear mass was transformed into energy. The discovery of nuclear fission was published in a scientific paper in January 1939 to coincide with the opening of the Fifth Washington Conference on Theoretical Physics. Thus far these discoveries were largely academic. Nevertheless it was clear at that stage that some form of chain reaction could be a possibility. The two critical developments in that process were attributable to the Danish physicist Niels Bohr. Bohr suggested that fission was not a characteristic of all uranium atoms but only of a certain kind known as uranium-235. His second proposition was that fission might be more likely if the bombarding neutrons could be slowed down. Bohr's theories were confirmed simultaneously by distinguished physicists working under Professor Frederick Joliot, Professor of Nuclear Chemistry at the Collège de France in Paris and, at Columbia University in New York, by a team led by Fermi and Leo Szilard, a Hungarian. The discovery of the possibility of a chain reaction revived the potential for a bomb and, for the first time, caused some scientists, particularly Szilard, to ponder the dangers of what they were doing and to question the wisdom of the open exchange of knowledge within the scientific community. Despite this concern the French researchers published their findings and the possibility of achieving a chain reaction became public knowledge some months before the outbreak of the Second World War.

Following the publication of the French paper, scientists in Britain, the United States and Germany alerted their governments to the military implications of nuclear research. President Roosevelt set up an Advisory Committee on Uranium on the advice of Szilard while, in Germany, a nuclear research office was set up within the Army Ordnance Department. The reaction in Britain was more dynamic, due largely to the efforts of refugee scientists. Sir Henry Tizard, Chairman of the Committee on the Scientific Survey of Air Defence, was persuaded to reserve stocks of uranium, should it prove possible to develop an atomic bomb. In early 1940, two refugee scientists working in Britain, Otto Frisch and Rudolph Peierls made an important theoretical breakthrough. They calculated that the amount of the rare uranium isotope U-235 needed to achieve a chain reaction was much smaller than hitherto supposed. They also proposed an industrial method for separating U-235 from U-238. This was the first practical proposal, in any country, for making an atomic bomb and it led directly to the establishment of the Military Application of Uranium Detonation (MAUD) Committee, a group of leading British scientists reporting initially to the Air Ministry and later to the Ministry of Aircraft Production. The MAUD Committee, unlike its United States counterpart, sought action. Professor Francis Simon of Oxford University was charged to examine the possibility of separating U-235 from U-238. He reported back in four months, a remarkable achievement. While the Oxford physicists were at work the British initiative was reinforced by the arrival of two of Joilot's team from Paris, now in the hands of the Germans, bringing with them the total world stock of heavy water. At the time heavy water was the best known, and most efficient, means of slowing down neutrons to enhance the process of uranium fission using unseparated uranium in a nuclear reactor. The new refugees, Halban and Kowarski, joined the Cavendish Laboratories in Cambridge and, working with British colleagues, soon discovered a new element named plutonium which appeared to have the potential to be as fissile as U-235. The report of the MAUD Committee in the summer of 1941 showed that an atomic bomb was possible using U-235 and that it may also be possible using plutonium. Ministers were convinced that the project should go ahead. Britain had established an early lead in atomic weapons research and the legacy of this was to have a significant effect on future political decision making.

Britain's pre-eminence, however, was relatively short-lived. Dr Vannevar Busch, President of the Carnegie Institute, persuaded President Roosevelt to establish a National Defence Research Council with himself as chairman. Busch received a copy of the MAUD Report in July 1941 and realised that British scientific thinking was well ahead of anything that the Americans were undertaking. Busch used the British findings to convince the President of the importance of the need for nuclear research and was given authority to discover whether a bomb could be made and at what price. Busch, realising the British lead, persuaded Roosevelt to write to Churchill to suggest that there should be a joint Anglo–American project. The British response was cool. Britain wished to retain control of its own programme and was willing only to share information with the Americans. This situation changed dramatically in December 1941 when the United States entered the war, following the Japanese attack at Pearl Harbor. Within six months the United States atomic weapons programme had outstripped the British and, when the United States Army took control of the project, now called Manhattan, the free exchange of information ceased. The British quickly realised that entry into the Manhattan Project was their only chance of staying in the forefront of nuclear development. Churchill persuaded Roosevelt to let Britain back in, basing his case on Britain's key initial role. In August 1943 at Quebec, after a year of hard diplomacy, Roosevelt signed a secret agreement reinstating the interchange of atomic energy information between the two countries.

The Quebec Agreement marked Britain's 'foot in the door' as far as nuclear weapons development was concerned. At the time Britain fully expected that the door would be opened and that the breakdown in Anglo-American collaboration was a bureaucratic inconvenience arising largely from the militarization of the Manhattan Project. In retrospect, however, it became clear that without the belated intervention of Churchill with Stimson, the United States Secretary of War, the United States was intent on proceeding on its own. The explanation of the situation is multi-causal. The key issues were the United States' suspicion of Britain's post-war intentions whereas Britain failed to understand the concerns of the United States Administration in relation to post-war accountability to Congress. Britain also failed to comprehend the rate of scientific progress that the Americans were achieving.[2]

The wording of the Quebec Agreement made the pre-eminence of the United States position quite explicit. Indeed the reluctance of the United States to enter into the Agreement is clearly visible 'between the lines' of the text.[3] Nevertheless the Quebec Agreement marked the formal recognition of a nuclear partnership that has survived the last 50 years.

The immediate effect was that some 50 British scientists and engineers moved to the United States to work on the Manhattan Project. Their work was confined to the uranium separation process as the British had no experience of plutonium production. The outcome, however, was practical co-operation in the race to develop a bomb. Historians differ about the importance of the British contribution but it certainly helped in solving the operational problems in the separation process that continued throughout 1944. The first test took place on 16 July 1945, just six days after the required amount of fissile plutonium became available, and gave a yield of 20 kilotons. A 13 kiloton, U-235, untested, bomb was dropped on Hiroshima on 6 August 1945 and, on 9 August, a 19 kiloton, plutonium bomb was dropped on Nagasaki. Japan surrendered five days later.

While the Quebec Agreement probably had little direct effect on the outcome of the Manhattan Project it was an event of considerable importance for Britain. It transformed Britain's capacity to produce nuclear weapons. It moved the special Anglo–American relationship into the nuclear field and, for both these reasons, it had major implications for British post-war policy making. At its simplest the Quebec Agreement moved the development of British nuclear weapons out of the field of scientific research and munitions production and into the arena of international relations. From then on political factors were to be of increasing importance in the development of Britain's independent nuclear capability.

In September 1944 Churchill reached an 'agreement' with Roosevelt aimed at retaining close post-war co-operation in the development of nuclear weapons. There is no documentary evidence of this agreement. It seems to have been no more than an understanding between the two heads of state. With Roosevelt's death in April 1945 and Churchill's fall from power shortly afterwards, this 'agreement' lapsed and when Attlee discussed nuclear co-operation with Truman in November 1945 no material progress was achieved.

What evidence there is suggests that Truman, although Roosevelt's deputy, was not party to all the nuclear information given to the President. His unwillingness to co-operate with Attlee may have been due, at least in part, to his lack of knowledge of the Roosevelt–Churchill 'agreement'. Much more significantly, on 22 June 1946, the United States government passed the McMahon Act. This was the first formal move towards nuclear non-proliferation, and it effectively stopped co-operation on nuclear matters with all other states, including Britain. Wartime partnership had ceased and, of necessity, Britain embarked upon an independent nuclear programme.

Attlee authorised the development of nuclear weapons in January 1947. Both domestically and internationally it was widely assumed that Britain, as one of 'The Big Three', would develop its own nuclear capability. Attlee's decision was essentially seen as a logical step that did not require justification vis à vis any specific threat. Indeed a ten-year no-war assumption had been adopted in the winter of 1946.[4] Conversely, it would be simplistic to suggest that contemporary events were unimportant. The war had ended and United States forces had largely returned home. The Red Army remained in Europe, the communists took power in Hungary in 1947 and in Czechoslovakia in early 1948. There was no NATO, although the Brussels Treaty was signed in March 1948; nor was there any United States nuclear guarantee. The first wing of the USAF strategic bomber force did not become fully operational until 1947 and the United States possessed fewer than 50 nuclear bombs until 1948. Against that background Attlee's decision could possibly be justified simply on the basis of Morgenthau's theory that the irreducible minimum of state policy is the need to survive. On the other hand it can equally be argued that Great Powers, and those states that consider themselves to be Great Powers, have always sought to possess the 'capital' weapons of their time. In this respect Britain had no intention of renouncing its nuclear birthright.

While the background to the British decision to develop nuclear weapons was important, the events leading up to the first British test in October 1952 were equally significant in influencing the development of British nuclear weapons policy. That critical five-year period saw the transition of the wartime alliance of 'The Big Three' into the bipolar confrontation of the Cold War. While the origins of the Cold War are to be found in the post-war division of Europe (the outcome of Churchill's famous 'percentage' agreement with Stalin in 1944) its development needs to be assessed against three key events: the announcement of the Truman Doctrine and the Marshall Plan, the Berlin blockade, and the outbreak of the Korean War.

On 23 March 1947 President Truman gave a firm commitment to the political leadership of what the United States administration regarded as 'the free peoples': 'I believe that it must be the policy of the United States to support free peoples who are resisting attempted subjugation by armed minorities or by outside pressures.'[5] Three months later Secretary of State Marshall unfolded a plan for financial aid in support of the new doctrine that was designed to ensure the recovery of the European economy: 'It is logical that the United States should do what it is able to do to assist the return of normal economic health in a world without which there can be no political stability and no assured peace.'[6] Although the Marshall Plan claimed that, 'Our policy is not directed against any country or doctrine, but against hunger, poverty, desperation and chaos', it nevertheless linked capitalist economic philosophy with Truman's political ideology. Thus the *ad hoc* wartime 'spheres of influence' agreement ossified into two politico-economic camps with irreconcilable aims.

The Berlin blockade began on 30 March 1948 in response to currency reforms within the three Western zones of Germany. Initially the blockade was spasmodic. On 24 June, however, in response to the West's decision to extend its currency reforms to West Berlin, all overland access to the city was denied. Rather than provoke a crisis on the ground, the West mounted a massive airlift which provided the city with all its needs until 12 May 1949 when the blockade was lifted. Soviet intransigence over Berlin had a profound impact in the West. In particular it reinforced the American perception that the Soviet Union was a belligerent, expansionist power. As a direct result of the crisis, the United States moved B-29 bombers to British bases and it was widely believed that these were armed with nuclear bombs. Although this was not correct it is significant to note that the bombers remained after the crisis and they were equipped with nuclear weapons by the middle of 1950. Although it was not an issue at the time it is of interest to recall that the decision to equip USAF bombers operating from British bases with nuclear, rather than conventional, bombs was a unilateral United States decision. From the summer of 1950, therefore, Britain became a United States strategic nuclear base not as a con- sequence of British or United States political policy but simply as a result of a change in the USAF's operational capability. Britain was therefore involved *de facto* in the initial operational deployment of a nuclear deterrent from the outset, albeit passively.

In June 1950 troops from North Korea invaded the South. At the time it was widely believed that the North Koreans were acting on orders from Moscow. The analogies between Korea and Eastern Europe seemed obvious, especially to the Americans, who dispatched a large force under the aegis of the United Nations to support the South Koreans. By the autumn the United Nations forces had driven the North Koreans back over the 38th parallel and were intent upon the destruction of the North Korean regime. At that point the Chinese came to the aid of the North Koreans. Rather than escalate the conflict, the United States, to the relief of its European allies, chose to limit it and the war petered out in July 1953. The recourse to nuclear war was avoided.

Although this eventuality was probably unlikely, the consequences of the conflict were important. The formation of the United Nation's force ensured the reactivation of Western Europe's military capability, albeit in many cases on an embryonic scale. More significantly it transformed the infant NATO into an operational military alliance.

In December 1950 Eisenhower was appointed the first Supreme Allied Commander in Europe (SACEUR) and was tasked with the creation of an integrated military structure for the Alliance. Four additional American divisions were deployed to Europe in the following year. In April 1949, when NATO was established it was estimated that the British, French and Americans could raise only four divisions in Germany compared with 175 Soviet divisions in Eastern Europe. American insistence on a German military contribution to NATO resulted in a significant build up of United States forces in Europe in 1951–52, in part at least, to reassure Paris against the consequences of a resurgence of German militarism. Thus it can be argued that the trigger for the institutional militarization of Western Europe was the outbreak of the Korean War.

There is one other important event that had its origins in the Korean conflict. In 1952 the NATO Council, meeting in Lisbon, set the incredible target of 96 divisions to secure the conventional defence of Europe. That target was never met. By 1954, when only 15 divisions were in existence, it was generally accepted that this conventional concept had failed. The unwillingness, or inability, of the West Europeans to address this conventional target gave birth to, and subsequently ensured the continuing need for, extended nuclear deterrence.[7] The politico-economic confrontation of the Truman Doctrine was now backed by military force in which the use, or the credible threat of the use, of United States' nuclear weapons was implicit.

The importance of these events is clearly unquestionable. In analysing them, however, it is relevant to remember that the wartime 'spheres of influence' agreement resulted from a British initiative with the Russians to the exclusion of the Americans. The Truman–Marshall initiative was an all-American concept, the Berlin blockade a unilateral Soviet action, while the Korean War developed into a major international event resembling a modern ideological crusade. Clearly concepts of importance varied according to the perceptions of the actors. The historiography of the political motives behind the Truman Doctrine is one of the great debates of modern history. The orthodox view sees the initiative as: 'the brave and essential response of free men to communist aggression'.[8] The revisionist position is that the United States, with a monopoly of nuclear power and unchallengeable economic paramountcy, sought to eliminate Soviet control of Eastern Europe by establishing capitalist, and therefore liberal democratic, countries up to the border of the Soviet Union.[9] Not surprisingly, the Soviet Union perceived this to be a deliberate act of political aggression. Whatever position one adopts, the impact of that event can hardly be judged as crucial as seen from West European eyes. It was an intellectual, ideological, economic debate that had no immediate impact on the war-weary Europeans.

The Berlin blockade coinciding, as it did, with the communist coup in Czechoslovakia, was dramatically different in its impact. The airlift was a full-scale military operation throughout which the threat of war in Europe was real, and the media ensured that this perception was widely understood. By contrast the Korean War, although an open conflict, was seen in Europe, although not in the United States, as something of an anti-climax. Limited war in the Far East was preferable to the daily threat of a holocaust in Europe. In summary, therefore, it seems likely that for the Soviet leadership the crucial event in the development of the Cold War was the declaration of the Truman Doctrine. Conversely, for the average American citizen, the advent of the Korean War was probably crucial. Undoubtedly, however, for Britain, and its West European allies, and the United States leadership, the crucial event in making the Cold War visible on an international scale was the Soviet blockade of Berlin. It was in this forum that Britain played a key political, strategic and operational role that strengthened its links, and prestige, both with the United States and its European partners. Equally significant is the fact that the Berlin blockade was the first political crisis of the nuclear era. It has been argued that the Berlin crisis was the first example of the failure of US nuclear supremacy to deter lower level confrontations.[10] Conversely Garden has argued that it is just as valid: 'to suggest that it was the nuclear element which deterred sufficiently to keep the conflict at a low level'.[11]

Irrespective of which view one favours, the important fact, in the context of this study, is that Britain was in a key position throughout the crisis to address this very issue. Although it is not possible to quantify the benefits of this experience it would be simplistic to ignore their significance. It is equally plausible, however, to hypothesise that Britain would still have sought to develop nuclear weapons had there been no Cold War backdrop. The perception that Britain was still a world power with global responsibilities was widely held, both at home and throughout the international community. The Cold War may have helped to justify the decision and probably added a degree of urgency to the decision-making process. The decision itself, however, was probably inevitable.

The first test of a British fission bomb took place in October 1952. The following decade was remarkable, both for the speed of technical and operational progress and, for the steady move towards closer co-operation with the United States. The 1946 McMahon Act's non-proliferation aim was largely ineffective as far as Britain was concerned. The 1952 Monte Bello test strengthened Britain's hand in negotiations on co-operation and, in 1954, a more permissive United States Atomic Energy Act was passed which enabled some limited exchanges to take place. There was a much more significant change following Britain's first thermonuclear test in May 1957. The 1954 Act was substantially amended in 1957 and the following August the Anglo–American agreement 'for Co-operation on the Uses of Atomic Energy for Mutual Defence Purposes' became effective. A further amendment to the Act in 1959 put Britain into a 'special' position for the purposes of nuclear weapons development: a position which remains unchanged today. One of the direct consequences of the discussions between Macmillan and Eisenhower was the agreement to allow 60 Thor Intermediate Range Ballistic Missiles (IRBMs) to be based on British soil under a dual-control system.[12] In early 1956, 238 Squadron RAF became operational with Blue Danube Britain's first fission weapon. As the bomb was too big for the Canberra bomber the RAF had to borrow USAF B-29s until its own V-bombers became operational. The V-bombers, which started to enter operational service at the end of 1956, were the world's first ever purpose built nuclear delivery system. They were, however, being developed at a time when the benefits of missiles over manned bombers were becoming increasingly obvious.

NOTES

1. Gowing M., 'Britain, America and the Bomb', in Dilks D. (ed.) *Retreat from Power*, Vol. 2 (London: Macmillan, 1981) p. 51.
2. For a full account of this critical phase in Anglo–American relations see Gowing M., *Britain and Atomic Energy, 1939–1945* (London: Macmillan, 1964) pp. 164–177.
3. For the text of the Quebec Agreement see ibid., pp. 439–440.
4. See Rosecrance R. N., *Defence of the Realm: British Strategy in the Nuclear Epoch* (New York: Columbia University Press, 1968) p. 10. Also Pierre A. J., *Nuclear Politics: The British Experience with an Independent Strategic Force 1939–1970* (London: Oxford University Press, 1972) p. 71.
5. *US State Department Bulletin*, 23 March 1947.
6. George Marshall, speech at Harvard, 5 June 1947.
7. For explanations of the concept of extended deterrence see Freedman L., *The Evolution of Nuclear Strategy* (London: Macmillan, 1989) pp. 424–6 and Baylis J., Booth K., Garnett J. and Williams P., *Contemporary Strategy Volume I: Theories and Concepts* (New York and London: Holmes and Meier, 1987) pp. 128–34.
8. Schlessinger A. Jnr, 'Origins of the Cold War', *Foreign Affairs*, Vol. 46 (October 1967) p. 23.
9. For a fuller treatment of the orthodox and revisionist arguments see ibid., pp. 21–52.
10. See George A. L. and Smoke R., *Deterrence in American Foreign Policy* (New York: Columbia University Press, 1974) pp. 134–6.
11. See Garden T., *Can Deterrence Last?* (London: The Royal United Services Institute for Defence Studies, 1984) p. 40.
12. See Pierre A. J., p. 140.

CHAPTER TWO

The Development of Nuclear Strategy

The question has been whether any useful purpose could be served by employment of devices which invited discussion using such words as 'holocaust', 'doomsday' and 'armageddon', and whether any employment could be sufficiently deliberate and controlled to ensure that political objectives were met. Which means that at issue has been whether a 'nuclear strategy' is a contradiction in terms.[1]

T HE ABOVE QUOTATION encapsulates the dichotomy that lies at the heart of the issue of nuclear strategy. Can any nuclear strategy be reconciled with rational political decision making and be amenable to practical political control? The term strategy derives from the Greek term meaning 'the art of the general' and, by implication, makes clear the distinction between the use of military force and political influence. Since Clausewitz, however, it has been accepted that military force is an extension of political influence, rather than a development beyond political control. Although Clausewitz's view that strategy was the art of achieving the aims of war through the use of battles lost much of its validity as a consequence of the First World War, it gained renewed utility with the development of air power.[2] Today Liddell Hart's definition of strategy as: 'the art of distributing and applying military means to fulfil the ends of policy', is widely accepted.[3] Three key elements of Liddell Hart's definition are important to the development of this chapter. First, the utility of military means is dependent upon the fulfilment of political policy. Second, the methodology of military means is not subscribed, other than by the need to achieve policy aims. Third, Liddell Hart's definition emphasises the pre-eminence of military means in the concept of strategy. This does not necessarily exclude the influence of economic, psychological and ideological factors but it places them on a different scale of importance. The critical role of military force in the concept of strategy is implicit in Professor Ken Booth's somewhat wry definition: 'Ultimately strategy is a continuation of philosophy with an admixture of firepower'.[4]

Strategy is the link between military power and policy objectives. Furthermore, since the advent of nuclear weapons, 'conflict avoidance' strategies have become increasingly important. Strategy has consequently become a multi-disciplinary subject in which the military have an important, but far from exclusive, role. Strategy is conceived of as 'theory' or 'doctrine'. Strategic *theory* is the non-normative, or pure, study of strategic concepts, for example balance of power; deterrence; arms control. Strategic *doctrine* is the application of these concepts to specific policies, for example containment; massive retaliation, flexible response; build down. The existence of a strategic doctrine provides a conceptual template, thus reducing the uncertainty of the 'special case'. Furthermore doctrine links policy with technology. A credible doctrine projects foreign policy goals and conveys an image of a state's perceptions. To be credible such a doctrine must be relevant to foreign policy objectives and receive the support of both the domestic public and allies. In practical terms a state's strategic doctrine is an amalgam of publicly declared policies, operational planning, and developments in weapons technology. These components are rarely consistent. If nuclear strategy had developed in an academic vacuum doctrine could be expected to develop from theory and political aims from operational capabilities, which, in turn, would be based on realistic assessments of technological advance. In the 'hurly-burly' of the international arena such development is likely to be influenced by a variety of factors that make an inherently complex issue even more problematic. The theoretical 'horse' is ever in danger of being overtaken by the doctrinal 'cart', with the attendant risk of creating self-fulfilling policies. This danger was made explicit by Reinhold Niebuhr: 'It is the business of military strategists to prepare for eventualities and it is the fatal error of such strategists to create eventualities for which they must prepare.'[5]

This chapter seeks to trace the development of nuclear strategy in the period from 1945 to 1970. Clearly the British experience has, from the outset, been influenced by the broad dynamic framework created by United States' doctrine. The detail presented here consequently draws upon developments in the United States to help explain the British experience. The chapter covers a quarter of a century that starts with the United States as the sole nation with a strategic nuclear capability. It ends with that nation's acknowledgement of the need to negotiate a strategic arms limitation agreement with the Soviet Union. The United States' experience over this period falls into four phases. From 1945 to the early 1950s, while nuclear weapons were still scarce, there was an understandable attempt to balance conventional and nuclear forces. From the end of the Korean War until the early 1960s the United States embraced the doctrine of massive retaliation. In 1962, in acknowledgement of growing Soviet capabilities, McNamara announced the adoption of flexible response. By the end of the period, the label widely used to describe the global strategic situation was mutual assured destruction (MAD).

The British experience also falls into four distinct periods. Britain was at the forefront of strategic thinking immediately after the war, yet it did not possess the means to embrace a credible doctrine of deterrence. Massive retaliation was formally, albeit briefly, adopted in 1957. By the mid-1960s, when the United States had moved to flexible response in recognition of the imminence of nuclear parity between the superpowers, Britain had neither a credible doctrine nor a deterrent. By the end of the period, however, Britain was back in the nuclear club with the commissioning of the Polaris fleet. The 'independence' of Britain's deterrent was a matter of debate but the credibility of Polaris as a 'second strike' deterrent system was unquestionable.

In the immediate post-war period the United States was simultaneously dismantling its military capacity and reviewing its international strategic philosophy. Its actions and its thinking were at opposite poles of the strategic spectrum. The move back to isolation was short lived, however. A report to President Truman in the autumn of 1946, made the new perception of the United States' role in the international community clear and highlighted the importance of its latent military power. The report stressed that military power was the only language that Soviet leaders understood and warned that compromise and concession would be interpreted as a sign of weakness.[6] With political assessments being couched in such conventional 'balance of power' terms it is unsurprising that there was no immediate post-war reassessment of the impact of nuclear weapons on the development of geopolitical strategy.

The British experience in the immediate post-war period was markedly different: isolation was not an option. Indeed Groom has argued that, in 1945, Britain was trying to contain Russian 'probes', just as it had done in the nineteenth century, with the same dilemma of resources. The options were seen to be to pass the responsibility to the United States or to embrace nuclear weapons. In the event Britain chose to do both.[7] There was never any doubt that Britain would continue to be a nuclear power in 1945. According to Rosecrance: 'Even during the war it was perfectly clear that the UK was thinking not only of a bomb that would defeat Hitler but also of bombs for the post-war period.'[8] There is also the general argument that Britain's historical experience in relation to a military supported, power-projection, foreign policy has made its acceptance of capital weapons, be these battleships or nuclear bombs, inevitable. Thus the 'decision' would have been to reject nuclear weapons, not to procure them. Against that background it was generally accepted that Britain would become the second member of the nuclear club – before the Soviet Union. This was considered to be politically important. The choice for Britain was not one of whether to become a nuclear power but rather of how that would be achieved. While the possession of nuclear weapons was seen as a symbol of Great Power status and, therefore, not a contentious issue, the development of a stance that was independent of the United States was more a force of circumstances than a deliberate policy choice. In April 1946

Attlee warned the United States ambassador that, if the McMahon Act was passed, Britain would establish its own military and civil nuclear programmes:

> We had to hold our position *vis à vis* the Americans. We couldn't allow ourselves to be wholly in their hands, and their position wasn't awfully clear always . . . at the time we had to bear in mind that there was always the possibility of their withdrawing and becoming isolationist once again. The manufacture of a British atom bomb was therefore at that stage essential to our defence.[9]

It is important to remember that this was said well before the emergence of NATO and the concomitant United States commitment to Western Europe. As far as Britain was concerned the possession of nuclear weapons provided the twin advantages of enabling it to counter the Soviet Union's military strength while simultaneously strengthening the British claim to a special relationship with the United States.

From 1945 to 1953, strategic thinking within the United States remained predominantly conventional and nuclear free-fall bombs were perceived largely as an extension of conventional bombing capabilities, particularly in military circles. The United States had no stockpile of nuclear weapons until 1947 but a number of factors influenced a rapid United States nuclear build up thereafter. On the international scene there was growing tension between the superpowers culminating in the Berlin crisis. In the United States, vested interests within the USAF were working hard to increase the operational capability of the strategic bombing force. Technological developments within the Soviet Union spurred further advances in the United States. In 1948 United States atomic tests indicated that it would be possible to manufacture a large stockpile of weapons that would be smaller, cheaper, more destructive and use less fissionable material than was hitherto thought possible. These tests revealed the possibility of harnessing the deuterium-tritium reaction, which is the basis of nuclear fusion, and paved the way for the development of the thermonuclear bomb which combines both the fission and the fusion processes. During the work on the Manhattan Project, Enrico Fermi, Edward Teller and others at the Los Alamos Weapons Laboratory realised that the temperatures reached in the explosion of a fission bomb might well be high enough to produce thermonuclear reactions.[10] The outcome of these tests was the first fusion explosion at Eniwetok Atoll in May 1951. In August 1949 the first Soviet atomic bomb test had ended the United States monopoly and these two events concentrated thinking within both the United States and Britain on the development of a nuclear strategy. Technology was leading both theory and doctrine.

Britain has been historically renowned for its operational military capability. Conversely its willingness, or ability, to conceptualise about strategic theory has been markedly different. Blackett encapsulated that position: 'Traditionally Britain has been averse to thinking about war in between fighting wars; once they are over we tend to forget them until the next time.'[11] The advent of nuclear weapons was to change this in the early 1950s, when the British contribution, even though it was made by a small élite, was seminal. Indeed, one of the paradoxes of this period is that British thinking was probably some way ahead of the United States, and certainly far ahead of British operational capabilities. The background to Britain's contribution was similar to that of the United States: hardware developments preceding doctrine and a worsening international situation presaged by events in Berlin and the Korean War. The need to prevent war by deterrence was first recognised in the 1946 Defence White Paper, yet the Attlee government did not base its defence policy on deterrence.[12] The concept of an independent British nuclear deterrent was born in the early 1950s. Although the Attlee government sanctioned the development of nuclear weapons it viewed them essentially as weapons of last resort. By contrast Churchill's Conservative government which came to power in 1951 transformed what Freedman has described as 'nuclear aversion' into 'nuclear bias'.[13] The economic consequences of the Korean War were a direct consequence, with rearmament being in direct conflict with Britain's need for exports to improve its balance of payments position. This led to the 'long haul' policy for defence spending. The overall conclusion was that large, balanced, well-equipped, conventional forces were not achievable in relation to Britain's economic prospects. That, in turn, provided the conceptual background for the 1952 Global Strategy Paper, prepared by Sir John Slessor, Chief of the Imperial General Staff, which resulted in Britain becoming the first nation to base its security policy on an acceptance of nuclear deterrence.

The key tenet of the Global Strategy Paper was the need for an open declaration that retaliation would be at the Soviet Union's heartland rather than at the point of conflict. Reliance on any such strategy, it was argued, would permit a considerable reduction in conventional forces. There were four critical deductions that led Slessor to his conclusion. First, the advent of nuclear weapons had abolished the utility of total war. Second, effective air defence against nuclear weapons was not feasible. Third, that situation resulted in the primacy of the jet bomber. Finally, since a nuclear air strategy plus a conventional land strategy was not affordable, priority lay with the development of a nuclear air strategy to provide the 'Great Deterrent'.[14] Slessor briefed the United States Chiefs of Staff on the rationale of the Global Strategy Paper in an effort to argue for a reduction in NATO conventional force goal levels. Although reservations were expressed at the time it is significant to note that, in December 1952, the NATO Council approved major force reductions to those agreed at Lisbon earlier in the year. Furthermore, the

United States' 'New Look' strategy, announced in 1953, embraced much of Slessor's philosophy.[15] The first national enunciation of a nuclear strategy was made in a United States report prepared by the State Department's Policy Planning Staff and presented to the National Security Council (NSC) in April 1950. The report, known as NSC-68, undertook a fundamental re-examination of the United States' strategic objectives. The underlying theme of the report was to portray the threat the Soviet Union posed to world peace, and the resultant importance of the United States' military preparedness. The report renounced the concept of a preventive war prior to the Soviet Union's acquisition of thermonuclear weapons. It also renounced the concept of a pre-emptive strike as an acceptable politico-strategic position. It did, however, endorse the idea that the United States should not renounce the first use of nuclear weapons until adequate conventional forces could be built up.[16] NSC-68 conveys an image of political unwillingness to resort to even the threat of the use of nuclear weapons. That position, however, may not have been shared by some senior military commanders. At a briefing held in May 1954, General Curtis LeMay, of the USAF Strategic Air Command, said that: 'If the United States is pushed in the corner far enough, we would not hesitate to strike first.' When it was pointed out that pre-emptive attack was not official policy, LeMay replied: 'I don't care. It's my policy. That's what I'm going to do.'[17] The apparent gulf between political strategic thinking and military planning was further evidence of the need for a clear and well-understood strategic nuclear doctrine. Nevertheless the intellectual background to NSC-68 clearly stems from traditional concepts of defence rather than even embryonic notions of deterrence. While the Soviet potential was acknowledged, it would have to become a reality before conventional intellectual barriers could be broken down to facilitate innovative conceptual thinking. Military technology was still in the lead but the need for a strategic doctrine, based on a valid theory, was becoming increasingly clear.

Notwithstanding the early inability of officials and the military to develop a practical strategic theory it would be wrong to conclude that this area was not the subject of serious thought. The threat of reprisal was part of the politico-military arsenal long before the advent of nuclear weapons. The notion of deterrence, and the importance of retaliation, were therefore clear to some even before the first atom bombs were dropped. In September 1944 a report of the Jefferies Committee of Manhattan Project Scientists noted:

> The most that an American nucleonic rearmament can achieve is the certainty that a sudden total devastation of New York or Chicago can be answered the next day by an even more extensive devastation of the cities of the aggressor, and the hope that the fear of such a retaliation will paralyse the aggressor.

The Committee, drawing on the experience of history, expressed its reservation about the likelihood of deterrence being effective.[18] Bernard Brodie, writing in 1946, stressed the crucial importance of developing an effective retaliatory force and simultaneously noted the new *raison d'être* for military force: 'Thus far the chief purpose of a military establishment has been to win wars. From now on its chief purpose must be to avert them.'[19] Although Brodie probably deserves the credit for being the first to articulate what had to be done it would be simplistic to suggest that the way ahead was clear. Undoubtedly the major difficulty in formulating a practical theory for the use of nuclear weapons stemmed from the understanding that the weapons had enormous offensive potential, especially if used in a pre-emptive strike. It was equally clear that defence seemed impossible, a conclusion exacerbated by the knowledge that the world's major cities were the inevitable targets. The world's most powerful liberal democracy, in pursuing a war to uphold liberty and freedom, seemed to have developed a weapon that, because of its pre-dominantly offensive potential, was politically unusable by a democratic state.

The Eisenhower Administration, which replaced Truman's in 1953, had a different view about the utility of nuclear weapons. In part this stemmed from the political requirement to restore the credibility of nuclear weapons following the experience of the Korean War. Of equal importance was the fact that by the end of 1953 the United States had developed a substantial nuclear stockpile with a range of capabilities that would soon be enhanced by a formidable fleet of strategic bombers. The standard bomber of the USAF Strategic Air Command in the early 1950s was the 4,000 mile range B-29, which relied on the use of overseas bases to extend its range. The B-52, which became operational in 1955, much enhanced this capability as it had a range in excess of 8,000 miles. The origins of 'The New Look' strategy, as it came to be known, were enshrined in a National Security Council Paper (NSC-162/2) on Basic National Security Policy.[20] A key element of the paper was the statement that it was considered essential for the future to develop and maintain a strong military posture with emphasis on the capability for inflicting massive retaliatory damage by offensive power. This new doctrine of massive retaliation was announced to the world in a speech by Secretary of State John Foster Dulles in January 1954, in which he declared that the basic decision had been made to: 'depend primarily upon a great capacity to retaliate, instantly, by means and at places of our choosing'.[21] The declaration of the strategic doctrine of massive retaliation placed the concept of deterrence at the centre of the United States' strategic theory. From the outset it was acknowledged that the doctrine of massive retaliation, or deterrence by punishment, was credible only until the Soviet Union could match the United States' nuclear capability. This gave added impetus to the theoretical debate about the credibility of deterrence. In turn, this suggested that the concept of dissuasion embodied psychological aspects that were irrelevant to conventional theories of defence. For deterrence to be credible perceptions are as important as operational capabilities. Thus, while the concept relies on communication, the essential ingredient is the level of ambiguity. The adversary must know what actions are forbidden, and have some realisation of the type of response that will be invoked, if the threat is ignored. The deterrer must be perceived as having the political and military capability to do what is threatened, and the overall scenario must be credible. The potential for deterrence is enhanced when the adversary is rational, though Herman Kahn has argued that low rationality can be offset by increasing the level of threat. The more strategists examined the theory of deterrence, the more flawed the doctrine of massive retaliation appeared to be. The fundamental question centred on the credibility of the concept. Would any rational power unleash nuclear weapons against limited incursions thousands of miles from its homeland? Liddell Hart was one of the first to point out that: 'to the extent that the H-bomb reduces the likelihood of full scale war it increases the possibility of limited war pursued by widespread local aggression'.[22]

The British adoption of massive retaliation was enshrined in the 1957 Defence White Paper, although the move towards that position was implicit in earlier White Papers. The 1954 Defence White Paper envisaged the next large-scale war as being nuclear and catalytic with nuclear weapons being used on both sides, while the 1955 White Paper argued that the use of nuclear weapons was the only means by which Soviet land forces could be countered.[23] The British position in 1957, however, was substantially different from that of the United States in 1953–54. Britain was suffering from both the political and economic consequences of the Suez crisis.

> Undoubtedly, the abortive Suez episode increased the psychological desire for independence of action while at the same time brutally demonstrating Britain's diminished capabilities.[24]

The constraint on freedom of action encouraged politicians to espouse policies that were more rhetorical than real, while the economic constraints made reliance on nuclear weapons a matter of political expediency rather than a credible policy of national defence. On the other hand, as far as the economic issue was concerned, Groom argued that massive retaliation was the only policy that had any semblance of being reasonable in relation to Britain's post-Suez position.[25] In 1958, however, Randolph Churchill told the American Chambers of Commerce in London:

> Britain can knock down twelve cities in the region of Stalingrad and Moscow from bases in Britain and another dozen in the Crimea from bases in Cyprus. We did not have that power at the time of Suez. We are a major power again.[26]

Britain adopted the doctrine of massive retaliation for reasons of perceived domestic economy and international prestige. Furthermore, while Britain possessed nuclear weapons and the means to deliver them at the time, it is doubtful whether Britain possessed an effective deterrent. The consequences for the future were ominous. In embracing massive retaliation Britain committed itself to ending national service, cutting the armed forces from 690,000 to 375,000 by 1962, and cancelling the development of a manned supersonic bomber force. Henceforth massive retaliation was to rely on long range ballistic missiles: a system still at the early stages of development. The British adoption of massive retaliation in 1957 was probably little more than a dangerous bluff. It is arguable that the 1957 Statement on Defence was no more than a political facade, probably aimed at concealing growing weaknesses from the electorate and allies as much as from potential enemies.[27] That the bluff was not called is almost certainly attributable to developments in the international arena rather than the efficacy of Britain's strategic policy.

Growing Soviet nuclear strength suggested that massive retaliation, as a practical doctrine, was fatally flawed. The first Soviet thermonuclear test was conducted in 1953 and by 1956 the Soviet Union had a strategic bomber force capable of reaching the United States. The following year the Soviet Union launched its first successful Inter-Continental Ballistic Missile (ICBM) and also achieved the first space launch with Sputnik 1. These two events had considerable impact within both the United States and Britain. The strategic thinker, Albert Wohlstetter, played a leading role in developing nuclear doctrine to match the new threat. Wohlstetter recognised the vulnerability of the United States strategic bomber force when on the ground and argued that, to deter a pre-emptive attack, there had to be some nuclear forces that could survive such a strike. This was the origin of 'second strike capability' and it marked the realisation that deterrence was not an absolute position but rather a variable relationship, dependent upon capabilities and perceptions. Wohlstetter's analysis stressed the crucial importance of concealment and invulnerability and thus conceptually heralded the move away from the strategic bomber to the silo, or submarine launched missile.[28] If doctrine had moved ahead of technology it was only by a short way. The first United States ICBM, Atlas, became operational in 1960 and the USN tested its first Submarine Launched Ballistic Missile (SLBM), Polaris. In the same year the United States developed the first Single Integrated Operational Plan (SIOP) to co-ordinate the nuclear targeting of all three services. The SIOP has remained the key document in relation to nuclear operational capability and is the primary source for demonstrating, or suggesting, differences between national strategic policy and operational planning. By 1959 the number of forces involved in nuclear operations was creating serious co-ordination problems. In 1960 the Secretary of Defense told President Eisenhower that he was unable to resolve basic differences between the armed forces over targeting. The Eisenhower administration managed to establish a new Joint Strategic Planning Staff (JSTPS) whose first task was to develop a National Strategic Target List. Eisenhower was horrified by the number of targets in the plan, believed to be some 2,600, and the level of overkill with total potential casualties estimated to be in the region of 360 to 425 million.[29] Significantly, however, when the United States nuclear monopoly was broken the nuclear guarantee to Europe began to be questioned, albeit *sotto voce* in public discussion. This situation raised the possibility of the British force being used to 'trigger' a United States response. This notion indicates just how far behind Britain had fallen in terms of developing a credible 'independent' deterrent.

The election of John F. Kennedy to the Presidency in 1960 marked an important political change, and the appointment of Robert McNamara as Secretary of Defense from 1961 to 1968 heralded a new intellectual and methodological approach to the development of nuclear strategy. There were two key factors that assisted the Kennedy administration in seeking a new approach, apart from its own dynamic charisma. The launch of Sputnik 1, and the development of Soviet ICBMs had convinced the population of the United States that the Soviet Union had caught up. The 'Missile Gap' had been a major electioneering issue, and Kennedy's candidacy had been enhanced by incorrect intelligence assessments that supported this assertion. It is now known that there was no such gap. The successful launch of United States SLBMs, on the other hand, was more factual and more significant. This was the technological development that would give credibility to second strike theories. The large appropriations voted to expand the strategic nuclear forces were doubtless justified largely on the basis of the erroneous 'Missile Gap'.[30] Notwithstanding these developments, Kennedy rejected the doctrine of massive retaliation, which he regarded as inflexible:

> We have been driving ourselves into a corner where the only choice is all or nothing at all, world devastation or submission – a choice that necessarily causes us to hesitate on the brink and leaves the initiative in the hands of the enemy.[31]

McNamara's task was to devise a strategy that allowed the President a range of options for decision making. It also had to be capable of remaining under effective political control in the context of a nuclear war. In a report to the House Armed Services Committee, in February 1961, McNamara explained that he wanted a strategic force: 'which will permit its use, in event of attack, in a cool and deliberate fashion and always under the complete control of constituted authority.'[32] McNamara announced his new doctrine of flexible response in a speech at Ann Arbor, Michigan on 16 June 1962.[33] A key concept that was inherent within flexible response was the move away from countervalue targets, namely cities, towards counterforce targets, namely targets essential to an enemy's war-fighting capability. McNamara also wanted to create what is known as intra-war deterrence. This was the ability to deter an enemy from continuing to escalate during the course of a nuclear war. Thus, even if deterrence failed to stop a nuclear war breaking out the concept could still be credible by limiting the conflict. The move to flexibility and counterforce targeting was communicated clearly by the Secretary of Defense:

> Our forces can be used in several ways. We may have to retaliate in a single massive attack, or we may be able to use our retaliatory forces to limit damage done to ourselves, and our allies, by knocking out the enemy's bases before he has had time to launch a second salvo. Our new policy gives us the flexibility to choose among several operational plans . . . The very strength and nature of the Alliance forces makes it possible for us to retain, even in the face of a massive surprise attack, sufficient reserve striking power to destroy an enemy society if driven to it. In other words we are giving a possible opponent the strongest possible incentive to refrain from striking our own cities.[34]

A number of key criteria had to be met for flexible response to be considered as a viable doctrine. Conventional force levels, and deployments, had to be considerably greater than the 'trip-wire' levels associated with massive retaliation. They had to be capable of resisting moderate-sized conventional attacks. It was argued that this would force the attacker to deploy sufficient strength to make the possibility of a nuclear response credible. A more sophisticated approach to targeting was essential. This, in turn, was dependent upon the development of satellite reconnaissance which began to provide photographic coverage of the Soviet Union in September 1961. Improved levels of intelligence had to be reflected in the SIOP to demonstrate a move towards counterforce targets. This had to be matched with a level of technological development that provided the accuracy levels that were essential for a counterforce policy to be effective. In the early 1960s the United States was beginning to be capable of this level of accuracy. Finally, and most important, for intra-war deterrence to be credible it was essential to have control mechanisms that remained viable after a nuclear exchange had taken place. This was, and remains, a controversial issue.

With the move to concepts of flexible response induced by the state of nuclear parity between the superpowers Britain ceased to be a key player in the development of nuclear strategy. Of necessity, its adherence to massive retaliation had been short-lived. By 1965 the V-bomber force lacked the ability to penetrate the Soviet Union's air defences. This, together with the cancellation of Blue Streak in 1960, and Skybolt in 1962, meant that Britain was to be without a viable nuclear capability throughout the latter half of the 1960s. The deterrent gap was acknowledged following the Nassau meeting. The 1963 Defence White Paper, however, announced measures to reduce this vulnerability. The life of the V-bomber was to be extended, and the Tactical Strike and Reconnaissance Aircraft (TSR-2), due to enter service in 1967, was given a new strategic role. However, in 1965, the TSR-2 development programme was cancelled, and it was argued that it would have been cancelled before the 1964 election had the 1963 White Paper not given it a strategic nuclear role.[35] Not surprisingly in these circumstances, the Defence White Papers of 1960 and 1961 made little contribution to theories of deterrence although, significantly, the 1961 White Paper introduced the notion of 'graduated deterrence'.[36] The official silence of the years immediately following the 1957 Statement on Defence may, itself, be significant. Groom certainly thought this was the case:

> However it is difficult to resist the notion that the silence covered a retreat by the Government from the doctrine of modified 'massive retaliation' as expressed in the much quoted paragraph 12 of the 1958 White Paper.[37]

The 1962 White Paper, however, rejected the theoretical basis that Sandys had used to place all Britain's defence eggs in a nuclear basket. The 1962 statement acknowledged that a state of mutual assured destruction meant that nuclear weapons were only usable as a last resort in deterring an attack against the homeland. Their utility in all other situations was questionable. Thus if Britain wished to play an influential role in the international arena it had to possess sufficient conventional forces as well as a strategic deterrent:

> We must continue to make it clear to potential aggressors, however, that we should strike back with all the means that we judge appropriate, conventional or nuclear. If we had nothing but nuclear forces, this would not be credible. A balance must be maintained, therefore, between conventional and nuclear strength.[38]

In 1957 Britain embraced massive retaliation with a nuclear force of doubtful credibility. In 1962 it acknowledged the strategic reality of power politics in the post-nuclear era but had neither the conventional nor the nuclear forces to make a credible contribution to the defence of its national interests, either abroad or at home. As the general election of 1964 approached the debate turned from considerations of nuclear strategy to the issue of whether Britain should retain a nuclear force. The Labour Government that came to power in 1964 decided, pragmatically, to continue with the Polaris programme although, at least partly to assuage its internal critics, it played down the 'independent' aspects of the nuclear force and maintained a policy of linking the British deterrent with the NATO Alliance:

The 1966 Defence White Paper stated that it was the Government's 'aim to internationalise our nuclear forces in order to discourage further proliferation and to strengthen the alliance'. Accordingly under its proposal for an Atlantic Nuclear Force the United Kingdom had offered 'to internationalise the bulk of our nuclear strategic forces, including the entire Polaris fleet, by committing them irrevocably to NATO for the duration of the alliance'.[39]

After early 1965 the great debate on the future of the British strategic nuclear deterrent faded away. Not surprisingly, little was said in public about how it might be used. The Wilson government's view was that silence was golden as far as nuclear strategy was concerned. According to Freedman:

> The response to the dilemma of constructing a strategic rationale that was more plausible but did not undermine the fundamental articles of faith of NATO came to be an embarrassed and resolute silence.[40]

Even if all the technological criteria could be met, flexible response still had inherent difficulties. For a counterforce strategy to be fully credible it had to be perceived as being capable of use as a pre-emptive strike. The Kennedy administration, however, would not publicly countenance such a policy. The reality may have been different.[41] Flexible response assumed that the Soviet Union would also abandon a strategy of massive first use or massive retaliation in favour of a flexible one. Soviet military doctrine, on the other hand, rejected the concept of limited war and it would seem improbable that this was not reflected in their strategic thinking. It is doubtful whether the Soviet Union's missiles had the accuracy necessary for a counterforce policy and it is equally unlikely that the Soviet Union possessed a sufficiently sophisticated command and control structure to operate a flexible response strategy. The requirement for sufficient conventional forces to raise the nuclear threshold meant that the new policy was inherently expensive and thus created domestic difficulties for the United States. The new policy also created Alliance problems. Indeed it has been claimed that the United States' proposals for a multilateral nuclear force (MLF) bedevilled West European defence politics in the early 1960s.[42] After announcing its new doctrine the United States put pressure on its European allies to increase spending on conventional forces. McNamara also wanted Britain and France to give up their independent nuclear weapons. The United States' intentions were regarded with suspicion, particularly by the French and Germans. The French strategic thinker, Pierre Gallois, argued that by increasing conventional force levels the Europeans increased the likelihood of a Soviet nuclear attack. Some went so far as to argue that the United States' concept of a limited war was a war limited to Europe and felt that the reason behind the new doctrine was that the United States wished to escape from its nuclear guarantee to Western Europe.[43]

The fundamental difference between the United States and the Europeans centred on the concept of *first use*. McNamara wanted to be able to counter a conventional attack with a level of conventional defence that would force the attacker into the first use of nuclear weapons. The Europeans doubted if such conventional force levels could be achieved and, even if they were, felt this policy would lead to the destruction of much of Western Europe. The Germans, who had most to lose, had always stressed the importance of keeping open the option of the early use of nuclear weapons. This was, and until 1990 remained, a key tenet of their strategic thinking.[44] Flexible response was not formally adopted by NATO until 1967. By then the French had left the Alliance's military structure and the doctrine, at the insistence of the British and the Germans, had been modified to allow the early use, or the threat of use, of tactical nuclear weapons. This revised version of flexible response remained the basis of NATO's nuclear strategy until 1990. Despite the difficulties, its great strength had been its political flexibility. The Americans and the Europeans were able to interpret it in different ways at different times. While it was conceived by McNamara as a rigorous intellectual concept, its subsequent pragmatic flexibility has done much to promote its political acceptability within the Alliance, and its credibility as a strategic doctrine.

McNamara's new strategy made it even more difficult for him to control the Services' demands for new weapons systems. Flexibility, especially within the USAF, meant having the capacity to use every option simultaneously. In 1968 McNamara attempted to stop this by trying to define, as accurately as possible, the level of damage the United States was seeking to achieve in order that weapons programmes could be matched to this outcome. McNamara called this the 'assured destruction' criterion, and defined it as the ability to kill 20 to 25 per cent of the Soviet Union's population and destroy a half to two-thirds, of its industry. McNamara's staff calculated that to achieve assured destruction it would be necessary to use weapons capable of delivering the equivalent of between 200 and 300 megatons.[45] Assured destruction was soon followed by the concept of mutual assured destruction as it became increasingly obvious that the Soviet Union could inflict unacceptable damage on the United States. McNamara acknowledged this balance of mutual vulnerability and argued that stability was better served by accepting the position than by embarking upon a further destabilising arms race.[46] Despite McNamara's attempts to convince the Soviet Union of the validity of this position the Soviet Union, at that time, did not accept the concept of mutual assured destruction. Within the United States it came to be realised that any mutual restraint would have to be negotiated. In acknowledging this, President Johnson made the first offer of talks on strategic arms limitation in February 1967.

The final paradox of Britain's involvement in the development of nuclear strategy in the period up to 1970 was that, just as the United States was acknowledging the need for strategic arms limitation talks, Britain was about to re-enter the nuclear arena with the deployment of the Polaris fleet. The four boats were commissioned between October 1967 and December 1969 and all four boats were operational by September 1970. In agreeing to provide Britain with Polaris, the United States endowed it with a system that was far more viable than the land based ICBMs that it had sought to develop as the basis of its deterrent force. The heart of the irony, however, was that McNamara, who was one of the first to acknowledge the importance of 'survivability' in nuclear delivery vehicles, was also a vehement advocate of limiting the possession of nuclear weapons to the superpowers. His efforts in respect of the latter were thwarted by his President's somewhat surprising decision to supply Britain with what turned out to be the ideal deterrent system for a small nuclear power. Polaris has been described by Freedman as: 'an exemplary second strike weapon'.[47] From 1970 onwards, although the independence of the British nuclear deterrent would continue to be a matter for debate, both in respect of independence of manufacture and independence of control, the ability of Polaris to provide a credible second strike capability was not in question. Britain, by its continued possession of a strategic nuclear deterrent, would thenceforth be able to retain a degree of influence in the international arena in conventional and nuclear matters that far surpassed its military potential. For Britain, the notions of perception and ambiguity had strategic, political connotations that were every bit as important as the possession of a defence policy, based upon a credible doctrine of second strike deterrence.

NOTES

1. Freedman L., *The Evolution of Nuclear Strategy*, 2nd Edition(London: Macmillan, 1989) p. xxi.
2. The Italian, Brigadier General Giulio Douhet, is usually acknowledged as the first writer to enunciate a strategic theory of air power; the basis of his thesis was the supremacy of strategic air bombardment. See Douhet G., *The Command of the Air*, translated by Ferrari D. (New York: Coward McCann Inc, 1942). Other useful sources are, Brodie B., *Strategy in the Missile Age*, (Princeton, NJ: Princeton University Press, 1959) Chapter 3; Higham R., *The Military Intellectuals in Britain: 1918–1939* (New Brunswick, NJ: Rutgers University Press, 1966) Appendix 3; Emme E. M., *The Impact of Air Power* (Princeton, NJ: Van Nostrand, 1959). Brodie broadly supports Douhet's thesis; Higham is critical while Emme provides a selection of readings.
3. Liddell Hart B. H., *Strategy: The Indirect Approach* (London: Faber & Faber, 1968) p. 334.
4. Booth K., *Strategy and Ethnocentrism* (London: Croom Helm, 1979) p. 9.
5. Quoted in Blunden M., 'Nuclear Strategy', Unit 7 of Open University Course D235, *Nuclear Weapons, Inquiry Analysis and Debate* (Milton Keynes: Open University Press, 1986) p. 38.
6. See report to the President by the Special Counsel (Clark Clifford), 'American Relations with the Soviet Union', 24 September 1946. Reprinted in Etzold T. H. and Gaddis J. L., *Containment: Documents on American Policy and Strategy 1945–50* (New York: Columbia University Press, 1978) p. 66. Quoted in Freedman L., p. 38.
7. See Groom A. J. R., *British Thinking About Nuclear Weapons* (London: Frances Pinter, 1974)

p. 23.

8. Quoted in Gowing M., *Britain and Atomic Energy 1939–45* (London: Macmillan, 1964) p. 323.

9. Williams F., *A Prime Minister Remembers* (London: Heinemann, 1961) pp. 118–19.

10. These events, and the debate about whether to develop a thermonuclear weapon, are documented in York H., *The Advisors: Oppenheimer, Teller and the Superbomb* (San Francisco: Freeman, 1976) Ch. 4.

11. Blackett P. M. S., *Studies of War* (London and Edinburgh: Oliver & Boyd, 1962) p. 115.

12. See Cmd 6743, *Statement Relating to Defence: 1946* (London: HMSO, 1946). Also Pierre A. J., *Nuclear Politics: the British Experience with an Independent Strategic Force 1939–1970* (London: Oxford University Press, 1972) p. 86.

13. Freedman L., *Britain and Nuclear Weapons* (London: Macmillan, 1980) p. 3.

14. For further background information on the intellectual debate behind the Global Strategy Paper see Groom A. J. R., pp. 55–65 and Pierre A. J., pp. 87–9.

15. See Huntington S. P., *The Common Defence* (New York: Columbia University Press, 1961) p. 118. Quoted in Pierre A. J., p. 88.

16. For a fuller appraisal of NSC-68 see Freedman L. (1989) pp. 69–71.

17. See Ford D., 'Reporter at Large: The Button II', *The New Yorker* (8 April 1985).

18. See Freedman L. (1989) p. 41.

19. Brodie B., *The Absolute Weapon* (New York: Harcourt Brace, 1946) pp. 88–91.

20. NSC-162/2 is reprinted in full in *The Gravel Edition, Pentagon Papers, Vol. 1* (Boston: Beacon Press, 1971) pp. 412–29.

21. Dulles' speech was reprinted as 'The Evolution of Foreign Policy', *Department of State Bulletin*, Vol. XXX, 25 January 1954, pp. 107–10.

22. Written shortly after the Dulles speech in January 1954 and quoted in Yergin D., *Shattered Peace: The Origins of the Cold War and the National Security States* (London: André Deutsch, 1976) p. 478.

23. For further details see Cmnd 124, *Defence: Outline of Future Policy: 1957* (London: HMSO, 1957); Cmd 9075, *Statement on Defence: 1954* (London: HMSO, 1954); Cmd 9391, *Statement on Defence: 1955*, (London: HMSO, 1955).

24. Pierre A. J., p. 96.

25. See Groom A. J. R., p. 558.

26. Reported in *The Times*, 14 November 1958.

27. Pierre has suggested that the dilemma underlying the situation was the requirement to recognise the increasing need for interdependence with the United States, as well as the continuing desire for independence. Pierre A. J., p. 100.

28. See Wohlstetter A., 'The Delicate Balance of Terror', *Foreign Affairs*, XXXVII (2 January 1959).

29. For further details see Rosenberg D. A., 'The Origins of Overkill: Nuclear Weapons and American Strategy, 1945–1990', *International Security*, Vol. 7, No. 4 (1983).

30. For further details on the background to the alleged missile gap see Snow D. M., *Nuclear Strategy in a Dynamic World* (Tuscaloosa: University of Alabama Press, 1981).

31. Quoted in Baylis J. et al., *Contemporary Strategy, Theories and Policies* (London: Croom Helm, 1975) p. 119.

32. Quoted in Kaufmann W. M., *The McNamara Strategy* (New York: Harper and Row, 1964) p. 53.

33. See McNamara R. S., 'Defence Arrangements of the North Atlantic Community' *State Department Bulletin*, No 49 (Washington DC, 9 July 1962) pp. 67–68.

34. Quoted in Kaufmann W. M., pp. 74–5 and pp. 114–20.

35. For TSR-2's strategic nuclear role see Cmnd 1936, *Statement on Defence: 1963* (London: HMSO, 1963) p.67. The TSR-2 issue is analysed in depth in Williams G., Gregory F. and Simpson J., *Crisis in Procurement: A Case Study of the TSR-2* (London: The Royal United Services Institute for Defence Studies, 1969).

36. Cmnd 952, *Report on Defence: 1960* (London: HMSO, 1960) and Cmnd 1288, *Report on Defence: 1961* (London: HMSO, 1961).

37. Groom A. J. R., p. 481.

38. Cmnd 1639, *Statement on Defence: 1962: The Next Five Years* (London: HMSO, 1962).

39. See Pierre A. J., p. 290.

40. Freedman L. (1980), p. 30.

41. One former McNamara aide acknowledged, 'If you are going to shoot at missiles you're talking about first strike.' Cited in Trewhitt H., *McNamara: His Ordeal in the Pentagon* (New York:

Harper and Row, 1971) p. 115.

42. See Buchan A., *The Multilateral Force: An Historical Perspective*, Adelphi Papers, No 13 (London: Institute for Strategic Studies, October 1964).

43. See Schwartz D. N., *NATO's Nuclear Dilemmas* (Washington, DC, 1983) p. 167.

44. For a detailed explanation of German thinking on this issue see, Kaiser K., Leber G., Mertes A. and Schultze F.-J., 'Nuclear Weapons and the Preservation of Peace', *Foreign Affairs*, Vol. 60, No. 5 (Summer 1982) and reprinted as Chapter 17 in Holyroyd F., *Thinking About Nuclear Weapons: Analyses and Prescriptions* (London: Croom Helm, 1985).

45. See Kemp G., *Nuclear Forces for Medium Powers, Part 1: Targets and Weapon Systems*, Adelphi Papers, No 106 (London: International Institute for Strategic Studies, 1974) pp. 25–6.

46. This position was enunciated in a speech made by McNamara in September 1967. See 'The Dynamics of Nuclear Strategy', *Department of State Bulletin*, LVII (9 October 1967).

47. Freedman L. (1980) p. 19.

CHAPTER THREE

The Decision to Deploy a British Strategic Nuclear Deterrent

Introduction

Much of Britain's post-war history – in foreign and defence policy, in its economic and social difficulties – has been reflected in the quest for, the achievement of, and the maintenance of a British nuclear deterrent, its warheads and delivery systems. This reflection is but partial, although its implication is that the policy of successive British governments towards the deterrent cannot be seen in isolation either from defence policy as a whole or from wider considerations.[1]

THE RÉSUMÉ OF the historical background in Chapter 1 ended with the deployment of the Polaris boats in the late 1960s while Chapter 2 examined developments in nuclear strategy until 1970. The two key issues on which that period ended were the adoption of flexible response by NATO and, in recognition of the nuclear equality between the superpowers, the United States' decision to take tentative steps towards strategic arms limitation talks.

The assessment of the decision to procure and deploy a British strategic nuclear deterrent will now be considered against this background. The assessment covers the period from the lead up to the Sandys 1957 White Paper to the Labour government's decision, in 1974, to go ahead with the Chevaline programme while simultaneously stating that it had no intention of moving to a new generation of strategic nuclear weapons. This assessment examines three conflicting perspectives: the strategic political goals, the operational military requirements and the economic realities and seeks to answer the nine key questions posed below.

The strategic political perspective

1 Did Britain need an independent strategic nuclear deterrent to protect its vital national interests?
2 Could the decision to procure and deploy a strategic nuclear deterrent be

justified in terms of its strategic political influence rather than the narrower parameters of defence?

3 Did the strategic rationale behind the procurement decision remain constant from the time it was made until it was necessary to consider the procurement of a successor system?

The operational military perspective

4 Was there a threat, or a potential threat, that could best, or only, be deterred by a strategic nuclear capability and, if there was, what was the minimum requirement for a deterrent force?

5 Did Britain procure the right delivery system to meet the perceived need?

6 Did the level of the deterrent's credibility remain adequate throughout the life of the programme?

The economic perspective

7 Was the British deterrent a cost-effective system?

8 What was the impact of expenditure on the deterrent in relation to total defence expenditure?

9 Was Britain's level of expenditure on defence justifiable?

The Strategic Political Perspective

This assessment of the strategic political perspective encapsulates three distinct post-war periods. First, Britain's perception of developments in the international arena in the period leading up to the 1957 White Paper on defence. Second, the significance of the Sandys' White Paper. Third, the impact of major international developments in the period from 1959 to 1974 on the utility of Britain's nuclear deterrent.

If the historiography of the First World War suggests that, as a consequence of the *diktat* of the Treaty of Versailles in 1919, Germany lost the peace disproportionately to its defeat in war then the reverse is certainly true of Britain in the Second World War. In a technical sense there can be no doubt that Britain was a victor in 1945. Nevertheless it is equally beyond question that Britain was unable to enjoy even modest fruits from its victory. The post-1945 period was not as unpredictable, nor as demoralising, for Britain as the post-1918 period had been for Germany. Nevertheless, for both nations, there was a traumatic gap between their understandable expectations and the political realities of the international situation. Britain's aspirations and actions in this period need to be assessed against that background. With the wisdom of hindsight it can be argued that Britain was not a rational actor in the period up to the mid-1950s. To explain Britain's actions it is therefore necessary to understand the influences that impacted on its decision making processes. Professor Northedge has argued that in the post-1945 period Britain gave defence requirements a higher priority than foreign policy objectives. As a consequence there was a general tendency to overestimate the threat to national security and to underestimate the economic consequences of defence spending.[2]

That Britain saw itself as a world power in 1939, and was acknowledged as such by the international community, is not in contention. In 1945 Britain possessed armed forces of just over five million and a further four million citizens were employed in supplying these forces. In these circumstances it is not surprising that the 1946 Defence White Paper identified seven major tasks that bore all the hallmarks of world power status.[3] British forces were to be responsible for the execution of the surrender of Germany and Japan; the occupation of Germany and Austria; the maintenance of law and order in Venezia Guilia and Palestine; the provision of assistance to Greece and the liquidation of Japanese occupation in parts of south east Asia. British forces would also continue to be responsible for the maintenance of order throughout the still substantial British Empire, the safeguarding of communications and the upkeep of British bases abroad. Although not specifically included in the White Paper there was no doubt about the willingness of the Labour government of the day, at least in principle, to contribute troops for peace keeping duties under Article 43 of the United Nations Charter in addition to its formidable array of formally declared politico-military strategic objectives.[4]

The decade from 1947 contained many significant developments that were to influence British thinking about the future use of nuclear weapons. The initial bipolar confrontation of the Cold War had been rendered permanent by the West's adoption of the Truman Doctrine and its acceptance of aid under the Marshall Plan. Thereafter the Berlin blockade had been followed rapidly by the Korean War and, in 1953, the Soviet Union had conducted its first thermonuclear test. By 1956 the Soviet Union had a strategic nuclear bomber force capable of reaching the United States and, in 1957, the Soviet Union launched both Sputnik 1 and its first ICBM. Any 'thaw' in East–West political relations seemed to be more than offset by the Soviet Union's burgeoning strategic nuclear weapons programme and its continuing massive conventional arms superiority in Europe. Against that background it was not surprising that Britain felt the need for 'capital' weapons to guarantee its own survival and to protect its strategic interests. It is illuminating to note that as early as 1947 the British Chiefs of Staff considered that: 'between 1952 and 1957, the possibility of attacks by weapons of mass destruction exists, but for a variety of reasons, we think the chances are slight. After 1957, this form of attack is a distinct possibility'.[5]

While the decade starting in 1947 saw some changes in British overseas commitments there was little to suggest that they were part of a conscious rationalisation of Britain's role as a world power; rather they appeared to be more an *ad hoc* response to pressures as and when they arose. At the beginning of the decade Britain handed over its responsibilities in Greece and Turkey to the United States, those in Palestine to the United Nations, and it relinquished its sovereignty over India. It is of interest to note that there is a body of opinion that claims the decision to give India its independence was based on socio-political considerations rather than any reappraisal of foreign policy objectives. Had the decision been based on the latter it would have embraced an assessment of Britain's objectives east of Suez, the fulfilment of which had traditionally been met largely from resources provided from the Indian Empire. The consequence of the independence decision was that Britain retained, for dubious reasons, commitments east of Suez that it would find increasingly difficult to meet and justify. This constitutes a classic example of the mismatch between strategic political objectives and military capabilities that characterised the post-war period.[6] Conversely, in the mid-1950s Britain entered into a number of agreements that increased the scope and complexity of its strategic political objectives. In October 1954 it agreed to station four Army divisions and a Tactical Air Force in West Germany, a commitment, in terms of manpower and foreign exchange costs, that was to have a critical impact on British defence capabilities for the remainder of the century. The decision to establish BAOR was based almost exclusively on political considerations, with the underlying reason being the need to assuage French fears concerning the rearmament of West Germany in order that the latter could contribute to the defence of Western Europe as a member of NATO. The force level, originally some 77,000, was derived largely from those then present in West Germany rather than any strategic assessment.[7] In the same year Britain helped to establish the South East Asia Treaty Organisation (SEATO) and in 1955 it signed the Baghdad Pact which established the Central Treaty Organisation (CENTO). Britain's conventional military commitment to these alliances was minimal as it preferred to base its possible contribution on the deployment and use of nuclear weapons. Navias, in his study of the primary sources, has expressed the view that:

> a review of the documents associated with British strategic planning in relation to the Baghdad Pact and the South East Asia Treaty Organisation during 1955–6 reveals that growing emphasis was placed on strategic and tactical nuclear weapons for deterrence and war fighting purposes.[8]

At the same time as Britain was entering into these new alliances, emergencies in Kenya and British Guiana were making further demands on conventional resources. Navias is in no doubt about the scale of Britain's political objectives in the mid-1950s:

> In short, an international alliance infrastructure which manifested itself in both declaratory commitments and actual deployments, reflected the British perception of herself as a world power and her willingness to project power globally if necessary.[9]

The 1956 Suez *débâcle* threw British strategic shortcomings into sharp relief. The ponderous military build-up demonstrated the inadequacy of Britain's conventional forces while Bulganin's threat of rocket-borne reprisals demonstrated Britain's strategic vulnerability. Of even greater significance was the realisation that Britain no longer possessed the economic power, or the political credibility, to operate in the international arena without, at an absolute minimum, the tacit support of the United States. The Suez crisis marked the lowest point in Anglo–American relations since the signing of the McMahon Act in 1946.

The British government had long been ambivalent about its relationship with the United States, particularly in the sphere of nuclear weapons co-operation. Central to this dichotomy was the political-philosophical issue of whether Britain required a strategic nuclear deterrent for political or military reasons. The outcome of that debate would indicate whether Britain required an independent deterrent, or whether its strategic interests could be achieved through the acquisition of an interdependent capability. Both the political potential deriving from the possession of nuclear weapons and the risks of undue dependence on the United States had long been realised. Before the end of the war the MAUD Committee reported that:

> Even if the war should end before the bombs are ready the effort would not be wasted, except in the unlikely event of complete disarmament, since no nation would care to risk being caught without a weapon of such decisive possibilities.[10]

On the military level, Britain's concerns stemmed from its view that the United States could not, in all circumstances, be relied on to use its strategic nuclear forces for the defence of Western Europe. This concern was inevitably reinforced in the late 1950s when the Soviet Union possessed a fleet of strategic nuclear bombers capable of reaching the United States. On this level Britain's fears could only be assuaged by the possession of a credible, truly independent strategic nuclear deterrent. On the political level, however, Britain was concerned that its diminishing military strength rendered it incapable of influencing the United States' strategic policies. Some politicians believed that this could be achieved provided Britain possessed sufficient strategic nuclear resources for the United States to consider its contribution 'significant'. Clearly this level of nuclear power could be very considerably less than that required to provide a fully credible independent deterrent and, importantly in this scenario, the potential existed to achieve this capability through a negotiated level of interdependence with the United States. Like full-blown deterrence, the credibility of a qualified nuclear capability, achieved through interdependence, would be determined as much by perception as reality. This hypothesis serves to illustrate the rationale behind the gap between Britain's declared policies and its actual capabilities. These were to be a key feature of the Sandys White Paper.

By 1957 Britain's military need for a strategic nuclear deterrent to meet the Soviet threat in Europe was matched by the requirement to rebuild its political influence as an international actor, especially *vis à vis* the United States. The importance of the political perspective was reinforced by the growing need to match national defence capabilities with realistic domestic economic policies, as well as the requirement to combine Britain's extra European strategic political objectives with credible force-projection capabilities. As far as the Macmillan government was concerned, there was a general view that increased conventional capabilities would add to Britain's economic problems with few, if any, benefits to its strategic political objectives. The alternative was to embrace as ambitious a strategic nuclear weapons deployment programme as could be afforded. This, it was hoped, would provide an enhanced, and cost-effective, military capability that would enable Britain to continue to exert considerable political influence in the international arena. References abound to Britain's enthusiasm for procuring nuclear weapons to enhance its political standing. Navias, in his review of the historical legacy leading up to the Sandys White Paper, states that:

> . . . by the mid-1950s, nuclear weapons were to become those armaments and nuclear deterrence based on massive retaliation that policy which was chosen to help ensure Britain's international standing, influence and security in an era in which its traditional power resources were being depleted as well as overtaken by others.[11]

The underlying theme of Clark and Wheeler's study of the period up to 1955 was that British policy-makers viewed nuclear weapons as necessary accessories to world power status and that Britain, which considered itself as such a power, could not be without them.[12] This view was expressed by individuals on the Right of the conservative party and by the Cabinet itself: 'It will seem that the hydrogen bomb, when we have it, will make us a world power again,'[13] and: 'unless we possessed thermo-nuclear weapons, we should lose our influence and standing in world affairs.'[14]

The 1957 Sandys White Paper has long been viewed as a turning point in British defence policy. However, Navias's detailed study, which draws extensively on the primary sources of the period, serves to highlight both continuities and discontinuities as well as illustrating gaps between declared policy and actual changes in capabilities. The major explicit continuity was the public articulation of the broad strategic concept on which the Paper was based, namely the twin pillars of deterrence, through a policy of massive retaliation, and the replacement of conventional fire power with nuclear weapons. Indeed many writers have expressed the view that the Sandys White Paper was an admixture of British strategic thought, emanating from the 1952 Global Strategy Paper, and the United States' declaration of a policy of massive retaliation as articulated in the adoption of the 'New Look' policy in 1954. Sir John Slessor expressed the view that the Sandys White Paper:

> Introduces no basic revolution in policy, but merely rationalises and (probably for the first time) explains in admirably intelligible form tendencies which have long been obvious and policies most of which successive British governments have accepted and urged upon their allies for some years.[15]

The second major continuity of the period, although more implicit than explicit, was the importance of economic considerations. Indeed, in the light of Navias' work it is arguable that the impact of economic considerations represented more than straightforward continuity but rather that economic realities became, increasingly, the determinants of strategic capacity. Navias' study, like Wheeler's doctoral thesis, concluded that:

> Nuclear strategic thinking was very much a secondary consideration in a larger formula that sought major financial savings. The strongest evidence of this is found in the Minister's almost single-minded focus on manpower reductions and the concern expressed in the Air Ministry over Sandy's approach to the deterrent.[16]

Indeed, viewed from this standpoint, Sandys' influence on defence policy can be seen to mark an attempt to return to rational economic decision making, with defence requirements being constrained by political judgements about domestic economic capacity. Despite this the reality was that it would be another decade before a determined effort would be made to match strategic political objectives with military capabilities. Conversely the major discontinuity emanating from the 1957 White Paper was the reduction in the level of conventional forces from 690,000 to 375,000 by 1962. The Macmillan government's success in ending the unpopular policy of conscription, against the wishes of the Service chiefs, ensured that there could be no return to a policy that relied on the substantial deployment of conventional forces other than in an acute national emergency. It is, however, the disparity between declared and actual policy that is of more relevance to this work – especially with regard to the declared emphasis on both 'massive retaliation' and 'independence'. These contrasted markedly with the unstated, yet increasing, move towards the reality of interdependence with the United States and the influence of this implicit policy on the quantitative aspects of the government's adherence to massive retaliation. The centrality of the concepts of massive retaliation and interdependence are enshrined in the White Paper:

> The only safeguard against major aggression is the power to threaten retaliation with nuclear weapons (and, consequently, Britain) must possess an appreciable element of nuclear deterrent power of its own.[17]

Notwithstanding these statements both Clark and Wheeler on one hand and Navias on the other concluded that the acceptance of the reality of interdependence with the United States was an underlying theme of British policy discussions. Implicit in an acceptance of that situation was the political realisation that the level of strategic nuclear capability necessary to embrace interdependence was economically achievable whereas there was a growing realisation that the adoption of true strategic nuclear independence was beyond Britain's economic resources, given its domestic welfare commitments. Clark and Wheeler concluded that:

> The erosion of British nuclear strategy was to coincide with the articulation of a public doctrine of independence, as in the White Paper of 1957.[18] (And), The conclusion was therefore reached that economically and militarily Britain's security interests were best served through conventional integration with NATO and nuclear integration with the United States.[19]

In the same context it is illuminating to note that a special Foreign Office Steering Committee set up to assess the Anglo–American relationship reported in January 1958 that:

> To adopt interdependence as a policy is to recognise interdependence as a fact and to decide to promote it as the only means of progress and safety. It involves taking a process which is happening anyway and turning it to advantage by extending, accelerating and proclaiming it.[20]

Furthermore Britain's adherence to nuclear weapons as a means of influencing United States policy, at minimum cost, is implicit in a question put to the Cabinet by the Chancellor of the Exchequer in late 1958:

> Even if the number of targets that can be successfully attacked is not directly proportional to the size of the bomber force, is it really clear that

a smaller force than 144UE would not suffice to secure us the co-operation of the United States – if indeed that is the true aim of the independent deterrent.[21]

At the end of the day Britain, unsurprisingly, adopted a pragmatic approach and settled for, 'the most credible deterrent posture that was economically feasible, politically effective and strategically realistic'.[22] The critical weakness of the Sandys White Paper was its failure to appreciate that the economic consequences of Britain's defence policy arose as a result of its continuing wish to embrace strategic political objectives that were beyond its means. Further-more, the Macmillan government's failure to understand that nuclear deterrence, despite its significance in relation to global warfare, had little, if any, utility in relation to Britain's extra-European commitments meant that Britain's adoption of a nuclear strategy for both total and limited warfare was fatally flawed. The decade following the Sandys White Paper was to demonstrate this weakness so vividly that, despite Wilson's aspirations east of Suez, his government had to announce a fundamental review of Britain's strategic political objectives in 1967. The outcome of that review, which was driven by economic necessity, due to the inherent conflict of priorities between defence and domestic objectives, was to mark Britain's transition from a global to a regional power.

From what has been established so far it seems reasonable to conclude that in the period up to the late 1950s Britain had good reason to believe that it required an independent strategic nuclear deterrent to protect its vital national interests. Such interests, although never clearly articulated, were probably at best the maintenance of the *status quo* in Western Europe and, as an absolute minimum, the continuing existence of Britain as an independent state. This position was based on two self-reinforcing perceptions. The military threat posed by the Soviet Union was both formidable and growing. Furthermore, whilst the Soviet Union's geopolitical intentions were less clear, its bellicose rhetoric seemed to suggest that it viewed decisions about the use of its military power solely as an issue of time and place. At the other end of the spectrum Britain had reasonable doubts about the total reliability of the United States as an ally, and there were clearly no other states which could take its place. Initially therefore the development and deployment of an independent strategic nuclear deterrent was as much a matter of perceived need as it was of choice.

Ironically, by the time Britain was deploying its deterrent the position was already changing. From the time of Suez onwards there seems to have been a growing realisation that Britain, for economic reasons, would increasingly be unable to match the nuclear capacity of the superpowers. As a consequence its strategic political objectives would no longer be attainable unless they were compatible with those of the United States. The implicit acceptance of that situation led to the questioning of the need for a truly independent deterrent and to an increasingly pragmatic interest in the concept of nuclear interdependence with the United States. From that time onwards the *raison d'être* for Britain's deterrent shifted away from the narrow concept of military power to political influence. This departure was only possible with the tacit support of the United States. The 1958 Anglo–American agreement on nuclear co-operation paved the way for this development and the British decision to purchase Polaris from the United States in 1962 marked the beginning of the end of a truly independent British nuclear deterrent. The primary role of the British deterrent was increasingly to be a facet of political influence over allies rather than solely an instrument of military power to deter Britain's enemies.

In drawing the strategic perspective to a close it is necessary to assess the constancy of the strategic rationale for the deterrent. The early 1960s seemed no less unstable than the previous decade on the surface, with the Cuban missile crisis of 1962 following close on the Berlin crisis of 1961. Nevertheless there were counter developments. The 'hot-line' agreement signed on 20 June 1963 between the United States and the Soviet Union was a direct consequence of the Cuban crisis. Furthermore the Limited Test Ban Treaty signed in August 1963 was a signal step, albeit more symbolic than significant. Of greater consequence was the development of the Sino–Soviet split which began in 1960 and assumed a different magnitude of importance when the first Chinese nuclear test was conducted on 16 October 1964. If the Soviet Union's strategic focus was diverted eastwards at this time so, too, was that of the United States. The first United States military units were deployed to Vietnam in 1965 and the war there was to end with a nationalist victory in 1975. Back in Europe the Soviet Union was more concerned with events within the Warsaw Pact countries than potential threats from the West. The Brezhnev Doctrine was enunciated in August 1968 and was immediately applied in the suppression of the 'Prague Spring'. The West's tacit acceptance of the Soviet Union's 'right' to intervene in Eastern Europe demonstrated just how far the *status quo* had become accepted. This position was reinforced with the appointment of Brandt as the West German Chancellor in October 1969 and the rise of the concept of *Ostpolitik*. The decade from the early 1960s marked a lessening of strategic tensions between the superpowers. This suggested that the need for an independent strategic nuclear deterrent was less necessary than it had been in the period up to 1962, either as a source of military power or as an instrument of political influence. Nevertheless its potential in the latter capacity was undoubtedly greater than in the former.

The Operational Military Perspective

Any valid assessment of the operational military perspective must be based on some understanding of the key features of nuclear weapons technology. Thus the current section begins with a brief overview of this subject which will serve as a background for this and the following chapter.[23] It is particularly apposite to introduce this here as the historical period under consideration covers the move from a strategic nuclear bomber force, via an unfulfilled aspiration to procure a missile system, to the deployment of a submarine-based deterrent. The reality, of course, is not that any one system is better than any other but that each has its own advantages and disadvantages. Both the superpowers maintained a triad of nuclear forces comprising manned nuclear bombers, land-based missile forces and submarine-based systems. Before drawing any conclusions about the utility of British systems it is necessary to understand the relative capabilities and limitations of the range of possible systems.

Nuclear weapon systems are classified as either offensive or defensive and there are both technical and system factors that impact on their effectiveness. The three critical technical factors are accuracy, reliability combined with availability, and penetration. As far as accuracy is concerned it is important to realise that improvements in delivery vehicles and platforms can have a significant impact on the effectiveness of warheads. Thus the introduction of stealth technology, i.e. the ability to penetrate enemy air space undetected, has given the B-1B strategic bomber a capability beyond the comprehension of those who designed the V-bomber. Similarly the introduction of NAVSTAR has given a major boost to the effectiveness of missile systems. NAVSTAR is a global positioning system that is based on 18 satellites orbiting the earth and emitting radio signals. Missiles receive these signals and use them to determine their own position. The system provides an accuracy of about 15 metres in position and 0.1 metres per second in velocity.

Such improvements in guidance technology have reduced circular error probability (CEP) from over a kilometer in Titan II and SS-11 systems, deployed in the 1960s to about 80 metres in the Minuteman system deployed in the 1970s. Due to the complexity of nuclear delivery systems it is not technologically possible to achieve 100 per cent reliability; indeed 80 per cent system reliability is regarded as exceptionally high. Normal peacetime ratios of system availability are in the region of 50 per cent for aircraft and 65 per cent for missiles. Furthermore it is not possible to validate operational systems fully in peacetime so system reliability has to be based largely on prediction and extrapolation. These limitations can only be overcome by engineering system redundancy into production programmes. This in turn leads to the need for planned 'overkill' in strategic armouries. While it is not possible to assess the relative impact of these limitations it is important to note that liquid fuel propellants, used in older missiles, were significantly less reliable than solid fuel systems.

The limited penetration capability of manned bombers was acknowledged as early as the mid-1960s. This led to an increasing interest in missiles and the move to develop stand-off weapons for use from bombers. The penetration capability of ICBM systems is generally regarded as high and the introduction of MRV, MIRV and the development of MARV technology has ensured that a very high proportion of warheads are likely to get through to their targets.

As anti-missile technology evolved it was realised that the predictable path of a single free falling warhead would make it vulnerable to attack from anti-ballistic-missile (ABM) defence systems. The introduction of multiple re-entry vehicles (MRVs) enabled the delivery vehicle to release a cluster of warheads over the target in an effort to saturate ABM systems. The next development was the introduction of multiple independently-targetable re-entry vehicles (MIRVs). These enabled a number of targets to be engaged by warheads from the same vehicle. This was done via a 'bus' released from the missile which had its own booster and guidance system. Warheads or decoys released from the 'bus' free fall to their target. The most recent development has been manoeuvrable re-entry vehicles (MARVs). These provide warheads or decoys released from a 'bus' with the capacity to control their descent to the target area. This initially involved relatively unsophisticated devices such as fins to enable courses to be altered to avoid detection. Recent developments envisage the use of terminal guidance systems which would provide pin-point accuracy. Cruise missiles, on the other hand, although difficult to detect, are much more vulnerable due to their slow speed and, at present, they possess only one warhead per vehicle. There seems little chance of ABM systems that would be effective in protecting area targets such as cities being deployed in the foreseeable future. An ABM point defence system for small hardened targets, such as missile silos, seems to be much more likely.

The system factors depend upon whether the system is offensive or defensive and the contribution of command, control, communications and intelligence (C^3I). An offensive system consists of the warhead; the vehicle (aircraft or missile); the platform (silo, submarine, motor vehicle or, in the case of SRAM or ALCM, the aircraft); the guidance system (inertial navigation, NAVSTAR) and the requisite command, control and information component. A defensive system consists of early warning (radar, infra-red and other sensors), interception (fighter aircraft or anti-missile missiles) and passive measures such as civil defence, dispersal of assets, deception and improved protection. The objective of a defensive system is to retain an effective second strike capability while the offensive system aims to achieve a disarming first strike. Two points are important. First, the complete strategic nuclear deterrent needs both a first and second strike capability. Second, neither aircraft nor submarines are likely to be able to provide a disarming first strike capability (due to limitations of speed and accuracy) but both can make a considerable contribution to second strike capability. From the above it is clear that any assessment of nuclear capability is a complex matter and that this complexity increases with developments in technology. An understanding of the hardware statistics and developments in technology should give an insight into relative military capability. It is, however, essential to realise that capability is a combination of accuracy and throw-weight, in other words a combination of the number of targets that can be attacked independently and the equivalent megatonage (EMT) of the warheads, rather than the numbers of vehicles.

It is appropriate, now, to return to the historical assessment of the operational military perspective. Despite what has just been said about the complexity of assessing nuclear capabilities, the initial position was fairly straightforward. In the early post-war period Britain decided to develop an atomic bomb and, subsequently, a thermonuclear bomb, together with a fleet of strategic aircraft capable of delivering free-fall nuclear bombs to the territory of the Soviet Union. The critical decision, however, was the number of bombs and aircraft necessary to achieve deterrence. Early estimates of the requirements for bombs were crude and were based on the assumption that they would be used to attack cities. In 1946 the Chiefs of Staff indicated that 'a stock in the hundreds rather than scores' of bombs would be needed.[24] In July 1947 a Defence Policy Committee put the requirement at 1000 bombs. The rationale for that decision, however, is more enlightening than the quantity. The Home Defence Committee had concluded that 25 atom bombs would be sufficient to knock out Britain and, as the Soviet Union was 40 times the size of the United Kingdom, it was assumed that 1000 bombs would be sufficient to ensure its destruction.[25] In 1964 it was estimated that the British nuclear stockpile was in the region of 1000 to 1500 warheads. A more recent assessment lends credence to these figures and suggests that the total warhead stock has not surpassed 2000.[26]

The decision-making processes behind the quantities of V-bombers required was no more impressive. Navias, having studied this issue in some detail, concludes that the decisions contained little, if any, operational rationale:

Of course, had there been consensus that the sole objective of procurement and deployment policy was the establishment of a British finite force – that is a force with the ability to destroy a very limited set of Soviet cities – then the pressures of economic stringency and political/military sufficiency could have been satisfactorily resolved. However, an analysis of the available documents reveals that there was no agreement on the requirements of such a capability and, more significantly British policy makers were not willing to relate procurement and deployment solely to minimum countervalue objectives.[27]

In 1954 the Swinton Committee estimated that by the late 1950s the Soviet Union would have a force of some 850 strategic bombers operating from 40 air-bases with the ability to operate from another 150 dispersal sites.[28] This assessment, together with Defence Minister Selwyn Lloyd's statement to the Defence Committee that the first objective of the V-bomber force was the destruction of Soviet air bases from which nuclear attacks on Britain could be launched, is evidence that Britain envisaged adopting a pre-emptive counter-force policy once the V-bombers were operational. The anomaly is that while the Swinton assessment indicates 190 primary targets the operational capability of the V-bomber force was estimated at 100 successful target engagements in the first sortie. That assessment was based on a total V-bomber force of 200 aircraft, a 75 per cent serviceability rate and, apparently, assumes that 66 per cent of the available aircraft would successfully engage their targets. It is not improbable, however, that all three assumptions are rather optimistic.[29] Clearly this was an inadequate force to make such a policy viable. The original V-bomber procurement plans envisaged the production of 327 aircraft with the aim of maintaining an operational fleet of 240 bombers. There is, however, no evidence to link these numbers with any specific operational capability. In the summer of 1955 Selwyn Lloyd was still committed to the provision of an operational force of 240 bombers. Yet by September 1956 the requirement had been reduced to 184 aircraft. Navias's detailed study of that period makes it clear that this decision was based on economic constraints. The operational military arguments were not refuted; they were deemed to be politically unimportant.[30] The slowness of the V-bomber production process remained in stark contrast to the operational need and it was not until 1963 that the force possessed 180 operational aircraft.

The British experience with missiles was even more problematic. Work began on missiles in 1947 but this was largely on surface-to-air systems. The difficulties were soon realised and in 1954 Britain entered into an agreement with the United States on joint missile development. The British development of Blue Streak, an Intermediate Range Ballistic Missile (IRBM), which began in 1956, was based on the American Atlas missile. Blue Streak was to have a range of 2,000 nautical miles and it was envisaged that 15 to 20 missiles would be operational by 1965. There was a growing awareness in the mid-1950s that the manned bomber would ultimately be replaced by the missile. Simultaneously there were increasing doubts about the ability of the V-bombers to penetrate Soviet defences from the mid-1960s onwards. The 1955 White Paper, while acknowledging that the strategic bomber remained the prime means of delivering the deterrent, admitted that one day it would need to be replaced by missiles. Britain was, 'therefore working on the development of such a rocket as an addition to our deterrent strength.'[31] The 1956 White Paper contained similar assurances and the importance of these developments was stressed by the Minister of Supply, Reginald Maudling:

> It seems fundamental that eventually it will be very difficult for any manned aircraft to penetrate enemy defences, and the real weapon is likely to be a ballistic missile. If we are going to develop a warhead of any kind there is no sense in doing that unless we have the means to deliver it.[32]

Thus the operational requirement was for a system that would replace the V-bomber force. Blue Streak, however, was cancelled in April 1960. At that stage the development costs had reached £65 million and the anticipated production costs were in excess of £600 million. Apart from the economic considerations there were increasing doubts about the system's survivability as it would operate from fixed sites and be propelled by liquid fuel. At the time the decision was taken it was tacitly acknowledged that Britain might not have a viable deterrent beyond the mid-1960s.[33]

The other major British missile development of the period was Blue Steel. This was to be an air-to-ground system designed to give the V-bomber a stand-off attack capability. The missile was designed for use with the Mark 2 V-bombers of which there would ultimately be 120. It could be fitted to the earlier versions of the bomber but only with a reduction in its operating range. The missile was operational by 1963 with a minimum range of 100 nautical miles but by then its efficacy beyond the mid-1960s was already in doubt. A Mark 2 version was cancelled in 1960 after £1 million had been spent on development. By that time Britain had agreed to purchase 100 US Skybolt missiles, to which British warheads would be fitted, and it was considered that this decision made further work on Blue Steel irrelevant. Skybolt, although it was an air-to-ground system, was being procured primarily for political reasons. Macmillan had persuaded Kennedy to authorise the sale of Skybolt in March 1960, just one month before the decision to cancel Blue Steel was announced. Skybolt, however, was not operational in 1960 and there are conflicting views about whether it would have been superior to the Mark 2 Blue Steel. Skybolt posed its own special problems for the V-bomber force. While Skybolt was fully compatible with the Mark 2 Vulcan this was not the case with the Victor. These problems proved to be short-lived as the US cancelled Skybolt in December 1962 leaving Britain without the means of retaining a viable deterrent beyond the mid-1960s. The only practical interim solution was for the V-bomber force to revert to low altitude attack. This, however, reduced the force's operating range from 2,000 to 1,500 nautical miles. As has already been demonstrated, the only long-term option was to procure Polaris from the United States and Macmillan achieved this in December 1962. The first Polaris boat, however, was not operational until 1968.[34]

There is one other system that requires consideration at this stage. An Anglo–American agreement was negotiated in 1957–58 which allowed the United States to base 60 Thor missiles in Britain. The missiles were operated by Bomber Command on a 'dual key' basis, whereby American and British authorisation was required before missles could be launched. Thor was a liquid fuel system with a range of 1,500 nautical miles and a one megaton warhead. The missiles were deployed in unhardened sites in eastern England and had a slow reaction time. They were operational from 1960 to early 1963 and, while they made a significant numerical contribution to Britain's strategic deterrent, there were always doubts about their utility as a second strike force.[35]

It is now possible to piece together the various systems to quantify the utility of the British deterrent. Although some Canberra bombers had been fitted with atomic bombs as early as 1954 these aircraft lacked the capability to reach the Soviet heartland, thus they were not strategic assets. In effect Britain's strategic nuclear deterrent did not become operational until the end of 1956 when the first Valiant squadrons were formed. This was two years after the Soviet Union had developed a similar capability against the United Kingdom with the operational deployment of the TU-16 Badger. Britain's capability grew steadily from 1956 reaching its peak in 1962 at the time of the Cuban missile crisis. At that time there were 170 operational V-bombers and 60 Thor missiles all capable of delivering one megaton warheads. As can be seen from Table 3.1 below the decline thereafter was both systematic and spectacular.

Table 3.1

Year	Total	V-bombers	Thor	Polaris missiles
1962	230	170	60	
1963	180	180		
1964	180	180		
1965	120	120		
1966	80	80		
1967	80	80		
1968	72	56		16
1969	48			48
1970	64			64

Source: Ball D. and Richelson J. (eds), 'Strategic Nuclear Targeting' (Ithaca & London: Cornell University Press, 1986) Table 5.1, p. 119.

In 1964 the Valiants were grounded because of metal fatigue and in 1965 it was reported that the Victors were being deployed to another role and that the total force would be reduced to 80 aircraft. The implication was that these aircraft were no longer considered viable as strategic bombers. This deduction is certainly consistent with the oft-expressed view that the V-bombers would lack penetration by the mid-1960s unless equipped with a viable stand-off weapon system.[36] The 1965 decision not to proceed with the fifth Polaris boat limited the total force to a target coverage of 64.[37] Furthermore the 1964 decision to purchase the Polaris A-3 missile with its three (not independently targeted) 200 kiloton warheads rather than the single one megaton warhead of the A-2 missile meant that, while there was an increase in defence penetration capability, there was a penalty in total megatonage. There was also an availability penalty. With a four-boat Polaris force only one, or possibly two, boats would be on station at a given time.[38] Exceptionally, in a long-warning scenario, three boats could be deployed. Thus, assuming total penetration of defensive systems, Britain, in 1962, had the capability of attacking 230 targets simultaneously with one megaton weapons while its maximum potential at the end of the decade was to engage 48 targets with 28.8 megatons.

The only improvement envisaged was the introduction of the Chevaline warhead whose production was authorised by the Conservative government in 1972 in recognition of possible enhancements in Moscow's ABM system. The initial decision was based on a five-year development programme with an estimated cost of £175 million. In July 1976, development funding was authorised for a further two years. At that stage the costs were estimated at £600 million with deployment as late as 1981. The detail of the Chevaline programme was not announced publicly until January 1980 and both the secrecy surrounding the project and the dramatic escalation in the costs were issues of considerable parliamentary concern. The system, ultimately designated Polaris A3TK, involved a manoeuvrable space vehicle with three re-entry vehicles and a large number of penetration aids. Each re-entry vehicle possessed a limited capacity to manoeuvre independently, enabling a single target to be attacked using a different angle of re-entry, speed and course. Since only one target could be covered by each missile the system was not a fully fledged MIRV although it was considerably more sophisticated than the MRV system it replaced. The new warheads began to be deployed on operational patrols in the autumn of 1982 at a cost of £1,000 million (1980 prices).[39]

Trying to translate this quantitative assessment into a qualitative one is fraught; nevertheless an attempt must be made. It has been suggested earlier that, at the time the V-bomber force was becoming operational, Britain was considering a pre-emptive counterforce policy. As has already been shown, the efficacy of that policy was questionable from the outset. Furthermore it seemed to be counter to the general British approach to nuclear targeting which had its roots in a counter city philosophy.[40] The increasing co-operation with the United States on strategic targeting that took place from the late 1950s led Britain to conclude that a considerable number of the targets that posed a threat to Britain were on the SAC target list.[41] This was reassuring as the number of these targets was clearly outwith the capacity of the V-bomber force. Thus it is not surprising that from 1958 the primary sources indicate a move to countervalue targets.

At this time it was the Air Ministry's view that the capacity to destroy 30 to 40 of the 131 major centres of Soviet industry and administration would constitute an adequate deterrent.[42] That this could be achieved by the late 1950s seemed a reasonable assumption. Understandably there is little available literature that gives an insight into the details of British nuclear targeting. There are, however, unofficial studies by Kemp and Smart that throw some light on this obscure subject.[43] Kemp's 1974 assessment concentrates on countervalue targeting and he clearly believes this to be the most practical policy for medium-sized nuclear powers. Kemp identifies four levels of destruction: the top 10 cities, including Moscow; the top 10 cities, excluding Moscow; the top 50 cities and the top 200 cities. He concludes that only the first two options are realistic. Nevertheless, targeting these cities would put 15 to 21 million people at risk and 15 to 25 per cent of the Soviet Union's industrial capacity.[44]

Kemp's figures suggest that a minimum of two Polaris boats would be needed to have any reasonable chance of destroying 10 cities. If the target configuration included Moscow, with its Galosh ABM system, Kemp considers that two Polaris boats would be needed to ensure the destruction of that city alone. Smart's later study reaches broadly similar conclusions. Both assessments stress the importance of retaining a capacity that would ensure the destruction of Moscow. Indeed the 'Moscow criterion' had remained at the heart of Britain's targeting policy from the inception of the deterrent and seemed throughout to be the irreducible minimum below which deterrence would not be perceived as being credible.[45] Furthermore the development of the Chevaline warhead was seen as a necessity if Britain was to be able to retain this capacity.[46]

It is now possible to conclude the assessment of the operational perspective. It has already been shown that up until 1960 the Soviet Union posed a threat that could only be deterred by the possession of a credible strategic nuclear deterrent. Thereafter there was an indication that the likelihood of that threat coming to fruition was diminishing, despite the fact that there was no reduction in the Soviet Union's strategic capability. Apart from a brief period around 1960, when the British deterrent was probably perceived as being credible by the Soviet Union, British capability was either marginal or inadequate. In particular it appears that in the period between 1965 and 1969

Britain was without a viable deterrent. Finally it is clear that if Britain ended up with the ideal second strike system in Polaris it reached that position almost entirely by accident rather than by design.

The Economic Perspective

There is a considerable body of evidence to suggest that in the post-war period British governments, of both political persuasions, spent more on defence than might reasonably have been expected, given their other, often more highly publicised, political priorities. Against that background it is arguable that Britain spent more on defence than it could reasonably afford. The underlying reason for that position was a political inclination to try to ignore economic realities in a vain attempt to retain political status. The primary source of Britain's problem was an inability to meet balance of payments costs because, despite improvements in its own economic situation, it was unable to match the economic growth of other nations. While Britain enjoyed the post-war boom its economic performance lagged well behind that of its major competitors.

Between 1952 and 1957 production in Continental Europe rose by 47 per cent while the rise in Britain was only 22 per cent. Similarly Britain's share of the value of world exports in manufacturing dropped from 25.5 per cent in 1950 to 10.8 per cent in 1970. In the same period France's proportion dropped from 9.9 per cent to 8.7 per cent while the corresponding rise in West Germany and Japan was from 7.3 per cent to 19.5 per cent and from 3.4 per cent to 11.7 per cent respectively. Between 1950 and 1973 Britain's growth in GDP per annum was 3.0 per cent compared with 3.7 per cent in the United States, 5.1 per cent in France, 5.2 per cent in Canada, 5.5 per cent in Italy, 6.0 per cent in West Germany and 9.7 per cent in Japan. Even allowing for the fact that most of Britain's competitors came from a lower economic base, these figures indicate a significant gap in performance.

Britain has consistently spent more of its national income on defence than its allies other than the United States. Between 1955 and 1970 Britain spent an average of 6.4 per cent of its GDP on defence. The comparable figures for its West European allies were, France 5.6 per cent, the Netherlands 4.3 per cent, West Germany 3.9 per cent and Italy 3.2 per cent. Britain's inability to meet the economic consequences of its political aspirations arose from an unrealistic adherence to five major commitments in her defence policy. First, the resolute, and ultimately foolhardy, continuance of its imperial role. Second, the decision to develop an independent nuclear force. Third, the substantial European commitment, entered into for sensible political reasons at the time but maintained long after both its economic and security rationale had become seriously flawed. Fourth, the 'special relationship' with the United States, and finally, the wish to retain self-sufficiency in arms production. Furthermore there is evidence to suggest that defence spending has contributed to Britain's relative economic decline in three ways. It has taken place at the expense of investment. It has used a disproportionate amount of high technology resources. It has seriously harmed the balance of payments situation by diverting resources from export industries while simultaneously requiring a high level of overseas expenditure. According to Chalmers:

> For the period 1958–81 Britain had an accumulated commercial surplus of £16,710 million offset by a government deficit of £30,000 million. Of this £9,790 million was the deficit in military spending overseas.[47]

De Grasse is one of a number of economists who have argued that there is a correlation between high defence spending and low economic growth. Both these features were present in Britain throughout the period from 1945 to 1970 and, as has already been made clear, national decision-making during that period was driven by economic necessity rather than political vision. The economic hypothesis advanced by De Grasse and his colleagues seems, therefore, to be borne out by the British post-war experience. De Grasse, following a study of 13 industrial countries for the period 1960–79, concluded that there was no clear statistical relationship between growth and either wages or civilian government spending. Only military spending was associated with lower economic growth, less investment and slower productivity growth.[48] Similarly a comprehensive study by Smith of data for 14 advanced Western countries during the period 1954–73 found that a change in the military's share of national output tended to be associated with an equal change in the share of investment, in the opposite direction.[49]

Between 1946–47 and 1950–51, British defence spending decreased from 16.1 per cent of GDP to 5.8 per cent. The outbreak of the Korean War in 1950, however, marked a dramatic change in the pattern of defence expenditure. Under pressure from the United States to contribute more to the war effort in Korea, Britain agreed to a substantial increase in defence spending. This resulted in the percentage of GDP spent on defence rising to 7.5 per cent in 1951–52 and to 8.7 per cent in 1952–53. Thereafter there was a slow decrease to 7.1 per cent in 1955-56. This resulted in defence expenditure being higher in 1955–56 than at any time since 1948–49. The Korean War rearmament programme dealt a serious blow to the British economy. Industrial production rose by less than 1 per cent between 1950 and 1952 compared with 30 per cent between 1947 and 1950. Inflation rose from 3 per cent in 1950 to 12 per cent in 1951 and a balance of payments surplus of £300 million in 1950 became a deficit of £400 million in 1951. In 1950 Britain's metal-using industries were responsible for two-thirds of all British exports. The rearmament programme consequently provided Britain's competitors in this area, namely West Germany, Japan, Switzerland, Sweden and Italy, with a significant and most timely advantage. Japanese exports grew by 61 per cent in a single year while Germany's exports of steel, heavy capital goods and machine tools quadrupled between 1950 and 1953. Perhaps the best illustration of the severity of the level of Labour's commitment to defence expenditure was Churchill's remark on his return to office in 1952 that they 'were utterly beyond our economic capacity to bear'.[50] Throughout the period 1956–57 to 1963–64 defence expenditure dropped from 7.2 per cent of GDP to 5.7 per cent. Throughout this period, therefore, Britain's defence expenditure remained around the level of 1948–49 (6.3 per cent), or more than twice the level of expenditure devoted to defence in the 1930s, and well ahead of that of Britain's European allies. That situation was all the more remarkable as the underlying theme of the 1957 White Paper had been the achievement of substantial cuts in defence spending. The 1957 White Paper was quite explicit about the consequences of excessive expenditure on defence:

> Over the last five years, defence has on an average absorbed 10 per cent of Britain's gross national product. Some 7 per cent of the working population are either in the services or support them. One-eighth of the output of the metal producing industries, upon which the export trade so largely depends, is devoted to defence . . . In addition the retention of such large forces abroad gives rise to heavy charges which place a severe strain upon the balance of payments . . . it is impossible to escape the conclusion that Britain has been bearing a disproportionately large share of the total burden of Western defence . . . It can safely be assumed that the new plan . . . will release skilled men including badly needed scientists and engineers, for employment in civilian industry. Both exports and capital investment will gain.[51]

The White Paper claimed that £200 million would be saved on the planned 1957–58 defence budget and that there would be further savings in subsequent years. In the event the 1957–58 budget was only £95 million less than the previous year and subsequent decreases were considerably smaller. There were two significant economic factors that weighed against the aims of the White Paper. As a consequence of Britain's wish to retain self-sufficiency in arms production it was forced to commit increasing sums of money to research and development. These costs grew from £69 million in 1949–50 (9.3 per cent of defence spending) to £204 million in 1956–57 (13.3 per cent of defence spending). By the latter period 40 per cent of all professionally qualified scientists and engineers in research and development were working on defence projects. Indeed in the period 1963–65, 34.5 per cent of the total sum spent on both private and public research and development was devoted to defence, a proportion surpassed only by the United States. This money was being spent in an area that had demonstrated a remarkable lack of success. It has been estimated that between 1945 and 1956 no less than 166 civil and military aircraft projects were started, 142 of these were discontinued, 16 partly succeeded while only eight were fully viable. The cost of these programmes was in the region of £1,000 million.[52] The other important factor was costs attributable to overseas commitments. The 1957 White Paper, as has already been stated, made no attempt to rationalise Britain's overseas commitments. Indeed, it was singularly unsuccessful in achieving its economic aims. Between the Sandys review and the last year of the Conservative administration (1963–64) real defence spending rose by almost 8 per cent and as a proportion of national income fell only 0.6 per cent. The crisis came in late 1964 when the balance of payments forecast was a deficit of £800 million, the largest ever in peacetime. While major causes were the high wage settlements of the Macmillan period and the large-scale purchase of foreign goods, overseas defence commitments were also an important factor. Chalmers estimated that, between 1958 and 1964, net military spending overseas increased by 90 per cent and that it accounted for one-third of the 1964 deficit.[53] Throughout this period Britain maintained bases in Hong Kong, Singapore, Aden and Cyprus in addition to forces stationed permanently in West Germany. Bartlett pointed out that, although the accounting systems used by the Services did not enable the costs of overseas bases to be accurately calculated, it was thought in 1964 that Singapore was costing about £70 million per year. Similarly 'Confrontation' in Malaysia was estimated to have cost £260 million per annum over the period 1963–66 of which nearly £100 million was attributable to foreign exchange costs.[54] Defence Minister Healey, speaking in the House of Commons in 1970, estimated that about one quarter of the 1964–65 estimates were devoted to the presence east of Suez.[55] Chichester and Wilkinson recorded similar reservations about the costs of British forces in West Germany:

> By 1965 the maintenance of some 62,000 uniformed personnel accompanied by an almost equal number of dependants and supported by some 35,000 civilians was costing the country £180 million per annum of which £85 million represented a heavy drain on our foreign exchange.[56]

Labour's 1965 National Plan was as unequivocal about the source of the problem as the Sandys White Paper had been eight years earlier: 'In 1964–65 £252 million of the defence provision was direct overseas expenditure; this is more than we can afford.'[57] Sadly, Wilson and Healey were no more inclined to tackle the root cause of the problem than Macmillan and Sandys had been. Not surprisingly, however, the problem did not go away.

The second half of the 1960s saw a steady, if unspectacular, decrease in defence spending from 5.6 per cent of GDP in 1964–65 to 4.6 per cent of GDP in 1969–70. Despite the fact that, by 1970, this represented a decrease of 1.7 per cent over the previous decade it made no difference to Britain's position in relation to its European competitors. The equivalent GDP expenditure figures for France and West Germany in 1970 were 4.2 per cent and 3.3 per cent respectively. While Labour had failed to seize the economic initiative in 1964, deepening economic deficits were soon to force a reconsideration of commitments. Chalmers estimated that by 1967 it was costing £257 million to keep 160,000 men overseas – as much, after allowing for inflation, as the £190 million that had been needed for 320,000 men 10 years earlier.[58] Consequently the period between 1965 and 1968 was one of more or less continuous review of defence commitments, driven essentially by economic weakness. The first phase was marked by the cancellation of a number of indigenous aircraft projects in favour of cheaper purchases from the United States. Subsequently the February 1966 Defence Review announced the eventual demise of the aircraft carrier while the sterling crisis later that year led to the announcement of the decision to withdraw from east of Suez. Finally the sterling devaluation of November 1967 influenced the decision to accelerate that withdrawal and, as a direct consequence, to the cancellation of the order for F-111 aircraft from the United States. The withdrawal from east of Suez marked a turning point, albeit a belated one. It achieved substantial savings in defence costs with 1969–70 spending £200 million below the original target of £2,000 million. Nevertheless the 1968 review, while undoubtedly successful in curbing increases, failed to make any significant cuts:

> The 1968 Defence White Paper had estimated that defence spending would fall to £2,014 million at 1968 prices (about £1,700 million at 1964–65 prices) by 1972–73. But despite these cuts, defence spending in 1972–73 was as high in real terms as in 1964–65.[59]

While there is no lack of information on Britain's post-war defence spending there is a dearth of specific information about the costs of the strategic deterrent prior to the deployment of Polaris. There are probably three main reasons for this.

First the early nuclear weapons programmes were shrouded in secrecy. Initially the costs of the programme were, for presentational reasons, absorbed under other headings in the defence vote. Such habits are difficult to eradicate and, not surprisingly, when such costs are subsequently disclosed there is always doubt about their validity.

The second issue centres on the allocation of research and development costs. In the 1950s it would have been difficult, and perhaps not very meaningful, to separate the very considerable expenditure on aircraft development programmes between nuclear and conventional projects.

The third constraint is similar in nature. While the V-bombers were clearly developed as nuclear-weapons carriers they were also capable of fulfilling conventional roles, and increasingly did so with the passage of time. Furthermore the fighter aircraft whose primary role was to defend V-bomber bases from attack clearly had a significant secondary role. Despite these difficulties both Bartlett and Chalmers agreed that, at the peak of the V-bomber project, the costs amounted to between 10 per cent and 20 per cent of defence expenditure, depending on whether the costs of fighters and missiles assigned to defend the force's bases were included.[60] Whatever the exact figures, there is no doubt that the costs of developing and deploying an independent deterrent were considerable. Furthermore, it can be argued that, because Britain viewed the deployment of its strategic nuclear deterrent as an incremental enhancement to its defence capabilities, rather than as an opportunity to conduct a fundamental reappraisal of its defence requirements, the deterrent simply reinforced Britain's perception of herself as a global power. This, in turn, encouraged Britain, and also made it easier for the United States to persuade it, to retain those commitments that were eroding its economic strength. Thus the costs of the deterrent went considerably beyond those of the system's materiel and manpower requirements.

The decision to procure Polaris, on the other hand, reduced the cost of maintaining a nuclear force, and provided the opportunity for Britain to remain a strategic nuclear power – something which, otherwise, would have been beyond its economic reach. There are two reasons for the relative cost-effectiveness of Polaris. First the political climate in which the agreement was reached enabled Macmillan to deal direct with Kennedy in circumstances where speed was important. All the anecdotal evidence suggests that Macmillan concluded an excellent economic deal in December 1962. On a more practical level, Britain was able to purchase Polaris on the basis that the research and development costs had already been met. This was a marked improvement on the earlier situation. Freedman has shown that while the strategic nuclear forces absorbed some 18.6 per cent of defence expenditure in the mid-1960s this had fallen to 8.8 per cent by 1966–67 and that the main reason for this reduction was the declining costs of the V-bomber force. Furthermore the proportion of the defence budget spent on nuclear weapons reduced steadily from 8.0 per cent in 1967–68 to 2.6 per cent in 1972–73.[61]

The evidence adduced throughout this examination of the economic perspective indicates two persistent parallel outcomes. First, all major changes in British defence policy were driven by economic constraints rather than political vision.[62] Second, Britain repeatedly spent more on defence than its continental allies which, of course, were also Britain's main economic competitors. These are powerful and consistent indicators that, in the first three post-war decades, Britain spent more on defence than it could afford, given its domestic political objectives. To spend more than you can afford is not necessarily a bad political decision, *per se*. The acceptability of such decisions depends upon their perceived legitimacy. Thus before making judgements on the validity of Britain's defence expenditure it is necessary to view these decisions in their appropriate political context. It is also important to realise that the true cost of defence spending is not simply the cost of military materiel and manpower, but rather the foregone opportunity to divert these resources to other, more productive areas. Thus the appropriate allocation of resources is the key issue at the heart of a successful defence policy. Too little investment can signal weakness to the international community while too much investment can result in unacceptable economic difficulties at home.[63]

In the first post-war decade Britain's defence spending remained high. At that time the international situation was tense. Consequently defence policy retained a prominent place within the nation's priorities. The impact of 'the nuclear age' indicated a need for substantial standing forces, rather than the earlier concept of a mobilisation base. Furthermore, Britain's wish to possess the new 'capital' weapon was a decision that was perceived as being politically legitimate. The advent of the Korean War, despite its severe economic consequences, was seen to justify Britain's defence priorities. In sum, Britain's level of expenditure on defence was perceived as being justifiable, and the increasing amount of the budget being devoted to the independent nuclear deterrent was perceived as being legitimate. Notwithstanding the general consensus, there were some in positions of influence, and with access to the best sources of information, who doubted the wisdom of the level of expenditure necessary to acquire strategic nuclear weapons from the outset. In 1958 Thorneycroft, who had recently resigned as Chancellor of the Exchequer, argued that expenditure on nuclear weapons was:

> a questionable policy. . . our prestige will be rated not by the bombs we make nor by the money we can spend but by the contribution we make to western solvency and economic strength.[64]

Perceptions changed in the decade following Suez. Suez demonstrated Britain's economic, political and military weakness, both at home and abroad. While the underlying tenet of the Sandys White Paper was the need to limit defence expenditure, Britain sought to achieve this through strategic rhetoric rather than via a pragmatic re-appraisal of its global interests. The international scene remained turbulent until the early 1960s, although it was less critical than during the preceding 10 years. The V-bomber force became operational towards the beginning of the decade and was already obsolete by the mid-1960s. At home Britain was becoming increasingly aware of its relative economic decline. Greenwood, describing the missed opportunities of the period, described 1955 as: 'the year when helmsmanship might have given away to navigation'.[65] The opportunity, however, was lost. In the second post-war decade, therefore, the level of expenditure on defence remained relatively high and its legitimacy was increasingly questioned. During this period it became abundantly clear that Britain's economic stature would never return to its pre-war position:

> In the late 1950s and early 1960s, the economy was the object of increasing concern. Between 1951 and 1960 British industrial production grew by 32 per cent while that of Western Europe grew by 86 per cent. By the early 1960s France and Germany had both overtaken the UK in national income per head for the first time in more than a century.[66]

Simultaneously both the credibility of the deterrent and the 'threat' seemed to be reducing. Inevitably this resulted in a questioning of defence expenditure and, as part of that process, the proportion of the budget spent on the deterrent was subject to increasing scrutiny. In the event Healey had little difficulty in persuading the government that, in economic terms, Polaris was a good deal, although he did cancel the option to build the fifth boat. He was also able to argue that the cancellation costs for the whole programme would be high, while the long-term expenditure on the deterrent was set to fall steadily. Despite this assessment, the longer term prognosis was problematic. In late 1964 the strategic inheritance of the new Labour government was described by *The Times* as:

> A prosperous island still detached from Continental Europe, preserved from the necessity of too much thought by the nuclear diplomacy of the United States, scattering its armed forces by handfuls to fight in the last remaining and least rewarding fragments of a once incomparable Empire.[67]

The third post-war decade marked fundamental change. Economic weakness led to economic crisis and, consequently, despite its avowed declarations and deepest wishes, the Wilson government decided to withdraw from east of Suez, apparently concluding that this was the least controversial of the political options. Despite its unwillingness to come to terms with reality, the Wilson government was not unaware of the prevailing situation. Labour's National Plan of 1965 argued that:

> If we endeavour to support too large a defence effort, it will create economic weakness which will, in the long run, frustrate our external policy as a whole no less than our internal policy.[68]

By the late 1960s economic reality had forced Britain to renounce its extra-NATO imperial role. The military threat to NATO was simultaneously decreasing while Britain was deploying a credible, and relatively cost effective, strategic nuclear deterrent; albeit one whose independence was conditional. By the mid-1970s Britain's military capability was essentially NATO orientated. And despite the fact that Britain's aspirations, in terms of political influence, knew no such boundaries, fulfilling NATO commitments was the primary, if not the sole justification, for defence expenditure. The exception was the strategic deterrent together with a limited residual out-of-area role. By that time, however, the Polaris boats were operational and proving to be relatively cheap to maintain. The potential costs of Chevaline were not yet public knowledge and the long-term future of the deterrent was not an issue as the Labour Government of the period had declared that Polaris would not be replaced. In the mid-1970s economic considerations were not a critical issue in relation to the utility of the deterrent.

Summary

It is timely, now, to summarise Britain's decision to deploy an independent strategic nuclear deterrent. It has been argued here that, certainly until the late 1950s, Britain was justified in seeking its own nuclear deterrent to protect its vital national interests. There were three key factors that contributed to this assessment. First, the Soviet Union was perceived to be a state whose dubious geopolitical intentions were rendered more threatening by its behaviour within its sphere of influence in Eastern Europe, its bellicose rhetoric in respect of matters outwith its sphere of influence and the burgeoning strength of its conventional and nuclear military power. Second, Britain was understandably dubious about the United States' continuing willingness to guarantee the security of Western Europe. The third factor was the impact of contemporary history. Britain had emerged from the Second World War as one of 'the Big Three' and its international prestige had probably never been higher. The events of the first half of the twentieth century had shown the British people the wisdom of the age-old adage of *si vis pacem, para bellum*. The continued possession of capital weapons was a direct material consequence of the acceptance of that concept. The influence of historical continuity was profound.

The position, however, became less clear-cut in the 1960s. Britain, albeit reluctantly and slowly, increasingly came to understand that it could not compete with the superpowers in economic terms. The geopolitical consequence of this position was the realisation that Britain's strategic political objectives would no longer be achievable unless they were compatible with those of the United States. As this awareness grew it became increasingly clear that an interdependent deterrent, rather than an independent one, would suffice. Simultaneously the *raison d'être* for Britain's deterrent moved from a notion of military power to a concept of political influence. The question, however, of whether the procurement and deployment of a strategic deterrent could be justified on the basis of its capacity for political influence cannot be answered in a practical sense in this period. The decision to procure Polaris had been made before Britain's reduced status was understood and the deterrent would be all but operational before Britain's diminishing role as a world power would be openly acknowledged. Nevertheless it was clear that the question was likely to have increasing relevance in the future.

If domestic economic developments were to limit the independence of Britain's deterrent in the 1960s, events in the international arena were simultaneously to curtail its potential utility. The United States' commitment to Europe was, by then, an established reality and that commitment embraced the notion of the 'nuclear umbrella'. The onset of nuclear parity between the superpowers had created a situation in which strategic arms limitation talks were certainly worth exploring. The United States was to become increasingly embroiled in Vietnam while events in China, including the acquisition of nuclear weapons by that state, were matters of increasing concern for the Soviet Union. Conversely the West had tacitly acknowledged the *status quo* in Eastern Europe and the prospects for conflict in Europe appeared to have receded steadily over the decade. Thus Britain's first viable deterrent became operational at a time when tension between East and West seemed to be lower that at any stage since 1945.

The effectiveness of the operational capacity of Britain's deterrent has to be assessed against an assumption of the damage criteria necessary to achieve 'success', notwithstanding the conclusion reached above that the government failed to apply such rigour in its own considerations. The best available criteria, therefore, are those contained in Kemp's assessment that the ability to destroy either the top 10 cities in the Soviet Union, including Moscow, or the top 10 cities, excluding Moscow, would suffice. Either option would put at risk some 15 to 21 million people and between 15 and 25 per cent of the Soviet Union's industrial capacity. Kemp's assessment is considerably lower than the Air Ministry's view, in the late 1950s, that Britain would need to be able to destroy 30 to 40 major centres of industry and administration in the Soviet Union. Kemp, however, writing in the mid-1970s, was able to benefit from more sophisticated approaches to this issue. Using these criteria it seems reasonable to conclude that, from the late 1950s to the early 1960s, the V-bomber force constituted a viable deterrent and that, in 1970, with the deployment of the fourth Polaris boat, Britain regained a credible deterrent. As has already been made clear, Britain obtained Polaris, which was to prove to be an ideal second strike system, for reasons of political expediency rather than as a consequence of rational decision making. Nevertheless it is salutary to realise that the reasons for the procurement of Britain's second generation of nuclear weapons may have had at least as much to do with Macmillan's short-term political survival as the nation's long-term security.

The economic analysis indicates that expenditure on the deterrent in the 1950s and early 1960s was relatively high, probably between 10 and 20 per cent of defence expenditure, depending on the economic definition of nuclear forces. Significantly defence expenditure as a whole during this period was high, only dropping to 5.7 per cent of GDP in 1963–64. This compared unfavourably with our European allies and competitors. It is not possible here to make any objective assessment of the lost opportunity costs of these policies. Nevertheless, Britain's comparatively sluggish economic development, during a period of sustained and significant growth throughout Western Europe, suggests that relatively high defence expenditure was one of a number of factors that contributed to Britain's poor comparative performance. All the indicators suggest that up until the mid-1960s Britain was spending more on defence than it could sensibly afford, given the conflicting requirements of its domestic policies. From the mid-1960s onwards that position was less critical, although it remained a matter of concern to successive governments. The proportion of the defence budget spent on Polaris reduced from 8 per cent in the late 1960s to under 3 per cent in the early 1970s. In the same period total defence spending remained below 5 per cent of GDP. It is, therefore, reasonable to conclude that Polaris was a relatively cost-effective deterrent and that the level of expenditure envisaged at the time the decision was made was justifiable.

The overall assessment is, of necessity, ambivalent. Britain's decision to procure an independent strategic nuclear deterrent in the 1950s could be justified in political and military terms. Nevertheless the reality was that, although Britain had made remarkable progress in developing nuclear weapons and the V-bomber force, it lacked both the technological ability and the economic base to develop appropriate systems to replace the manned aircraft. Conversely, by the time the more economical and militarily more credible Polaris force was operational, the strategic political threat had diminished, despite the fact that the Soviet Union's operational capability was still growing. Furthermore Polaris was an interdependent deterrent rather than an independent one. That this constraint was of no practical political or operational significance was due entirely to the convergence of Anglo–American strategic political goals – a convergence that, from Britain's perspective, despite its uncontroversial convenience was, at its irreducible minimum, an acknowledgement of *Realpolitik*. Interdependence was the price of remaining a nuclear power and the British government and people, albeit tacitly, considered that the price was worth paying.

NOTES

1. Groom A. J. R., 'The British Deterrent' in Baylis J. (ed.), *British Defence Policy in a Changing World* (London: Croom Helm, 1977) p. 120.
2. See Northedge F. S., *Descent from Power: British Foreign Policy 1945–73* (London: Allen and Unwin, 1974) p .271.
3. Cmd 6743, *Statement Relating to Defence* (London: HMSO, 1946).
4. See Northedge F. S., p. 276.
5. DEFE 5/6 COS 263 (47), 11 December 1947. Quoted in Navias M. S., *Nuclear Weapons and British Strategic Planning 1955–58* (Oxford: Clarendon Press, 1991) p. 17.
6. See Northedge F. S., p. 277.
7. The details of this Agreement were embodied in Article VI, Paris Agreements, 23 October 1954 and are published in *NATO Facts and Figures* (Brussels: NATO Headquarters, 1971) Appendix 10.
8. See Navias M. S., p. 39.
9. Ibid, p. 38.
10. Quoted in Gowing M., *Britain and Atomic Energy 1939–45* (London: Macmillan, 1964) p. 395.
11. Navias M. S., p. 14.
12. See Clark I. and Wheeler N. J., *The British Origins of Nuclear Strategy 1945–1955* (Oxford: Oxford University Press, 1989).
13. Julian Amery, House of Commons, Vol. 549, Cols 1091–2, 28 February 1956.
14. CAB 128/27 CC48 (54) 2, 8 July 1954. Quoted in Navias M. S., p. 22.
15. Slessor J., 'British Defence Policy', *Foreign Affairs*, 35, No. 4 (1957) p. 551. Similar views have been expressed by Groom A. J. R., *British Thinking About Nuclear Weapons* (London: Frances Pinter, 1974) p. 207; Darby P., *British Defence Policy East of Suez 1947–68* (London: Oxford University Press, 1973) p. 95 and Martin L., 'The Market for Strategic Ideas in Britain: The Sandys Era', *American Political Science Review*, 56, No. 1 (1962) p. 27.
16. Navias M. S., p. 248. See also Wheeler N. J., *The Roles Played by the British Chiefs of Staff Committee in the Development of British Nuclear Weapons Planning and Policy Making 1945–55*, Ph.D.Thesis, Department of Politics, University of Southampton, 1988.
17. Cmnd 124, *Defence: Outline of Future Policy* (London: HMSO, 1957) paragraphs 6 and 14.
18. Clark I. and Wheeler N. J., p. 16.
19. Navias M. S., p. 248.
20. FO 371/132330, Steering Committee, Planning Paper on Interdependence, 27 January 1958. Quoted in Navias M. S., p. 247.
21. CAB 130/20, D (58) 69, 11 November 1958. Quoted in Navias M. S., p. 247.
22. Ibid, p. 252.
23. For a more comprehensive introduction to nuclear weapons technology see Naughton J., Penrose O., Greene O. and Dyer G., *Nuclear Weapons Technology*, Block II, Unit 5 of Open University Course U235, *Nuclear Weapons: Inquiry Analysis and Debate* (Milton Keynes: The Open University Press, 1986). For a much more detailed analysis see Smart I., *Advanced Strategic Missiles: A Short Guide*, Adelphi Papers, No 63 (London: The Institute for Strategic Studies, 1969). Also Kemp G., *Nuclear Forces for Medium Powers: Part 1: Targets and Weapons Systems*, Adelphi Papers, No 106 (London: The Institute for Strategic Studies, 1974).
24. See Freedman L., *British Nuclear Targeting*, in Ball D. and Richelson J. (eds), *Strategic Nuclear Targeting* (Ithaca and London: Cornell University Press, 1986) p. 110.
25. See Gowing M., *Independence and Deterrence: Britain and Atomic Energy 1945–1952, Vol. 1 Policy Making* (London: Macmillan, 1974) pp. 169, 175 and 188–9.
26. See Beaton L., *Would Labour Give Up The Bomb*, Sunday Telegraph pamphlet, 1964 and Gallacher J., *Nuclear Stocktaking: A Count of Britain's Warheads*, Bailrigg Paper on International Security, No5, University of Lancaster (1982).
27. Navias M. S., p. 102.
28. CAB 129/71, C 54 (329), 3 November 1954. Quoted in Navias M. S., p. 105.
29. The V-bomber force capability source is DEFE 5/69, COS (56) 269, 11 July 1956. Quoted in Navias M. S., p. 105.
30. For a detailed account of the competing political, military and budgetary criteria that determined the size of the V-bomber.force see Navias M. S., pp. 100–19.
31. Cmd 9391, *Statement on Defence* (London: HMSO, 1955) paragraph 74.
32. House of Commons, Vol. 549, Col. 1226, 29 February 1956.

33. For further information on Blue Streak see Navias M. S., pp. 119–24. Also Bartlett C. J., pp. 109, 134, 148, 153–6 and 174 and Groom A. J. R., pp. 525–33.
34. For further information on Blue Steel see Navias M. S., pp. 168–9. Bartlett C. J., p.180. Groom A. J. R., pp. 521–4 and p. 532.
35. See Groom A. J. R., pp. 524–5 and Bartlett C. J., pp. 151–2.
36. There are many general references to the growing vulnerability of the V-bombers to the Soviet Union's air defences with some estimates giving a penetrative capacity of only three per cent. See McInnes C., *Trident: The Only Option?* (London: Brasseys, 1986) p.2; Pierre A. J., p. 151 and Groom A. J. R., p. 523.
37. For an account of the Labour government's decision to continue the Polaris procurement programme see Freedman L., *Britain and Nuclear Weapons* (London: Macmillan, 1980) pp. 31–40.
38. See Ball D. and Richelson J. (eds), p. 118.
39. For a useful summary of the vicissitudes and complexities of the Polaris Inprovement Programme (Chevaline) see McInnes C., pp. 4–10.
40. See Navias M. S., p. 211.
41. Ibid, p. 212.
42. CAB 131/20 D(58)69, 17 November 1958. Quoted in ibid., p. 213.
43. See Kemp G. and Smart I.
44. Kemp G., ibid., Part 1, p. 27.
45. For a more detailed exposition of the 'Moscow criterion' see Freedman L., pp. 47, 54 and 60; Smart I., 'Beyond Polaris', *International Affairs*, Vol. 53, No. 4 (October 1977) p. 563; Pym F., *Britain's Strategic Nuclear Force: The Choice of a System to Succeed Polaris*, Defence Open Government Document 80/23, Ministry of Defence, July 1980 and Kemp G., Part I, pp. 12–13.
46. See Freedman L., pp. 41–51.
47. Chalmers M., *Defence and the Economy* (Stoke-on-Trent: Information Education Ltd, 1991) p. 210.
48. See De Grasse R. Jnr., *The Cost and Consequences of Reagan's Military Build-Up* (New York: Council on Economic Priorities, 1982). Quoted in Chalmers M., p. 193.
49. See Smith R., 'Military Expenditure and Investment in OECD Countries 1954–73', *Journal of Comparative Economics*, Vol. 4.1 (1980). Quoted in Chalmers M., p. 193.
50. Quoted in Bartlett C. J., p. 79.
51. Cmnd 124, p. 10.
52. See Bartlett C. J., pp. 133–4.
53. See Chalmers M., p. 104.
54. See Bartlett C. J., p. 186 and p. 190 and Chalmers M., p. 220.
55. See Bartlett C. J., Note 19 to Chapter 6, p. 281.
56. Chichester M. and Wilkinson J., *The Uncertain Ally: British Defence Policy 1960–1990* (Aldershot: Gower, 1982) p. 4.
57. Cmnd 2724, *The National Plan* (London: HMSO, 1965) p. 19.
58. See Chalmers M., p. 96.
59. Chalmers M., p. 117.
60. See ibid., p. 26 and p. 72. Chalmers records that, in the early 1950s, the Labour government anticipated spending some £600 million on the V-bomber force over a period of 15 years while in relation to 1960 Bartlett describes the V-bomber force as a £500 million asset. Bartlett C. J., p. 155.
61. The figures are derived from Freedman L., *Britain and Nuclear Weapons* (London: Macmillan, 1980) Appendix 3, p. 144.
62. Greenwood, in an assessment of Britain's defence priorities in this period, suggests that it was not until the third post-war decade that Britain began to develop a coherent set of strategic priorities for a defence posture commensurate with its economic capacity. See Greenwood D., 'Defence and National Priorities since 1945', in Baylis J. (ed.), '*British Defence Policy in a Changing World*' (London: Croom Helm, 1977) p. 184.
63. The new Conservative government made the balance between civil investment and defence expenditure explicit in the context of increased defence spending at the time of the Korean War. 'Any further substantial diversion . . . from civil to military production would gravely impair our economic foundations and, with them, our ability to continue with the . . . programme.' Quoted by Snyder W. P., *The Politics of British Defence Policy 1945–62* (Columbus, OH: Ohio State University Press, 1964) pp. 195–6.
64. Quoted in Bartlett C. J., p. 149.

65. Baylis J. (ed.), p. 188.
66. Chalmers M., p. 101.
67. *The Times*, 30 September 1964. Quoted in Chichester M. and Wilkinson J., p. 8.
68. Cmnd 2724.

CHAPTER FOUR

The Decision to
Replace Polaris

Introduction

> The decision to maintain or discontinue an independent
> strategic nuclear deterrent will have a political significance out
> of all proportion to the military power involved.[1]

CHAPTER 3 ASSESSED the rationale behind Britain's decision to procure and deploy the four-boat Polaris fleet and, in so doing, covered the period from the mid-1950s to the early 1970s. This chapter assesses the decision to procure and deploy a successor system to Polaris and covers the period from the early 1970s to the mid-1990s. It examines the strategic political goals, the operational military requirements and the economic constraints, and seeks to answer the seven questions posed below:

The strategic political perspective

1 Did Britain have a continuing need for an independent strategic nuclear deterrent to protect its vital national interests?
2 Could the decision to procure and deploy a successor to Polaris be justified in terms of its strategic political influence rather than the specific parameters of defence?

The operational military perspective

3 Was there a threat, or a potential threat, that could best, or only, be deterred by a strategic nuclear capability and, if there was, what was the minimum requirement for such a deterrent force?
4 Did Britain procure the right delivery system to meet the perceived threat?

The economic perspective

5 Was the successor system cost-effective?

6 What was the impact of expenditure on the deterrent in relation to total defence expenditure?

7 Was Britain's level of expenditure on defence justifiable?

The Strategic Political Perspective

Similar questions to those posed above were addressed by Garnett in *The Defence Debate* as early as 1965. A brief consideration of the issues that he felt were salient, at that time, to the utility of the British strategic nuclear deterrent will help to set the scene for the assessment that follows.[2] Garnett considered that there were three fundamental questions that had to be answered:

> First will the proposed policy succeed in achieving the task for which it is intended? Second is the proposed policy technically, economically and politically feasible? Third, is the task it performs important enough to warrant the kind of expenditure necessary to implement the policy?[3]

In considering the first of these questions Garnett suggested a number of possible functions of the deterrent.

First, *to bolster Britain's declining image as a great power*. The underlying assumption here was that nuclear power is the ultimate symbol of true sovereignty. It can, however, be argued that in the thermonuclear age the concept of the truly independent state is obsolete. Nevertheless, within the international community perceptions of sovereignty are essentially value judgements and the impact of nuclear status on these considerations is probably more significant than is justified. There is, however, an alternative view that argues that possession of nuclear weapons diminishes British standing by draining its financial resources. It would consequently gain more international esteem from the renunciation of nuclear weapons.[4]

Second, *to increase Britain's bargaining power in negotiations for nuclear test agreements and disarmament*. The hypothesis here was that the views of nuclear powers are disproportionately influential at international conferences. Furthermore, as nuclear powers have something to give up they can expect to receive some form of compensation if they agree to renounce some of their nuclear capacity.

Third, *to increase Britain's influence within NATO and, in particular, with the United States*. This argument also has strengths and weaknesses. It is generally accepted that Britain's day-to-day influence within NATO is disproportionate, largely for historical reasons. The handling of the Cuban crisis, however, and the events that led to the Kennedy–Macmillan meeting at Nassau, indicate the limitations on British influence in a crisis. Anglo–French relations have, however, been hampered by the possession of nuclear weapons and this influenced the question of Britain's entry into the European Community. Anglo-American relations have also been strained by the nuclear issue as McNamara made clear in his Ann Arbor speech: 'limited nuclear capabilities, operating independently, are dangerous, expensive, prone to obsolescence, and lacking in credibility as a deterrent.'[5] Furthermore it can be argued that the value of the British deterrent to the United States is diminished, if not negated, by the inflexibility of Britain's weapon system and its anti-city targeting policy. Proliferation of sources complicates both planning and control. It is also pertinent to note that Garnett expressed the view that Britain's influence on both the United States and NATO would be enhanced more by a greater conventional capability, rather than a nuclear capability, on the basis that, at that time, there was a greater need for increased conventional strength. In making that assertion Garnett was accepting the premise that the more you contribute to the cause of allies the greater is your potential to influence their policies.

The fourth task enunciated by Garnett was *to provide increased military power to support political policies outside the NATO area*. This was probably an untenable position. Britain would be likely to incur massive domestic and international opprobrium if it were to threaten the use of nuclear weapons outside the NATO area.

The fifth task was *to prevent nuclear blackmail by the Soviet Union*. Clearly the validity of that option centred on the combined political and military credibility of Britain's deterrent which, in turn, hinged on the significance of the issue at stake. Garnett provides two illustrations. In the first scenario the Soviet Union threatens nuclear blackmail to stop Britain pursuing an independent foreign policy that is against the Soviet Union's interests. The supposition is that Britain is able to call the Soviet Union's bluff because of Britain's independent ability to retaliate. The theory may be plausible but it seems unlikely that a British government would pursue such a high-risk strategy. In the second scenario the Soviet Union threatens to use nuclear weapons against Britain to provoke its surrender. The supposition is that Britain can resist because of the power of its deterrent. Again this theory may be plausible but, in practical terms, it could also be a prescription for assured destruction. Despite these objections both situations could appear credible to a potential aggressor; indeed they probably would appear credible to a nuclear state that possessed neither the territorial mass, nor the nuclear arsenal, of the Soviet Union. The critical issue, however, is whether Britain can be relied on to act rationally. The international community probably saw little rationality in Britain's decision to go to war in 1914 and in 1939 or over the Falklands.

The final task suggested by Garnett was to provide Britain with a guarantee that if war were to break out in Europe the United States would be involved. This is the concept of the small, but significant, British deterrent acting as the 'trigger' for United States' strategic participation. This notion is flawed by the very assumption on which it is based. Why should Britain's response to an attack on European NATO, excluding Britain, be any more credible than the concept of a United States response to an attack by the Soviet Union in Europe? Garnett sums up his appraisal of the possible tasks of a British deterrent by concluding that:

> it may be said that although nuclear power may confer some practical advantages on the state controlling it, these advantages are by no means as numerous or as certain or as valuable as is sometimes suggested.[6]

Nevertheless he shies away from renunciation on two counts:

> The statesman should not judge the usefulness of the British deterrent solely on the advantages on which it confers on Britain today, but should note the possibility of adverse changes in the international situation, and should attempt to assess the value of the British deterrent in the light of those possible changes.[7]

Significantly, but not very scientifically, Garnett backs Hedly Bull's assertion that: 'no longer to have any say in the disposal of nuclear power is to slip away from the mainstream of events.'[8]

Chapter 3 has shown that Britain's actions and aspirations in the first post-war decade were those of a world power. Furthermore Britain's behaviour was seen to be as rational by the international community as it was at home. By the mid-1970s Britain's position was very different. Quantitatively, at least, its armed forces were of a different order, and they were organised and deployed on a wholly different basis. The future of its strategic deterrent, whose existence was due more to American goodwill than domestic capacity, was in doubt. In economic terms it was no longer a European leader and, while its international stature remained disproportionate to its domestic power base, its ambit was, and would clearly continue to be, increasingly Eurocentric. Greenwood, in a review of Britain's defence experience over the 20 years up to the mid-1970s, indicated that there were two key aspects of continuity and two salient aspects of change that marked that period.[9] He suggested that these could be important indicators for assessing the shape and direction of future security dispositions. The two areas of continuity were Britain's commitment to the strategic nuclear deterrent and its substantial ground and air force contribution to NATO's Central European Command as well as maritime forces to the North East Atlantic Command. The aspects of change were the progressive disengagement from post-imperial and extra-European commitments, ending in all but total withdrawal and, ultimately, to a contraction not only into, but also within, the NATO area. These four indicators clearly illustrate the fundamental change in Britain's defence priorities between the mid-1950s and the mid-1970s and set the domestic realities of the strategic scene.

It is timely now to assess Britain's position *vis à vis* the international community in the decade leading up to the announcement of the replacement decision. While there is no doubt that Britain's position had changed, it is equally clear that there had also been substantial changes within the international arena. Some of these developments had potential for increased stability and security while others had potential for the opposite.

The decade began with the move towards *Ostpolitik* following the election of Brandt as West German Chancellor in October 1969. While this departure had little immediate impact on superpower relations, it marked the beginning of a growing pan-European dimension in security policy whose impact, 20 years later, was to be profound. Rather more tangibly, although ultimately less significant, the 1970s saw a proliferation in arms limitation agreements.[10] In 1971 the Sea Bed Arms Control Treaty was concluded as was an agreement between the United States and the Soviet Union on measures to reduce the risk of nuclear war. The following year saw the SALT I ABM Treaty, the SALT I Interim Agreement to freeze the number of ICBMs and SLBMs at current levels for five years, and the establishment of the US–USSR Standing Consultative Committee to discuss apparent violations of the SALT I treaties. In 1973 the Geneva Conference on Security and Co-operation in Europe (CSCE) opened in Helsinki and was concluded in the 'Final Act' on 1 August 1975. The Threshold Test Ban Treaty limiting underground tests to 15 kilotons was concluded in 1974 and, although it was not ratified, its conditions were observed. The 1976 Treaty on Underground Nuclear Explosions for Peaceful Purposes also remained unratified although the agreed limits were observed. On 1 July 1978, at the first United Nations special session on disarmament, all governments agreed, in principle, to abolish weapons of mass destruction and to move to general and complete disarmament. The decade ended with the signing of the SALT II Agreement which put ceilings on strategic weapons. Notwithstanding these developments, the fact remained that both superpowers continued to possess massive nuclear arsenals. Against that background the motivation for these developments probably had more to do with a need to reduce expenditure than a semi-altruistic wish to improve stability.

There were contrary developments. In 1970 the first United States MIRVed ICBMs became operational. Britain's Chevaline programme started in 1973. The Soviet Union first tested MIRV warheads in 1972 and they became operational in 1975. In 1974 the Schlesinger doctrine, embracing the use of nuclear weapons for limited war, or counterforce purposes, was announced. In the same year India conducted its first nuclear explosion and Greece withdrew from NATO's military structure. The United States withdrew from Vietnam in 1975, acknowledging defeat at the hands of a pro-communist, nationalist movement. In 1978 the Soviet Union deployed SS-20 missiles in Eastern

Europe and the Afghan government was overthrown by a pro-Soviet faction. The period ended in December 1979 with the NATO Council agreeing to deploy GLCMs and Pershing II missiles in Europe in response to the Soviet Union's SS-20s and the Soviet Union's invasion of Afghanistan. While the deployment of the SS-20 missiles in Eastern Europe was a matter of considerable concern at the time the key indicator of the decade was India's move towards nuclear status. The critical question thereafter had to be: 'who will be next?' The answer could reasonably have included Pakistan, Israel and South Africa.[11] If that were only the tip of the nuclear iceberg the prospects for increased global security and stability in the twenty-first century appeared bleak.

While Britain was undoubtedly constrained and influenced by external events it was also actively seeking to influence its own position and relationships. It was eventually successful in joining the European Community in 1972 and its increasingly European perspective concerning international events influenced its perceptions of its own role, and of its allies and potential adversaries. Throughout the 1970s NATO increasingly became the explicit focus of Britain's security policy and consequently the centre of its political and economic activity. By then the Alliance was a symbol of permanence and political stability and it provided a forum that was more pertinent to Britain's future than her former links and interests outwith the NATO area. This brought Britain more directly, and more frequently, into contact with the major European powers. Specifically, it provided increased potential for Britain to play a classical balance of power role between France and Germany and, in this arena, Britain's nuclear status was clearly significant. This potential was enhanced by the return to a more nuclear bias within NATO in the 1970s. European doubts about the validity of the United States nuclear guarantee, which were strong in the 1960s, had subsequently subsided but these gained new significance in the late 1970s as a consequence of the impressive growth in Soviet military capability at that time. In that context the NATO dimension of Britain's 'independent' deterrent was of increased significance as a political lever, both within Europe and between NATO Europe and the United States.[12]

A key difference between Britain's initial decision to procure and deploy nuclear weapons and the decision to replace Polaris was the influence of timing on the latter. Nailor has pointed out that:

> the question of what might supersede the Polaris weapon system as the basis of the British strategic capability became a matter for speculation soon after the submarines, in which it is mounted, were deployed.[13]

If the 1947 decision was bereft of any substantive debate or assessment, the opposite was true in respect of the question of replacement. The date that a decision had to be made about whether to continue or renounce a nuclear capability was reasonably predictable. Furthermore the passage of time had ensured that the strategic, technological and economic issues were all amenable to analysis at a level of detail that was not possible in the early 1950s. A seminal study into the question of replacement was conducted by Chatham House in 1977.[14] Ian Smart, in an article that emanated from this study, concluded that, in his view, the sole strategic purpose that would justify the replacement of the Polaris force was the continuing need to deter the Soviet Union's nuclear threat to British territory, or to territory that Britain had a legal obligation to defend. Furthermore Smart considered that:

> the only credible justification for a British nuclear deterrent must assume that an effective American nuclear guarantee may not, in some plausible circumstance, be available.[15]

Not all assessments were so categorical. Nailor, in a paper published just prior to the announcement of the replacement decision, suggested three reasons why Britain might choose to give up its nuclear deterrent and three reasons why it might wish to retain that capability.[16] Nailor's arguments against replacement were that possession of the deterrent was ethically wrong and that simultaneously it made Britain less safe; that the deterrent was no longer in keeping with Britain's reduced international role, and, thirdly, that the security of Britain and its allies would be better served by diverting the costs of the deterrent to conventional defence. Nailor's views, however, were not welcomed by the government and Defence Secretary Mulley refused to allow him to give evidence to the Defence and External Affairs Sub-Committee when, in January 1979, it began an inquiry into the implications of the choice of a replacement for Polaris. Nailor's arguments in favour of replacement have their basis in history and the acceptance of the realistic perspective of international politics. First, Britain was an early contributor to nuclear weapons development and therefore the continuity argument was powerful, with the burden of proof lying with those who advocated discontinuity. Coupled with the continuity argument was the acceptance that Britain remained an actor in a hostile environment and, in keeping with its past, it wished to exert whatever influence it could in that environment. Second, Britain increasingly saw its future linked to that of the United States and Britain perceived that relationship as adding to the credibility of its own deterrent while simultaneously increasing its influence on the United States and Britain's standing in NATO. The third argument is the pragmatic acknowledgement that, as nuclear weapons became more powerful, Britain's return on her political and economic capital would increase disproportionately as long as Britian retained its minimum deterrent programme. This was especially true of a programme that embodied the cost-effective benefits of a continuing close relationship with the

United States. In essence there are three strands to the arguments in favour of replacement: *continuity*, based on a desire to remain in the first division of states capable of strategic power projection; *precaution*, based on a pragmatic acceptance that political alignments are not constants; and *status*, based on a wish to retain distinctive attributes and exacerbated by the wake of Empire and membership of 'the Big Three'.

While the evidence suggests that there was an uncontroversial political consensus surrounding the 1947 decision to procure nuclear weapons, both the main political parties, the academic community and the public were divided over the issue of replacement. In the late 1960s and early 1970s both the Conservative and Labour parties publicly raised the possibility of a more European dimension for the British deterrent, including some form of co-operation with France. These statements raised concerns in Washington. This approach appears, however, to have been superficial and was not pursued after Britain gained entry into the European Community in 1972. The Conservative government, which took office in 1970, remained committed to the deterrent and, despite exploratory talks with the French, continued to pursue the special nuclear relationship with the United States. The possibility of procuring the more advanced Poseidon SLBM was examined jointly with the United States.[17] In the early 1970s, however, Britain decided to upgrade the Polaris warhead on the basis of a national research programme that later became known as Chevaline. In the interests of keeping the nuclear programme out of the domestic political arena both parties saw the rejection of Poseidon as more politically significant than their support for Chevaline. The Labour government that succeeded the Conservatives in 1974 decided, shortly after taking office, to continue the Chevaline programme. On the other hand Labour's 1975 Statement on Defence declared that:

> The Polaris force, which Britain will continue to make available to the Alliance, provides a unique European contribution to NATO's strategic nuclear capability out of all proportion to the small fraction of our defence budget which it costs to maintain. We shall maintain its effectiveness. We do not intend to move to a new generation of strategic nuclear weapons.[18]

Notwithstanding the Labour government's statement, which was essentially a non-decision, the evidence was increasingly pointing to the fact that a positive decision would have to be taken around the end of the decade either to replace Polaris or to renounce the capability for nuclear deterrence. There were a number of factors that were growing in significance. It was expected that the United States would withdraw its remaining Polaris submarines from service in the early 1980s. As a consequence, in the late 1970s the Labour government ordered a further 31 Polaris missiles for delivery in the early 1980s. Once the

USN was no longer operating Polaris boats, Lockheed, the sole manufacturer of the missiles, would have no need to keep open its production line. Consequently there was increasing pressure on the need for timely decisions to purchase additional missiles or essential spares. The critical factor, however, was the shelf-life of the solid fuel propellant which was limited to a few years.[19] It was acknowledged, at the same time, that the overall cost of the Polaris force could rise by up to 20 per cent once the USN's Polaris fleet had been phased out.[20] The timing of a decision, however, was dictated not by the availability of missiles but by the serviceability of the submarines. There were two aspects to this issue: first, the operational life expectancy of the Polaris boat hulls and, second, the lead time necessary to procure a successor system. Both these factors pointed to the need for a decision to be made no later than the early 1980s. The original official estimate of the operational life of the Polaris boats was 20 years, and on that basis they would have needed to be replaced around 1990. It was subsequently accepted that this was an unduly conservative estimate. The view at the end of the 1970s was that an operational life of 25 years was quite probable.[21] On the other hand, maintenance of older boats takes longer and is more expensive. Older hulls are inevitably more noisy and thus reduce operational flexibility. All these factors indicated that if a decision was to be made in support of replacement there was much to be said in favour of avoiding undue delay. The other aspect was the lead time required to deploy a replacement system. All four Polaris boats were operational within eight years of the procurement decision being made. That was generally considered to be an impressive achievement. A period of 10 years would be a reasonable assumption for a new submarine, even with extensive reliance on the transfer of American technology. It remained possible, however, to procure an alternative system in less time.[22] The independent report published by the Royal Institute of International Affairs in October 1977 raised public awareness of the issues and drew attention to the need for a decision. It concluded that:

> If the British choice is to be the best and freest possible, it must be made . . . in at least some sense, by about 1980. Any delay beyond that time will entail increasing constraints, increasing costs and increasing risks.[23]

The Labour government refused, at least in public, to acknowledge the urgency surrounding a decision. Fred Mulley, Secretary of State for Defence, told the House of Commons in March 1978 that: 'In our view the existing Polaris fleet will be effective for many years and, that being the case, there is no need to take a decision on whether any other arrangements would have to be made'.[24] Two months later Lord Winterbottom reiterated that view in the House of Lords: 'The Polaris fleet has many years of effective life ahead of it. There is no need for a decision to be taken about what may happen thereafter.'[25] These views, however, were almost certainly due more to the prospect of a general election than to any substantive evidence that a decision could profitably be deferred. The Labour Party clearly did not intend to make a decision prior to the election. Indeed it would almost certainly have preferred that a decision could have been postponed beyond 1985 in order that the replacement issue could have been left out of its manifesto. The fact that the Labour Party found it impossible to defer the question of replacement was ample evidence of the need for an early decision.

The Conservative victory in May 1979 brought back to office a government committed to the future of the deterrent. In October of that year the Defence Secretary promised that:

> We will go on improving the Polaris force so that it will remain an ultimate deterrent to aggression in the 1990s. Furthermore consideration is already being given to the action that will be necessary to continue our strategic deterrent capability for as long as is necessary thereafter.[26]

On 15 July 1980 the government published the text of letters exchanged between the Prime Minister and President Carter confirming that Britain would purchase the Trident I missile for a force of British-built ballistic missile submarines to replace the Polaris fleet. The new Trident force was to be acquired, committed and operated on the same basis as its predecessor. The government simultaneously published a document outlining its reasons for the decision.[27] That document is illuminating at least as far as the Government's declaratory policy was concerned. It stressed that the Trident decision was one that was commensurate with a policy extending back over 40 years and had been embraced by both Conservative and Labour governments. Nevertheless it sought to reinforce the validity of its decision by claiming that it was made against a background:

> much less favourable for Western security than when the V-force and Nassau decisions were taken – there is for example a changed strategic balance and much stronger and more versatile all-round Soviet military capability than before, wielded moreover with the growing adventurism highlighted in Afghanistan.[28]

The document is quite explicit about the fact that the Soviet Union was the target for the British deterrent and, by implication, the only target. Britain's continuing commitment to match the 'Moscow criterion' is also implicit in the document: 'The Government thinks it right now to make clear that their concept of deterrence is concerned essentially with posing a potential threat to key aspects of Soviet state power.'[29] Furthermore paragraph 17 of the document makes reference to Chevaline's ability to penetrate anti-ballistic missile defences into the 1990s.

One of the most interesting aspects of the document is the extent to which the European dimension of the deterrent is stressed. The fact that the Trident force would be committed to NATO was clearly uncontroversial. However much emphasis was placed on the importance of the 'Second Centre' concept and there was a clear implication that Britain might decide to use its deterrent in defence of NATO Europe ahead of a United States strategic strike. While both these issues clearly have some potential to enhance the overall credibility of a NATO deterrent, their potential for enhancing Britain's status in relation to its European allies is more significant and much more obvious. Substantial sections of the document appear to have been drafted to impress NATO politicians and electorates rather than to confound Soviet defence analysts. Smart, Nailor and Alford all drew attention to the significance of the political implications of the decision. Smart set out the questions but offered no answers. He asked whether a replacement decision would be seen as a move towards greater commitment to Western Europe or as a gesture of continuing independence. On the other hand, if Britain decided not to replace Polaris, he asked whether that would be interpreted as an acknowledgement of reduced political status or taken as an indication of Britain's determination to maintain effective conventional forces.[30] Alford expressed the view that the deployment of SS-20 missiles, targeted on locations in Western Europe, raised the importance of the British deterrent. He concluded that such a situation indicated:

> the growing importance the West European allies are likely to attach to the continuance of a British deterrent and that the political consequences for Britain's relations within the Alliance of a decision to opt out of a strategic nuclear role would be rather far reaching.[31]

Nailor, on the other hand, suggested that the United States was coming to accept a future that embraced a European political community that included a strategic nuclear capability:

> A basic premise of American foreign policy over the last generation has been the emergence of a stronger and more unified Western Europe and as things now are, it is entirely conceivable that the United States is already reconciled to the emergence in the longer term of a Western European political entity that will have, as one of its attributes, a nuclear capability.[32]

It is time now to provide answers to the questions set at the beginning of this chapter. First it is clear that the British government's declared policy was to base the justification for the replacement decision on the threat posed by the Soviet Union to its vital national interests. That threat was not perceived as being restricted to an attack on British territory but rather it extended to an attack on NATO Europe. Clearly the extent to which an attack on the NATO European mainland might pose a threat to Britain's vital national interests was likely to be conditioned by the scale and location of such an attack. That distinction, however, must remain a matter for speculation. The claim that the perceived threat was greater in 1980 than had been the case in the 1950s and 1960s is arguable, certainly from the perspective of assessed Soviet intentions. Nevertheless there is ample evidence to indicate that, by 1980, Soviet military capability was considerable and it certainly had the potential to pose a significant threat to NATO Europe. That imbalance was exacerbated by the deployment of Soviet SS-20 missiles in the late 1970s. It would be difficult to provide substantive evidence to refute the government's declared perception of the threat. Whether that threat was greater than in earlier decades is not relevant to the justification of the decision. The critical issue is whether it was credible at the time the decision was made. Notwithstanding the weight given to the threat, the British case made much of the issue of continuity. In that respect it would seem prudent to assume that continuity will be of increasing importance with the passage of time. A future assessment could be structured on the premise that continuity is a constant while the threat is perceived as the critical variable. Providing an answer to the question of whether the replacement decision could be justified in terms of its strategic political influence rather than the specific parameters of defence is more complex. That complexity stems from the inter-relationship between defence, deterrence and political relationships: 'A deterrent is, after all, a political instrument, at least in the sense that psychology is the other face of politics.'[33]

What does seem clear is that there was considerable political awareness, both within NATO Europe and the United States, of the potential benefits of a British deterrent as an attribute for the collective defence of Western Europe. This perspective was not apparent at the time the Polaris decision was made. There were, therefore, indications that the concept of strategic political influence was of increasing importance, albeit on the basis of a concept that envisaged Britain acting, perhaps as *primus inter pares*, within an informal NATO European grouping. Such a position clearly has advantages for Britain both within Europe and, in concert with its European partners, *vis à vis* the United States. This, like the continuity argument, would seem to provide a continuing political basis for a British deterrent in the future.

There is a final consideration for which it is difficult to adduce any evidence: the issue of nuclear proliferation. While British governments can be expected to be reasonably explicit about threats posed to NATO, wider international concerns remain shrouded in secrecy. That, however, should not be taken to imply that these issues are not kept under constant and critical review, both nationally and internationally. It is apposite here to remember Garnett's rejoinder, quoted at the beginning of this chapter, that the utility of Britain's deterrent should not be assessed solely on present need: 'but should note the possibility of adverse changes in the international situation.'[34] Alford supports that position. He acknowledged the seriousness of the Soviet military threat to Western Europe and also, 'a general trend towards nuclear proliferation.' It would seem to be sensible to conclude that, while Britain's declared reasons for deciding that a successor to Polaris was necessary can be defended in the context of the NATO Alliance, there may well have been wider issues that were essentially national concerns of the type that are neither discussed with allies nor even implied in official documents.

The Operational Military Perspective

This assessment of the operational perspective can be based on the following strategic assumptions: that Britain required a successor system because the Polaris boats, unlike missiles, had a finite operational life that would not extend much into the 1990s; that the successor system would need to be perceived as a credible deterrent *vis à vis* the Soviet Union; that, if Britain did have another, undeclared, need for a nuclear deterrent, it would also be met, by any strategic nuclear force that could threaten the Soviet Union. That narrows the focus of what follows to an examination of the destructive power required, in terms of throw-weight megatonage, to achieve that level of destruction and to the selection of the most appropriate strategic system to deliver that megatonage.

In the period leading up to 1980, each Polaris boat was fitted with 16 A-3 missiles with a range of 2,500 nautical miles. Each missile was capable of delivering three warheads with a yield of 200 kt providing a destructive capacity per boat 150 times greater than that used against Hiroshima. These warheads were not independently targetable, nor would they become so with the introduction of Chevaline, although that enhancement would considerably improve their ability to penetrate defensive systems. It was generally accepted that, from the time the Polaris fleet became operational, that capacity provided Britain with an adequate, albeit minimal, second strike deterrent, provided it remained committed to countervalue targets and provided that the fleet continued to consist of four serviceable boats. 'Adequate' had traditionally been accepted as being capable of successfully attacking Moscow, while 'successful' had implied the capability of killing tens of millions of Soviet citizens or destroying a substantial proportion of the Soviet Union's industrial capacity. Smart made this explicit by expressing the view that two Polaris boats had the potential to kill up to 15–20 million Soviet citizens while, for a single boat, the figure was probably in the region of 10–15 million. Furthermore, he argued that, with only slightly different targeting, the Polaris force could probably destroy one quarter of the Soviet Union's industrial capacity. Implicit in that equation was the view that Moscow remained at the heart of

Britain's targeting policy, despite the existence of the Galosh ABM defences. (There were 64 launchers with a range of at least 200 miles until 1978–80 when they were reduced to 32.) In 1974 Michael Quinlan, then Deputy Under-Secretary of State at the Ministry of Defence, confirmed the importance of the Moscow criterion in Parliamentary evidence:

> There is a concept which Chevaline makes clear, that Governments did not want to have a situation where the adversary could have a sanctuary for his capital and a large area around it.[35]

Although Moscow has consistently been regarded as a high-value target it has always been accepted that its destruction would require the bulk, if not the whole, of the available Polaris force. This has been a major limitation of Britain's targeting policy.[36] Furthermore, while the introduction of Chevaline improved the penetration of Polaris warheads, it did not improve the flexibility of the force as a whole. Polaris has meant, *de facto*, that Britain has had no option but to retain a countervalue strategy which, in turn, has meant targeting Moscow. Thus the credibility of operational deterrence has been based solely on a massive capacity to kill Soviet citizens.

Against that background it can be argued that the capacity of Britain's deterrent, prior to a replacement decision being made, was adequate and, consequently, a successor system need not embrace any significant enhancement over the potential of Polaris. On the other hand it would be reasonable to suggest that a successor system should, as far as is possible or practical, demonstrate the potential to retain, for the foreseeable future, the equivalent of Britain's *current* deterrent capability. Any successor system ought, at least, to possess more deliverable warheads as well as some further enhancement in penetration capability. Furthermore there would be clear operational advantages in a successor system that, in fleet size, was rather less exiguous and possessed increased targeting flexibility. As a minimum, enhancements of this nature would serve to provide Britain with a deterrent that possessed some degree of system redundancy, to ensure its longevity, without significantly increasing its potential destructive power. It would also make sound operational sense to procure a successor system that possessed some additional capacity to meet unforeseen needs, especially if that could be achieved without incurring disproportionate costs or other penalties.

While the choice of Polaris was reached more by force of circumstance than as a consequence of rational decision making, the issue of replacement was addressed against a very different background. Despite the Labour government's ambivalence about the replacement issue it instigated a Parliamentary Committee to explore the subject and, following the election of a Conservative administration in May 1979, this work was continued. Parallel studies were carried out by the academic community and, although there is little evidence of formal co-operation, it seems inevitable that each side was influenced, to some extent, by the other. From the outset there seems to have been agreement that manned bombers dropping gravity bombs were not a viable delivery system. In the late 1970s the Soviet Union possessed over 2,500 interceptor aircraft and some 10,000 surface to air missile (SAM) launchers. As a consequence of that situation the United States had abandoned plans to introduce the new B-1 bomber. Clearly the problems posed by defence penetration issues made it inevitable that the delivery system would have to be some kind of missile. While there remained some choice over the question of a launch platform the technological debate at the centre of the replacement decision concerned the relative merits of cruise versus ballistic missiles.

The cruise missile is a modern development of the flying bombs that were used during the Second World War. The technology had been under development by both the United States and the Soviet Union since the 1950s. Prior to 1970 the missiles remained inaccurate, easy to detect and destroy, and cumbersome to operate. The United States saw the possibility of overcoming these disadvantages in the 1970s with breakthroughs in high energy fuel chemistry, munition design and the introduction of new guidance systems. Although the cruise missile was not operational in the 1970s considerable development work was undertaken in the United States by both General Dynamics and McDonnel Douglas and all the indications were that an ALCM would be in operational service with the United States forces in the early 1980s. The cruise missile flies through the atmosphere using its own continuous power source together with the aid of wings to give it lift. It is therefore capable of being guided throughout its flight. Unlike the ballistic missile it is relatively slow; a typical cruise missile speed is 550 mph, or 250 metres per second, compared with 7,000 metres per second for a ballistic missile. This gives rise to two difficulties. The cruise missile requires a highly sophisticated guidance system and, although small and difficult to detect, it is relatively easy to shoot down once located. The first of these problems was overcome by the combination of inertial navigation and Terrain Contour Matching (TERCOM). While the former can ensure that the missile comes reasonably close to the target area the latter enables the missile to recognise the ground contours in the target vicinity and thereby steer itself to within metres of its intended point of impact. On the other hand while problems of vulnerability can be reduced by increasingly sophisticated ECM techniques, they cannot be eliminated. Thus target penetration relies more on saturation than defence suppression.[37]

Clearly the advent of the cruise missile demanded careful consideration especially as it seemed, in some configurations, to provide a cost-effective alternative to the ballistic missile.[38] The leading protagonists of a cruise missile system as a successor to Polaris were Bellini and Pattie. They made much of the fact that cruise could be a cheap option:

Compared to the estimated costs of Trident deployment, a credible cruise-missile system is within the capacities of any government which could produce, say, a Mirage V or a Harrier. Indeed it is a cost effective replacement.[39]

Although their economic argument seemed to be based more on assertion than substance they also claimed, and here they were on better ground, that the cruise missile had the added advantages of embodying a technology that was within Britain's capacity and that the system could fulfil a number of operational roles, both conventional and nuclear. Others did not share Bellini's and Pattie's view about the cost-effectiveness of cruise as a strategic deterrent. Smart, having acknowledged the inherent problem of cruise's vulnerability, as well as the low cost of the missile itself, suggested an operational comparison. If cruise were to be deployed in submarines, which gave it the best option for survivability, then 17 cruise missile submarines would be needed to replace the destructive power of the four-boat Polaris force.[40] Despite the relative cheapness of cruise compared with ballistic missiles this type of comparison certainly suggested that cruise was not necessarily a cost-effective alternative. Clearly a cruise system could be deployed in a variety of delivery vehicles. Nevertheless the constraints of survivability of platforms and penetration of delivery systems demanded increased numbers to achieve the same results as those achieved with a SSBN/SLBM system. Smart concluded that there would probably be little difference in the cost of providing sufficient cruise missiles to achieve the same effect as that achievable by ballistic missiles.[41] Alford, having acknowledged that the two viable options were to continue with ballistic missiles or to adopt cruise, comes to a roughly similar conclusion:

> Yet the arguments for an alternative to the present technological structure of British deterrent forces, while not negligible, seem insufficient to warrant a major departure from the pattern and infrastructure established over the past two decades.[42]

Freedman offers a compelling piece of commercial collateral for that position from the testimony of British Aerospace Dynamics to the Parliamentary Expenditure Committee. British Aerospace were confident that they could develop a viable cruise missile system. Nevertheless they concluded that: 'On the information available to us at present, we would expect that a ballistic missile would be more likely to be the one more appropriate to the needs of the UK.'[43] McInnes, writing some five years later, while acknowledging the uncertainties and risks of any cruise system, held the view that the best option could be SSCN/SLCM using converted Resolution class boats which, he claimed, could be achieved at half the price of Trident. The tenor of his argument, however, is more that this option should, at least publicly, have received more consideration, rather than an assertion that it was a better option. A detailed assessment of the various options available was carried out by Alford. In his summary of these issues he highlighted the following implications for Britain. The threat posed by Soviet IRBMs and aircraft would render deterrent systems launched from airfields or fixed-base missile sites ineffective. British nuclear forces acting alone would have little impact against counterforce targets, although ballistic missiles would continue to be effective against countervalue targets. However, a British cruise missile strike, launched on its own, would suffer heavily from Soviet defensive systems. Future developments within SALT could restrict, or stop, Britain benefiting from United States assistance in developing long-range cruise missile systems for independent use. This could have important economic consequences. Similarly, SALT developments could, at some stage in the future, include constraints against increased numbers of cruise missiles. The reliance of cruise systems on target saturation to penetrate defence systems made this an important consideration. Finally, while the ability of SSBNs to evade detection would continue, the technological gap between the hunter and the hunted would reduce. For that reason, and because of the Soviet Union's growing number of SSNs, the possibility that British SSBNs acting alone would be detected and destroyed by Soviet SSNs would increase.[44] Alford considered the arguments to be close but came down in favour of retaining a submarine-launched ballistic missile deterrent.

Against that background it is not surprising that the British Government chose to replace Polaris with Trident. Nevertheless the evidence suggests that all the viable options for both delivery vehicles and launch platforms were explored, albeit to varying levels, before a decision was announced.[45] Land-based delivery systems, both static and mobile, were ruled out at an early stage due to their vulnerability. The same limitation was deemed to be crucial in respect of missiles launched from aircraft, whether these were to be launched from new dedicated bombers or from existing aircraft which had been re-roled or given a dual role. The former would be expensive, slow to develop and extremely vulnerable on the ground. While launched aircraft are less vulnerable such postures are very expensive and lack the operational flexibility that is essential in second strike deterrents. Using Tornado in a dual role capacity was also considered. While this must have proved to be a relatively cheap option it suffered all the inherent problems of dual roling, these being exacerbated significantly by the importance of dedicating aircraft to the strategic deterrent role before hostilities commence. There were also limitations of range. Finally any decision to choose an air-launched system was also, of necessity, a decision to opt for a cruise missile system.

Similar limitations applied to the use of surface ships as launch platforms. For a comparable performance with submarines in terms of endurance, speed and missile capacity, surface ships were not markedly cheaper, yet they were significantly more vulnerable and, if dual roled, although theoretically more cost effective, they suffered from the same operational inflexibility as aircraft. For all these reasons Britain considered that submarines continued to provide the best launch platform and the government's statement made it clear that it gave the survivability of the force, together with the ability to retain its operational and technological lead in submarine warfare, a high priority. The possibility of deploying the deterrent in diesel-powered submarines was also examined. Superficially this appeared a cheaper option but again there were limitations. Diesel-powered submarines, although inherently quieter than nuclear-powered boats, must surface to recharge their batteries. Furthermore they lack the sustained speed and endurance of nuclear-powered submarines. This limits their operating areas, thus increasing their vulnerability as the proportion of their time spent in coastal waters heightens the chances of detection as well as the risk of damage from mines or collision. Finally diesel-powered submarines of the required size, and with the necessary electrical power, had not been built, nor had the United States shown any interest in undertaking development work in that area. Thus for reasons predominantly of invulnerability, but also of reduced technological and economic risk, it was decided to retain a sub-surface, nuclear-powered, ocean-going, launch platform.

The Government's assessment of the relative merits of cruise and ballistic missile systems seems to have been no less thorough.[46] While it was acknowledged that cruise technology was within Britain's capacity it was noted that the United States, although about to introduce both ALCM and GLCM systems, had reached no decisions about SLCM systems. (For Britain the parallel with Skybolt was obvious.) There were other more practical limitations. Range, although expected to be in excess of 1,500 miles, would provide no improvement over Polaris. This gave rise to two important considerations; the operating area for boats on station would be limited and the inertial navigation systems used by cruise could limit the off-shore range of boats at launch.[47] Considerable concern was expressed about the potential for improvement of Soviet air defence systems. This made it very difficult to predict the quantity of missiles required to saturate defences well into the twenty-first century. In this respect the fact that each Trident missile could carry eight, separately targetable, warheads compared with only one for cruise made the comparison, and therefore the cost, less favourable. The 'shoot and scoot' comparison was even more invidious. Polaris can fire a salvo every 14 seconds, and even that can be bettered in extremis. To launch an equivalent megatonage of cruise missiles, using torpedo tubes, the only proven technology at that time, would have taken hours during which the boat would be at severe risk. The conclusion reached was unequivocal:

For a given weight of striking power and a given level of probability of delivering it successfully, cruise based forces are in fact much more expensive. For example, eleven boats each capable of carrying eighty cruise missiles would give less assured deterrent capability than a force of five boats each with sixteen Trident ballistic missiles; and it would cost at least a third as much to acquire and about twice as much to run.[48]

Despite a clear preference for a SLBM system there was consideration of systems other than Trident. The possibility of developing a British strategic missile was discounted, not because it was deemed to be beyond the capacity of domestic industry but because of a combination of cost, time-scale and technical risk. The idea of retaining Polaris for use in new submarines was discarded. Despite the fact that the costs of that option would rise disproportionately with the life of the system it could, overall, be some 40 per cent cheaper than procuring Trident. The problem was that this option was only viable if it could be assumed that Polaris would continue to provide a viable deterrent beyond 2010. That was a high risk strategy that the government was not prepared to pursue.

Retaining Polaris and developing it to meet future needs was ruled out on grounds of costs. All the research and development overheads of this option would fall on Britain and the indications were that a British, improved, Polaris might cost twice as much as a Trident missile. Poseidon was also considered. It was deemed to be an effective system. Nevertheless it delivered a smaller yield than Polaris and produced no significant improvement in range. Critically, however, it had been in service since 1971 and would be phased out by the USN at the same time as it could be entering operational service with the Royal Navy.

Trident won the argument on three important counts. It had been deployed on operational service by the USN since 1979; consequently there was no technical risk and there was every reason to believe it would remain in service for some considerable time. It seemed to offer an attractive economic package over the life of the system. Its eight independently targetable warheads with a range in the 4,000 to 5,000 nautical mile bracket gave it considerable built-in system redundancy to absorb Soviet advances in ASW and ABM capabilities. In particular the range of the Trident missile increased the area of ocean from which an offensive strike could be launched from around 7 million square nautical miles to about 20 million square nautical miles, thus increasing the surface area in which an SSBN could to be concealed by a factor of three.[49]

The final issue concerned the size of the force. The two key criteria here were the number of submarines and the number of missiles per submarine.[50] Two self-evident points are worth stating. First, there is an arithmetical relationship between the number of boats and the number of missiles. Second, once the Trident decision had been made the arithmetical outcome was largely inevitable. It would of course have been possible to start with the arithmetic and assess the issue backwards from the deliverable megatonage required on the target. That would have been a logical course to adopt. Whether it would have been a common sense approach, bearing in mind that some of the factors were unknown variables while others were absolute givens, is arguable. The important issue, in the context of this analysis, is that the British government, by accident or design, arrived at the arithmetic of force size via decisions to opt first, for an SLBM and, thereafter, for Trident as the preferred delivery vehicle. In essence the British case in respect of boats was that four was the minimum required to maintain at least one boat on operational patrol at all times. The government's statement made it clear, however, that it would prefer to procure a five-boat fleet, arguing that a 25 per cent increase in fleet size could be obtained for a 15 per cent increase in costs. Nevertheless the conclusion reached in 1980 was to defer a final decision on the option of a fifth boat until 1982 or 1983. The arithmetic behind the decision to opt for 16 missiles per submarine was less convincing. The government's statement claimed that it had considered configurations of 8, 12, 16 and 24 missiles per boat. The only reason that it offered for its choice of the 16 missile option was that it was: 'the number used in our present force, the French SLBM force, and the United States Polaris and Poseidon forces (and also most of the Soviet SLBM force).'[51] This seemed to imply that nuclear deterrence was being played by the Marquess of Queensberry's Rules. The reality was that a Trident boat, equipped with 16 C-4 missiles, each with eight independently targetable warheads with a nominal yield of 100 kt, could launch 12.8 mt at 128 individual targets. This represented a one-third increase in deliverable yield and an eight-fold increase in targeting capacity. Freedman summed up the position thus: 'this extra flexibility and scope was not sought and seems to have been acquired without any clear sense of how it should have been employed.'[52] The operational logic of that position was to become even more flawed when the Government chose to purchase the D-5 missile in 1982.[53] This would enable each Trident boat to attack up to 192 targets with a maximum yield of 19.2 mt, a 200 per cent increase in yield and a twelve-fold increase in targeting capacity over Polaris.[54]

The information assessed above suggests that the best operational option for a successor system would make use of a submarine as launch platform and a ballistic missile delivery system. The experience gained from operating the Polaris fleet indicates that a deterrent capability can be maintained with four boats. It seems reasonable to assume that the reliability of Trident will be no less than that of Polaris. Indeed total system reliability should be considerably better and that, together with increased operational endurance, should lead to four Trident boats providing a higher proportion of operational serviceability than was achievable with the Polaris fleet. On this basis there appears to be no substantive case for a fifth boat. Clearly a successor system should embrace available enhancements in technology such as a MIRV capability for warheads and increased range for missiles. Furthermore it would be imprudent not to seek some increase in targeting capacity. Arriving at a precise figure is more difficult. The starting point for this perspective was that a 16-target capacity per Polaris boat was probably an absolute minimum. Doubtless it could be argued that a 32-target capacity would be sufficient for Trident. On the other hand it may be prudent to assume that a 50 per cent missile attrition rate may be achievable by the end of Trident's operational life. On that basis a per boat capacity of 64 targets, half that sought by the government in 1980, would seem to meet the operational requirement and include a not inconsiderable proportion of system redundancy. That suggests that a four-boat force with either eight C-4 missiles with eight warheads or 12 C-4 missiles with six warheads would fully meet the operational requirement. On that basis there would seem to be no operational case for the purchase of the D-5 missile.

The Economic Perspective

There are two important facts against which the economic perspective of the replacement decision must be judged. First Polaris, with operating costs running at about 1.5 per cent of the total defence budget, was a very cost-effective deterrent. Second it was clear that the 5.5 per cent of GDP being spent on defence in the late 1970s was envisaged by both the major political parties as being a maximum. Indeed the basic structure of the defence budget for 1980–81 was set in accordance with the Labour government's defence review of 1974–75 which was aimed at reducing the proportion of GDP devoted to defence.[55] As a consequence of statements made while in opposition it was widely believed that the Conservative government would increase spending on defence, possibly substantially. That expectation was not fulfilled as can be seen from the document laid before Parliament in April 1980.[56] Furthermore, at the time the Trident decision was announced the Conservative government had given no substantive commitment to increasing defence spending in the immediate future, contrary to contemporary popular expectations. Both these considerations indicate that, whatever the absolute costs of any successor system, the chances of its comparing favourably with Polaris in economic terms, either directly as a weapon system or as a proportion of the overall defence budget, were minimal. Clearly judgements about the successor system's cost-effectiveness need to be determined against that background.

As with the other perspectives examined in this study there is significantly more comparative information available about the economics of the replace-

ment decision than there was for the procurement of Polaris. The logical starting point is the information provided in the government's announcement in
July 1980:

> In broad terms, however, we assess the likely order of capital cost for a
> four-boat force, at today's prices, at around four-and-a-half to five billion
> pounds, spread over some fifteen years.[57]

Of the total costs 12 per cent was for missiles (the C-4), 30 per cent for submarines, 16 per cent for weapons, 12 per cent for shore construction and the
remaining 30 per cent for warhead design and production, miscellaneous costs
and contingency funding. Over 70 per cent of the total was to be spent in the
UK, the remainder in the United States. The government's statement made a
number of other illuminating claims. First, it claimed that the Trident programme was unlikely to absorb, on average, more than 3 per cent of the total
defence budget between 1980 and 1995. Second, it claimed that the capital
costs associated with Trident would be considerably less than those of the
V-bomber force, and less than those envisaged for the Tornado programme.
Third, it claimed that the Trident force would be 'notably inexpensive' to
operate 'probably well below 2% of the defence budget from the mid-1990s'.[58]
The government's statement, however, gave no information on the possible
costs of alternative systems. Furthermore, all costings and relative comparisons were based on a four-boat force notwithstanding the government's
explicit wish to procure a five-boat fleet.

The most illuminating contemporary source on the economic perspective
was that provided by Greenwood in the spring of 1980, just prior to the government's decisions being announced.[59] Greenwood built on the earlier analytical
work undertaken by Smart and Alford and constructed a comparative economic
analysis of six replacement options using the 1980–81 Defence Estimate prices
as a baseline. The assessment concluded with an illustrative cost-benefit
analysis, an aspect not addressed in the government's statement. Indeed the
government's line throughout was to avoid the issue of opportunity costs:

> There are so many variables and uncertainties that even if we could
> assume that the total defence budget would in the future be the same
> without Trident as with it, any attempt now to calculate the effect of
> Trident in terms of a comprehensive and specific list of repercussions
> would not be meaningful.[60]

Greenwood sought to answer two questions: first what might a successor
system cost and, second, what might the impact of that expenditure be on
other defence programmes. He began by constructing a benchmark programme for defence expenditure from 1980–81 to 1994–95 which showed that
if Polaris remained in service, and was not replaced, the cost of the deterrent

would not exceed 2 per cent of total defence expenditure before the system was withdrawn from service in the early 1990s.[61] He then calculated the relative costs, and constructed expenditure profiles, for six alternative systems. These are shown at Table 4.1 below. Options 1 and 2 are Smart's original illustrations, constructed on the basis of equal strategic benefit, with the costs updated by Greenwood, and indicate that, for a submarine launched system, the ballistic missile is a more cost-effective option than cruise. Options 3 and 4, based on alternative launch platforms, were prepared by Alford for the 1978–79 Parliamentary inquiry.[62] These show that air or surface ship launched cruise systems were substantially cheaper than submarine systems although, as Greenwood points out, the surface ship system, based on hovercraft or fast patrol craft, was technically unproven. Option 5 was included by Greenwood to demonstrate that the use of an existing wide bodied commercial jet as a launch platform was probably the most cost-effective option although it seemed to have been given little serious consideration in the British studies.[63] While the development and procurement costs for this option appear to be slightly higher than Alford's options the operating costs are appreciably lower making this option cheaper over the life of the whole programme. Option 6 is based on Trident, the government's preferred choice. The estimated development and procurement costs of the six options are summarised below.[64]

(1) A new five boat SSBN/SLBM force with 16 MIRVed missiles per boat. Development and procurement costs £4050–£5250 million.
(2) A 17 boat SSCN/SLCM force with 24 single-warhead missiles per boat. Development and procurement costs £4950–£6150 million.
(3) A force of 18 fast ship-launched cruise missile carriers (FCMC) based on hovercraft or patrol boats. Development and procurement costs £750–£3000 million.
(4) A force of 25 high performance aircraft carrying ALCMs. Development and procurement costs £1000–£3000 million.
(5) A force of 15 wide bodied commercial jets, sufficient to maintain an alert force of six aircraft, each carrying 25–30 ALCMs. Detailed development and procurement costs were not available for this option but Greenwood's predictions indicated that the development and procurement costs would be comparable with Options 3 and 4 while the operating cost would be lower.
(6) A Trident programme based on C-4, and later D-5, SLBMs from the United States and a new SSBN fitted for 16 missiles. Development and procurement costs £5500–£6500 million. Greenwood's estimate of the breakdown of these costs indicated that the construction of five submarines might cost £2000–£2500 million, depending on whether one or two shipyards were used: £1250 million for the purchase of 125 missiles:

Table 4.1

ESTIMATED EXPENDITURE PROFILES FOR SIX POLARIS SUCCESSOR OPTIONS
(£ millions at 1980–81 Estimates prices)

System	1980–81	1981–82	1982–83	1983–84	1984–85	1985–90	1990–95	Total
1. (Smart) 5 × SSBN/16 × SLBM	105	250	450	400	500	725	275	6705
2. (Smart) 17 × SSCN/24 × SLCM	110	300	525	475	550	850	650	9860
3. (Alford) 18 × FCMC	25–100	50–200	75–300	75–400	88–510	110–200	110–230	1413–3660
4. (Alford) 25 × HP/ALCM	25 × 100	50–200	75–300	100–400	125–525	150–200	125–225	1750–3650
5. (Greenwood) 15 × WB/ALCM	25–100	50–200	75–300	125–425	150–550	175–225	100–200	1800–3700
6. (Trident) 5 × SSBN/16 × SLBM	50	150	300	300	400	625	400	6325

Source: adapted from Greenwood D., *The Polaris Successor System: At What Cost?* (University of Aberdeen: Aberdeen Studies in Defence Economics, No 16, Centre for Defence Studies, Spring 1980) Table 3, p. 23.

Table 4.2

THE BENCHMARK PROGRAMME (IE EXCLUDING TRIDENT COSTS)

(£ millions at 1980–81 Estimates prices)

PROGRAMME	1980–81	1981–82	1982–83	1983–84	1984–85	1985–90	1990–95
Nuclear Strategic Force (Polaris)	165 1.5%	180 1.6%	200 1.7%	220 1.9%	240 2.0%	250 1.9%	(120) (0.9%)
Navy GP Combat Forces	1461 13.6%	1525 13.7%	1600 14.0%	1650 14.0%	1700 14.0%	1840–1890 14.0%	1890–2080 14.0%
European Theatre Ground Forces	1746 16.1%	1775 16.0%	1825 14.0%	1885 14.0%	1940 16.0%	2300–2360 17.0%	2360–2600 18.0%
Air Force GP Forces	1865 17.3%	1940 17.5%	2060 18.0%	2240 19.0%	2430 20.0%	2300–2360 17.0%	2360–2600 18.0%
Other Army Combat Forces	105 0.9%	105 0.9%	100 0.9%	100 0.8%	100 0.8%	100 0.7%	100 0.7%
Support Programmes	5443 50.5%	5585 50.2%	5655 49.4%	5695 48.3%	5735 47.0%	6360–6540 48.0%	6540–7350 50.0%
Total	10785	11110	11440	11790	12145	13150–13500	13500–14850

Source: adapted from Greenwood D, *The Polaris Successor System: At What Cost?* (University of Aberdeen: Aberdeen Studies in Defence Economics, No 16, Centre for Defence Studies, Spring 1980) Table 2, p. 12.

£1750–£2000 million for the warheads and £500–£750 million for other research and development costs. He also suggested that the running costs for each submarine in commission might be £40–£50 million per annum.

Greenwood then proceeded to use the Option 6 (Trident) figures to illustrate the impact of the replacement decision on other aspects of the defence budget. He did this by constructing two tables. The first was a functional analysis of defence programme expenditure up to 1994–95 excluding the costs of a replacement deterrent. He called this the 'Benchmark Programme'. The second was the same data modified to include two illustrations of how the costs of the Trident option might impact on other programmes. Table 4.2 above and Table 4.3 below are based on Greenwood's original tables. These show that the peak was due to occur in the second half of the 1980s when annual average expenditure would be around £625 million (at 1980–81 Estimates prices). This would amount to about 4.75 per cent of the defence budget. However the costs of nuclear strategic forces as a whole – the 'running out' Polaris force and the 'running in' Trident force – would total around £825 million. That would be over 6 per cent of the total defence budget (and, therefore, around 12 per cent of the funds allocated to the front line or mission programmes). Greenwood's tables also indicated that once the procurement and development costs had been met the operating costs of the Trident fleet would stabilise at about 3.5 per cent of the budget: slightly more than double the operating costs of Polaris. The impact of that expenditure on the other major mission programmes would be substantial as Table 4.3 illustrates. If the Trident costs were borne by a combination of the budgets allocated to the European Theatre Ground Forces and the Air Force General Purpose Forces, these would have to be reduced by some 15 per cent throughout the late 1980s when the programme was due to 'peak'. In the early 1990s, when the force was due to be operational, its operating costs would result in a reduction of some 9 per cent to these programmes. Alternatively if these costs were to be offset by reduced expenditure in the Navy and Air Force General Purpose Forces the reduction would amount to some 17 per cent in the late 1980s, reducing to around 10 per cent in the early 1990s. Either option would result in a significant reduction in the equipment procurement programme for two of the Armed Services and, consequently, a proportionate reduction in their operational effectiveness. Greenwood predicted that the scale of these reductions could be of the order of several frigates or squadrons of aircraft or the reduction of 1st British Corps from four to three armoured divisions.[65]

Before drawing conclusions about this perspective it is necessary to advocate a degree of caution about the robustness of the figures used as the basis of the above assessment. With very few exceptions these were informed guesses rather than estimates, at least in the accountancy sense in which that term is

Table 4.3

HYPOTHETICAL DEFENCE PROGRAMMES
WITH PROVISION FOR TRIDENT SYSTEM
(£ millions at 1980–81 Estimates prices)

Programme Options	1980–81	1981–82	1982–83	1983–84	1984–85	1985–90	1990–95
Nuclear Strategic Forces							
–Polaris	165	180	200	220	240	200	100
–Trident	50	150	300	330	400	625	400
–total	215	330	500	550	640	825	500
% of total defence expenditure	2.0%	3.0%	4.4%	4.7%	5.2%	6.2%	3.5%
Option 1 – Navy GP Forces +Air Force GP Forces	3276	3315	3360	3590	3730	3565–3675	4000–4300
Reduction from Table 4.2	1.5%	4.5%	8.9%	8.4%	10.7%	17.2%	9.0%
Other Mission Programmes	1851	1880	1925	1985	2040	2400–2460	2460–2700
OR							
Option 2 – European Theatre Ground Forces + Air GP Forces	3561	3565	3585	3825	3970	4025–4145	4470–4820
Reduction from Table 4.2	1.4%	4.2%	8.3%	7.8%	10.0%	15.2%	10.0%
Other Mission Programmes	1566	1630	1700	1720	1800	1940–1990	1990–2180
Support Programmes (as Table 4.2)	5443	5585	5655	5695	5735	6360–6540	6540–7350
Total	10785	11110	11440	11790	12145	13150–13500	13500–14850

Source: adapted from Grenwood D., *The Polaris Successor System: At What Cost?* (University of Aberdeen: Aberdeen Studies in Defence Economics, No 16, Centre for Defence Studies, Spring 1980) Table 4, p. 24.

used. At the time the replacement decision was made there were few detailed costs available, not least because many of the decisions about specific aspects of the programme had not been taken, such as the number of missiles to be purchased. It is also prudent to remember that major new defence programmes rarely remain within their initial budget projections, especially those that embrace a significant proportion of new technology. Furthermore, as earlier parts of this study have already made clear, British governments have rarely been successful in estimating their overall expenditure and the usual consequence of that situation has been further reductions in defence spending. Finally, while programmes that include significant purchases from the United States benefit from reduced unit costs, these remain subject to the vagaries of the exchange rate. All these factors suggested that both the absolute costs of the Trident programme, and the proportion of the total defence budget allocated to Trident were likely to rise. The inevitable result could only be further reductions on other defence programmes. Greenwood, in his assessment of Secretary of State for Defence John Nott's Parliamentary statement on 25 June 1981, noted that, in the review of Britain's defences, the Trident programme had come out unscathed. Nevertheless he suggested that instead of the government's figure of £5,000 million at mid-1980 prices the capital costs of the Trident programme spread over 15 years could be in the region of £6,000 to £7,000 million on the same price basis.[66]

Greenwood's prediction proved to be correct with the publication of the government's statement on the implications of the decision to procure the Trident D-5 missile and the concomitant requirement to build Ohio class hulls.[67] The government's statement made clear the increases in the forecast costs of Trident, some of which arose as a consequence of the D-5 decision and some of which were attributable to a combination of domestic inflation and the exchange rate with the dollar. The estimated cost of the original Trident C-4 programme, at September 1980 prices, was £5,125 million, at the top end of the original estimate of £4,600–£5,125 million. By the spring of 1982 the following additional costs had been identified. £475 million to build Ohio class hulls (the original estimate was based on modified 640 class hulls which were adequate for the C-4 missile), an increment of £390 million to purchase the D-5 missile rather than the C-4. Changes in the exchange rate had added a further £710 million and inflation another £800 million. The total cost had risen to £7,500 million, an increase of £2,375 million.[68] While these additional costs were, at least in part, expected they nevertheless indicated the fragility of estimates of defence expenditure.

In summing up there is a need to suggest answers to three questions. Was Trident a cost-effective successor system? What would the impact of Trident's costs be on other defence programmes? Was the level of expenditure on Trident justified?

If one accepts that the British government perceived a need for a strategic nuclear deterrent that would remain effective until at least the first decade of the twenty-first century then the evidence suggests that the choice of a SSBN/SLBM system was the correct one. That system, although not the cheapest available, provided greatest invulnerability and made best use of technologies and operating procedures that were already well understood. Similarly the decision to procure missiles from the United States, and to construct hulls using United States designs, made economic sense by reducing technical risks as well as research and development and unit production costs.

It was clear from the outset that Trident was going to cost more than its predecessor. The estimates available at the time the decision was made indicated that Trident's costs might amount to rather more than 6 per cent of the defence budget, a little more than double the costs of Polaris but less than the Tornado programme. The indications, however, were that this proportion would rise, at least during the early part of the programme. Nevertheless if Trident had the potential to contribute significantly to deterrence, as the government claimed, and the evidence suggests that this was the case in 1980, 6 per cent, or even 9 per cent, does not seem to be an unbearable insurance premium. Trident was probably the best buy available.

Trident would clearly have a significantly greater impact on other defence programmes than Polaris. This would inevitably mean some contraction of Britain's conventional contribution to NATO. In terms of ground and air forces this was likely to be a bigger political problem than a military problem as there was no technical reason why these commitments could not be assumed, or subsidised, by Britain's NATO allies. From a national point of view, therefore, it seemed to make sense to spend more on Britain's capital weapon, especially as it would be assigned to NATO, rather than committing a greater proportion of the defence budget to European theatre programmes that were inherently less flexible and provided less direct defence for Britain on a pound-for-pound basis.

In 1980 there was an adequate, but not overwhelming, political and military justification for the replacement of Polaris. Furthermore part of that justification rested on the need to possess a deterrent capability that could have potential in situations that might arise over the next three decades. Trident would have a degree of strategic and operational flexibility unmatched by any of Britain's other defence programmes. The ability to maintain a reserve that can be moved quickly, preferably without detection, and strike when and where required remains a key military attribute. The thinner one's forces are deployed, the greater the need for such a reserve. If Trident can fulfil that role then the level of expenditure might well be justified. Indeed failure to meet that requirement could negate all the expenditure on other defence programmes. Even if Trident's costs were to rise significantly the future validity of the programme is unlikely to be seriously questioned solely on economic grounds.

Summary

In summarising the key issues that influenced Britain to seek a successor system to Polaris a comparison is now made with the factors that were critical in influencing the initial decision to procure and deploy a strategic nuclear deterrent.

As with the Polaris decision the perceived threat posed by the Soviet Union was a key factor in the replacement decision. That issue figured highly in statements emanating from the government. There were, however, significant differences of emphasis. While the Soviet Union's potential, in terms of military capacity, to damage Britain's vital national interests was at least as great in the 1970s as it had been in the 1950s, there was less need for concern about the Soviet Union's political intentions. Nuclear stalemate, *inter alia*, had contributed to a degree of stability in Europe. Notwithstanding that overall assessment there can be little doubt that the deployment of SS-20 missiles in Eastern Europe in early 1978 did much to exacerbate threat perceptions. Conversely there were some substantial differences. The United States was no longer a dubious ally and Britain's European NATO allies' ability to contribute to the conventional defence of Europe had increased markedly. Throughout the 1970s, the likelihood of a Soviet attack against NATO Europe, perhaps with the exception of limited incursions on the flanks, had reduced. On balance Britain was probably justified in the late 1970s in considering that it continued to need an independent nuclear deterrent to protect its vital national interests. Nevertheless it seems probable that the threat, at least in political terms, was less than it had been in the 1970s.

Britain's declared policy revealed two additional and illuminating differences. First, Britain stressed the contribution that its deterrent would make to the Alliance. This had not been considered necessary, nor appropriate, at the time the Polaris decision was made. Second, much was made of the continuity factor in arguing for a replacement. Both these issues seemed to indicate an increasing acknowledgement of the deterrent's political influence. There is, therefore, some semblance of a pattern, which appears to suggest that while the highly visible and openly acknowledged threat posed by the Soviet Union might have declined, there is growing emphasis on the importance of the deterrent as an instrument of political influence, especially with regard to allies. Finally, despite a lack of empirical evidence, there remains a suspicion that Britain may have had reasons for wishing to retain its contemporary capital weapon system that were not, and indeed could not, be articulated publicly.

The operational perspective is more straightforward. All the available evidence, and there is much of it, suggests that the best strategic deterrent available to a medium power is a second strike capability that combines a nuclear-powered submarine launch platform with a ballistic missile delivery system. In this respect there is no change over the situation pertaining to the Polaris decision, despite the fact that Polaris was procured in desperation while the decision to replace it with Trident was reached through a process of comprehensive and rigorous assessment. It seems beyond reasonable doubt that Britain procured the best system available to meet its perceived needs. Conversely Trident is manifestly not a minimum deterrent. The vast increase in Trident's targeting capacity and deliverable megatonage seems to have been obtained by accident. There is no evidence to suggest that it was sought and the evidence that does exist indicates that Trident's potential destructive power is far greater than is necessary to meet Britain's needs, irrespective of how these are determined. There are no discernible trends in respect of the operational perspective. Whether the submarine ballistic missile combination retains its pre-eminence for second strike deterrent forces depends upon its continuing ability to avoid detection. As the increase in Trident's destructive power seems to have resulted more from accident than design it has been assumed that this development should not be regarded as an indicator for the future.

The economic perspective is also fairly straightforward. From the outset it was acknowledged that Trident would cost about twice as much as Polaris. Nevertheless the replacement system was expected to account for little more than six per cent of the total defence budget. Furthermore, by procuring a system from the United States Britain was able to minimise both costs and technical risk. On balance it seems reasonable to conclude that Trident was a cost-effective deterrent. The system was considerably more expensive than Polaris and so its costs had significantly more impact on other defence programmes. On the other hand reductions in Britain's conventional contribution to the Alliance could be offset, or accepted, by its allies on the basis that the British deterrent would provide the Alliance with a strategic asset out of all proportion to the conventional capability that could be procured for the same amount of money. Britain could also reduce its conventional contribution to the Alliance without that reduction having any direct consequences on Britain's own defence while its strategic influence, both within and beyond the Alliance, would be maintained and possibly enhanced by its possession of Trident. During the life span of Trident Britain planned to spend proportionately only slightly less on defence than it had spent during the Polaris period. It remains, therefore, arguable that Britain's overall level of expenditure on the strategic deterrent was justifiable. Irrespective of the outcome of that argument, it seems clear that Trident offered more 'bang per buck' than other programmes. In short, if that case is proven, it is an argument for reducing expensive conventional programmes, such as Tornado, rather than cutting back, or cutting out, the strategic deterrent.

There are three clear economic indicators for the future. First, the cost of the deterrent is increasing both in terms of total expenditure and as a proportion of the defence budget. Second, if Britain wishes to continue to possess a strategic deterrent, its conventional capability will have to be reduced at an increasing rate to offset the costs of the nuclear programme. Third, Britain's deterrent would have cost significantly more had Britain been unable to purchase much of it from the United States. It seems beyond doubt that, in the future, Britain will be unable to afford its own deterrent unless it can be obtained on similar terms. That constraint will probably continue to bind Britain to the United States although collaborative development with another medium-size power could be an alternative.

There are three overall trends. Britain seems to be placing more emphasis on the political benefits of its deterrent over time and giving less credence to the visible threat. Britain's declared policy suggests that Trident is to be perceived as more of an Alliance asset than was the case with Polaris. Finally, the costs of the deterrent are rising, both in absolute terms and as a proportion of total defence costs. While Britain will probably manage to afford Trident, any decision to progress to a fourth generation of deterrence systems may ultimately be determined by cost.

NOTES

1. Nailor P. and Alford J., *The Future of Britain's Deterrent Force*, Adelphi Papers, No. 156 (London: The International Institute for Strategic Studies, 1980) p. 1.
2. See Garnett J. C., 'The Defence Debate', *International Relations*, Vol. II, No. 12 (October 1965) pp. 813–29.
3. Ibid, p. 813.
4. See King-Hall S., *Power Politics in the Nuclear Age* (London: Gollancz, 1962) p. 13.
5. See McNamara R. S., 'Defence Arrangements of the North Atlantic Community', *State Department Bulletin*, No. 49, Washington, DC, 9 July 1962, p. 67.
6. Garnett J. C., p. 824.
7. Ibid, p. 825.
8. Bull H., 'Inconsistent Objectives', *Spectator*, 4 January 1963.
9. See Greenwood D. and Hazel D., *The Evolution of Britain's Defence Priorities 1957–76* (Aberdeen: Aberdeen Studies in Defence Economics, No. 9, 1978) pp. 58–9.
10. For fuller details of arms control agreements see pp. 99–107 in Chapter 5 below.
11. For a detailed exposition of proliferation see McGrew A., *Nuclear Proliferation and Global Security*, in Open University Course U235, *Nuclear Weapons: Inquiry Analysis and Debate*, Block IV (Milton Keynes: The Open University Press, 1986) pp. 107–61. Also pp. 108–11 in Chapter 5 below.
12. For a fuller explanation of these issues see Freedman L., *Britain and Nuclear Weapons* (London: Macmillan, 1980) pp. 101–2.
13. Nailor P. and Alford J., *The Future of Britain's Deterrent Force*, Adelphi Papers, No. 156 (London: The International Institute for Strategic Studies, 1980) p. 2.
14. The outcome of the Chatham House study was documented in a report by Smart I., *The Future of*

the British Nuclear Deterrent: Technical, Economic and Strategic Issues (London: Royal Institute of International Affairs, 1977). Smart's paper ensured that the replacement decision became a matter for public debate. Furthermore it is noteworthy that while Smart claimed to have had no help from the Ministry of Defence the reality was that his arguments were remarkably similar to those of the government. See McInnes C., *Trident: The Only Option?* (London: Brassey's, 1986) p. 12.

15. Smart I., 'British Foreign Policy to 1985. I: Beyond Polaris', *International Affairs*, Vol. 53, No. 4 (London: Chatham House, October 1977) pp. 561–2.
16. Nailor P. and Alford J., p. 2.
17. For a good *resumé* of the Poseidon option see McInnes C., pp. 42–5.
18. Cmnd 5976, *Statement on Defence Estimates: 1975*, (London: HMSO, 1975) para. I, 25d.
19. The figures on orders of Polaris missiles come from Department of Defense Security Assistance Agency, Foreign Military Sales and Military Assistance Facts, Washington, DC, December 1978. See Freedman L., Chapter 6, Note 5, p. 151.
20. Twelfth Report from the Expenditure Committee, Session 1978–9, (London: HMSO) pp. 9, 1.
21. In the event 25 years appears to have been an absolute maximum for the hull life of the Polaris boats. *HMS Revenge* was withdrawn after only 22 years' service. In theory the remaining three boats completed 25/26 years' service. However, towards the end of her service, *HMS Renown* spent four non-operational years in refit to give her a final three years of operational service. That situation almost certainly influenced the decision to cancel *HMS Resolution's* refit in 1993 and her subsequent withdrawal from service shortly afterwards. At the end of 1996, Britain's strategic deterrent capability rests solely on the first two Trident boats and is likely to remain with them until the end of 1998 at the earliest. It is inconceivable that the original replacement plan was based on that dangerous assumption. Had the Cold War not ended when it did the credibility of the British deterrent would have been a matter for considerable concern in the mid-1990s.
22. For a fuller exposition of these issues see Freedman L., pp. 56–9 and McInnes C., pp. 12–14.
23. Smart I., p. 71.
24. *Hansard*, Vol. 946, Col. 1315, 21 March 1978.
25. Hansard (Lords), Vol. 391, Col. 601, 18 May 1978.
26. Francis Pym, Speech to Conservative University Students, Nottingham, 26 October 1979. Quoted in Freedman L., p. 63.
27. Pym F., *Britain's Strategic Nuclear Force: The Choice of a System to Succeed Polaris*, Defence Open Document 80/23 (London: Ministry of Defence, July 1980).
28. Ibid., paragraph 3, p. 3.
29. Ibid., paragraph 12.
30. See Smart I., pp. 569–70.
31. Nailor P. and Alford J., p. 28.
32. Ibid., p. 14.
33. Smart I., p. 569.
34. See Note 7 above.
35. House of Commons Defence Committee, Strategic Nuclear Weapons Policy, 1974, p. 107.
36. See Freedman L. in Ball D. and Richelson J. (eds), *Strategic Nuclear Targeting* (Ithaca and London: Cornell University Press, 1986) pp. 122–3.
37. For further details of the technical aspects of cruise missiles see Freedman L., pp. 69–70; Nailor P. and Alford J., pp. 18–22 and Naughton J. with Penrose O., Greene O. and Dyer G., *Nuclear Weapons Technology*, Unit 5, Course U235; *Nuclear Weapons: Inquiry Analysis and Debate* (Milton Keynes: The Open University Press, 1986) pp. 94–5.
38. For a thorough analysis of the cruise missile option alternative see McInnes C., pp. 100–58 and especially the details on Force Size and Costs, pp. 138–52.
39. See Bellini J. and Pattie G., *A New World Role for the Medium Power: The British Opportunity* (London: Royal United Services Institute for Defence Studies, 1977) p. 39. Chapter 6, pp. 37–42 deals with this issue generally.
40. See Smart I., pp. 51–3 and Freedman L., pp. 74–5. Conversely McInnes has suggested that an adequate strategic deterrent could be provided by 5 SSCN each equipped with 80 cruise missiles. See McInnes C., pp. 149–50.
41. See Smart I., p. 566.
42. Nailor P. and Alford J., p. 36.
43. Freedman L., p. 75.
44. For a more detailed exposition of the arithmetic behind this argument see Nailor P. and Alford J.,

p. 24.

45. For a concise yet comprehensive *résumé* of the British Government's assessment of the options for launch platforms see Pym F., paragraphs 22–33.

46. For the British government's assessment of the relative merits of cruise and ballistic missiles see ibid, paragraphs 34–53.

47. See ibid, paragraph 41 for further details of this limitation.

48. Pym F., paragraph 43.

49. Figures derived from Bellini J. and Pattie G., Note 1, p. 42.

50. For a valuable *résumé* of the force size arguments and arithmetic see McInnes C., pp. 54–7.

51. Pym F., paragraph 55.

52. Freedman L. in Ball D. and Richelson J. (eds), p. 126.

53. Although government costings had all been based on the C-4 missile, the Ministry of Defence had been aware for some time of the possibility that the United States might retire the C-4 early. The decision was announced in October 1981, considerably earlier than expected. Clearly the operational logic in opting for the D-5 was essentially similar to the case in favour of procuring Trident rather than Poseidon or retaining Polaris. Support for the decision was nevertheless far from universal both within government circles and with the public. See McInnes C., pp. 24–5.

54. It is of more than passing interest to note that when the decision to opt for the Trident D5 missile was made, the government acknowledged that each missile had the ability to carry up to 14 warheads. Thus the decision to procure the D5 missile could have provided an ability for each Trident boat to attack 224 targets with a maximum yield of 22.4 mt, a 233 per cent increase in yield and a fifteen-fold increase in targeting capacity over Polaris. On the other hand, when announcing the D5 decision the government stated that: 'we feel it right to make clear that the move to Trident D5 will not involve any significant change in the planned total number of warheads associated with our strategic deterrent force in comparison with the original intentions for a force based on the C4 missile system'. See Nott, F., *The United Kingdom Trident Programme*, Defence Open Government Document 82/1 (London: Ministry of Defence, March 1982) paragraphs 29–30.

55. For background on this subject see Greenwood D. and Mason R., 'Setting British Defence Priorities', *Survival*, September–October 1974.

56. See Cmnd 7826-I, *Defence in the 1980s* (London: HMSO, 1980) especially Chapters 1–4 and 8.

57. Pym F., p. 25.

58. Ibid, p. 26.

59. Greenwood D., *The Polaris Successor System: At What Cost?*, Aberdeen Studies in Defence Economics, No 16, Centre for Defence Studies, University of Aberdeen (Spring 1980).

60. See McInnes C., p. 66.

61. See Greenwood D., Table 2, p. 12 from which these figures can be calculated.

62. Ibid, p. 20 and Note 19, p. 31.

63. Further details of these options can be found in Nailor P. and Alford J., pp. 30–3.

64. These details have been gleaned from Greenwood D., pp. 17–22. For a similar appraisal conducted some five years later see McInnes C., pp. 138–52.

65. For further explanation of the impact of the Trident programme's costs on other aspects of the defence budget see Greenwood D., pp. 40–2. Again, McInnes's research benefits from being conducted some time after the replacement decision had been made and is therefore able to draw on reality rather than prediction. For an excellent exposition of the 'funding gap' and possible opportunity costs see McInnes C., pp. 69–77.

66. Greenwood D., *Reshaping Britain's Defences*, Aberdeen Studies in Defence Economics, No 19, Centre for Defence Studies, University of Aberdeen (1981) p. 25–6.

67. See Nott J., *The United Kingdom Trident Programme*, Defence Open Government Document, 82/1 (London: Ministry of Defence, March 1982).

68. For further details see ibid., Part 4 – 'Resources' and the associated tables. See also McInnes C., pp. 64–7. McInnes draws attention to the fact that only 55 per cent of the revised costs would be spent within the UK compared with over 70 per cent of the original costings.

CHAPTER FIVE

Arms Control:
Problems, Progress and
Proliferation

Introduction

> The risks of retaining nuclear weapons, with all the possibilities
> which that entails . . . is significantly greater than the danger
> that the abolition of nuclear weapons could increase the likeli-
> hood of war and that their abolition might not prove complete or
> permanent.[1]

W HILE THERE IS widespread agreement that nuclear war should be
avoided, there is no general agreement about how that is best achieved.
Most countries, including Britain, claim to support the total abolition of
nuclear weapons. Their behaviour in practice, however, has been markedly
different and early commitments to disarmament have given way to policies
based on the concept of arms control. Arms control is one means of reducing
the probability of war. Arms control shares the same aim as the concepts of
disarmament, transarmament and arms racing but the means to that end are
different. Arms racing seeks to reduce the probability of war by achieving a
substantial measure of military superiority over opponents and is based on the
uncomfortable assumption that the dominant power will not itself initiate war.
Transarmament seeks to minimise the risk of conflict by concentrating on
defensive, rather than offensive, military systems while disarmament seeks to
achieve the total elimination of weapons systems. The concept of arms control
rests on the assumption that the global growth of weapons systems cannot
be reversed or stopped and therefore the best practical option is mutually
negotiated limitation. Arms control is essentially concerned with pragmatic
security enhancement rather than with making political concessions or the
adoption of a moral position. Invariably a state's policy on arms control is
formulated in the overall context of its approach to national security and, as
such, it is shaped by the influences of economics, foreign and defence policies
and domestic politics. As arms control takes a pragmatic approach to security it
accepts the logic of deterrence and seeks simply to reduce the risks inherent in

that concept. Nevertheless arms controllers are not unanimous about how best to achieve their aims. Some, especially those who fear a nuclear conflict or accident, see arms control as a matter of urgency. Others, who may share these concerns, acknowledge the inescapable complexity of the concept of arms control and accept that progress is never likely to be fast but nevertheless strive for whatever improvements can be achieved. Against that background this chapter examines the problems inherent in arms control, the progress made so far and the potential dangers of nuclear proliferation.

Problems

Despite widespread support for nuclear disarmament throughout the international community, arms control has only made modest progress. The reasons for this are both technologically and politically complex. Arms control is an inherently weak political goal. It is based on an acceptance of nuclear deterrence and therefore has no moral base. To be successful it requires some degree of co-operation with enemies or rivals concerning major issues of national security and is therefore always vulnerable to domestic political pressures as well as the vagaries of other states. Progress is inevitably achieved through a process of bargaining with internal military and scientific interests as well as by external negotiation. These procedures can raise concerns, both at home and with allies, that political concessions are being offered contrary to military and scientific advice. Conversely because negotiations tend to be protracted the process can engender public cynicism, especially amongst those most anxious to achieve progress who may conclude that governments involved in arms control negotiations are insincere. At the external level there is always the suspicion that the other side is cheating. Furthermore it has proved impossible to divorce the technical process of arms control from the much wider issue of political relations. The mere fact that arms control discussions are taking place can lead members of the public to believe that tensions are reducing whereas the opposite might be true. Arms control is needed most when tensions are greatest, possibly because one or both parties believe that the arms race is about to escalate to new heights. Finally, and perhaps most importantly, arms control can never be a solution in itself but only a step, probably a small one, towards a solution. For all these reasons, therefore, arms control negotiations may increase both internal as well as external tensions rather than alleviate them. The process is politically fraught, especially for democratic states.

Progress in arms control is made even more problematic by the pressures created by the burgeoning progress of technology. The impact of that constraint means that negotiations require constant rethinking. Advances in technology may be potentially destabilising. An example of this might be improvements in missile accuracy that increase the vulnerability of targets. Other advances, such as improved satellite surveillance systems, may have the opposite effect. Cruise missiles, on the other hand, fall into a third category, these are too slow to be used as first strike systems yet because they are both small and numerous they are difficult to count and consequently their inclusion in arms control agreements is inherently problematic. For the reasons outlined above arms control agreements tend to be transitory in their effect and that can leave them vulnerable to speculation that the security gains made do not offset the overall political costs.

There are other more practical problems to be overcome before arms control agreements can be successfully concluded. These issues include the difficulty of agreeing effective verification procedures and in deciding what sanctions might prevent an agreement being broken. There are also problems relating to the links between nuclear and conventional forces. As long as international relations continue to be conducted within an anarchic arena there will be distrust between states. Consequently arms control agreements need to embody appropriate verification procedures in order that the signatories can deter cheating by enforcing agreed detection procedures.

These tend to consist of three phases, first *the collection of information* (monitoring), second *the analysis of that information* and, third, *decision taking*. No verification system is foolproof, but signatories must believe that the verification procedures that have been agreed reduce the risks to an acceptable level. Not all forms of monitoring depend upon co-operation, however. Effective verification needs to embrace co-operative monitoring with technical monitoring. Technical monitoring has advanced dramatically with the development of satellite surveillance systems. These systems can provide detailed images (using optical, infra-red, microwave or other wavelengths), detect radiation emissions (such as the heat from missile exhausts or the flash of a nuclear explosion) and use radar to monitor or probe emissions from known or suspected test sites.

These data can be supplemented by other forms of electronic intelligence gathering as well as by the monitoring of seismic waves and human intelligence-gathering methods. Technical monitoring can detect nuclear submarines in harbour, missile sites, nuclear bombers on airfields and much else besides. There is much that it cannot achieve, however. In particular, technical monitoring cannot count nuclear warheads or stocks of fissile materials. Effective verification requires technical monitoring to be enhanced by the addition of specific co-operative monitoring procedures. These, in ascending order of intrusion, could include the use of fixed seismic recorders and cameras, regular inspection of sites and their records, challenge inspections whenever a violation is suspected, the right to unannounced inspection and, finally, continual monitoring by resident inspectors. As things stand today, despite some dramatic advances in arms control procedures, highly intrusive inspection remains a remote prospect with regard to nuclear weapons. Put at its simplest the nuclear weapons states are not prepared to grant such facilities, whatever the alternative risks appear to be. On the other hand, even with the use of highly intrusive measures monitoring cannot be foolproof and therefore some risk of nuclear escalation remains possible for the foreseeable future.

Agreements between adversarial states need to be backed by some form of sanction so that one party has a means of punishing the other should it abrogate the agreement. When the stakes are high, as they always are in arms control agreements, so is the requirement for effective sanctions. Nevertheless it is even more difficult to guard against abrogation than it is to establish effective verification procedures. The normal sanctions used by the international community – political isolation or economic sanctions – are unlikely to be effective. They did not deter Hitler or Mussolini, nor did they persuade Stalin to make concessions in Eastern Europe in the 1940s despite the United States' nuclear monopoly at that time. In theory the abrogation of international law should be punishable by the United Nations either directly or via an agent. That procedure was adopted effectively during the Gulf War but the punishment of a nuclear armed state for abrogating a nuclear arms control agreement would seem certain to create the very situation that the agreement was designed to avoid. The threat of that type of sanction could only be plausible if the United Nations itself had recourse to nuclear weapons. This, however, would be a prescription for a nuclear monopoly rather than a step towards increased nuclear stability. So far the only practical sanction has been the threat of a continuation of the nuclear arms race and, although that may at first sight seem to be singularly inappropriate, it has achieved some success in the past.

The final problem that is inescapably linked to nuclear arms control agreements is the interface between nuclear and conventional weapons. Many facilities and weapons systems have two roles. For example, SSBNs share shore facilities with conventionally armed warships and some military aircraft can be deployed on both nuclear and conventionally armed missions while operating from the same base as non-nuclear armed aircraft. The second issue is even more fraught. For some decades the United States provided extended deterrence against both conventional and nuclear attack for its European partners within NATO. The reduction of United States' strategic nuclear weapons beyond a certain level might trigger increases in conventional weapons or, if the reductions went far enough, encourage other states, for example Germany, to develop their own nuclear weapons. Similar scenarios could be applied to the Far East in relation to less formal extended deterrence provided by United States nuclear weapons to Japan and South Korea.

Progress

Despite the problems described above, a considerable number of nuclear arms control treaties have been negotiated between the United States and the former Soviet Union over the last four decades. Several of these treaties have included Britain as well as other signatories; indeed Britain has been an active participant in arms control negotiations. The main treaties and agreements are summarised in the table below and it is clear, even from a cursory glance, that although early achievements were modest, relatively uncontroversial, and aimed at limiting peripheral potential problems, recent agreements have been successful in agreeing major reductions within the superpowers' arsenals on a scale, and in a manner, that would have seemed impossible two decades ago. This section describes the major implications of these developments.

During the 1950s there was growing public concern about the effects of radioactive fallout from nuclear weapons tests. This led to the United Nations considering the feasibility of a comprehensive test ban and to a voluntary moratorium on tests from 1958 to 1961. The moratorium was first broken by the Soviet Union but this was swiftly followed by the resumption of tests by the United States. It was against that background that the three nuclear weapons states, the United States, the Soviet Union and Britain, signed the 1963 Limited Test Ban Treaty which limited future tests to underground sites. The treaty had little impact on the ability of the nuclear weapons states to continue their development programmes. Nevertheless it ended 'dirty' atmospheric tests and, more significantly, it was the first agreement between the superpowers designed to limit nuclear competition. Its timing, just a few months after the Cuban missile crisis, was immensely significant. It demonstrated the superpowers' willingness to negotiate and also established arms control as an agenda item for the future.

The next major development was the opening of the SALT I talks in 1969 which led to the signing of two treaties between the superpowers in 1972. The ABM treaty limited each signatory to the ABM defence of only one site. The Soviet Union earmarked its network for the defence of Moscow while the United States nominated its for the defence of an ICBM site – although that work was discontinued. The superpowers had sound economic reasons for signing the treaty as, at the time, it was not technically possible to construct a fully effective ABM site and the available predictions suggested that the costs of further development were likely to be prohibitive. Nevertheless the treaty was important because it sought to limit the effectiveness of defensive systems which, in theory at least, had the potential to destabilise the strategic balance and therefore upset the assessed risks on which mutual nuclear deterrence rested. For that reason the treaty marked the first nuclear arms control

Table 5.1[2]

Year	Treaty
1959	Antarctic Treaty. Prohibited the militarization of Antarctica. Ratified by 25 states including US, USSR and UK.
1963	US–USSR 'Hot Line' Agreement.
1963	Limited Test Ban Treaty. Limited testing to underground sites. Original signatories US, USSR and UK. Treaty subsequently ratified by over 100 states. Notable exceptions were France and China.
1967	Outer Space Treaty. Forbade the militarization of space. Ratified by 81 countries including all NATO and former Warsaw Pact states.
1967	Treaty of Tlatelolco. Forbade the deployment of nuclear weapons in Latin America. Ratified by all Latin American states except Argentina (signed but not ratified), Cuba and Guyana.
1968	Nuclear Non-proliferation Treaty. Non-nuclear states agreed not to acquire nuclear weapons and nuclear armed states agreed not to supply them. Initially ratified by 118 countries including all NATO and former Warsaw Pact states. Notable exceptions Argentina, Brazil, India, Israel, Pakistan and South Africa.
1971	Sea Bed Treaty. Forbade deployment of nuclear weapons on sea bed. Ratified by 70 countries including all NATO and former Warsaw Pact littoral states.
1971	'Accidents Measures' Agreement. Sought to minimise the risk of an accidental nuclear war between the US and the former USSR.
1971	US–USSR 'Hot Line' Modernisation Agreement.
1972	SALT I. Consisted of two major treaties between the US and the USSR – the ABM treaty and the Interim Agreement on Strategic Offensive Arms. The former limited the further deployment of ABM systems while the latter froze the current number of ICBMs and SLBMs for a five-year period.
1974	Threshold Test Ban Treaty. US and USSR agreed to limit underground tests to yields not exceeding 150 kilotons.
1979	SALT II. US and USSR agreed to a ceiling of 2,250 strategic launchers with effect from 1981 – launchers exceeding total to be destroyed by the end of 1981. Treaty not ratified but observed.
1987	INF Agreement. US and USSR agreed to eliminate all ground-launched missiles with a range between 500 and 5,500 kilometres within three years of ratification. Treaty ratified by both states in May 1988.
1991	START I. US and USSR agreed to reduce 'accountable' strategic warheads to 6,000 each.
1993	START II. US and Russia agreed to reduce strategic warheads to 3,000 to 3,500 each within a 10-year period.
1995	Indefinite extension of the Nuclear Non-Proliferation Treaty. Extension signed by 182 states. Only nine states remain outside the NPT including three threshold states India, Israel and Pakistan.

agreement that sought simultaneously to maintain the nuclear balance and reduce the risks of nuclear war. The ABM treaty was not time limited.

The second SALT I treaty was the so-called 'Interim Agreement' which sought to introduce a temporary freeze on ICBM arsenals during the period from 1972 to 1977. The 'Interim Agreement' was little more than a primitive start, but it was nevertheless a start. The agreement did not specify the exact size of the superpowers' arsenals nor did it limit warheads, only launchers. Perhaps unsurprisingly the treaty quickly came under attack in the United States where it was argued that it guaranteed the Soviet Union's superiority for the next five years. Superficially that argument was correct insofar as the Soviet Union possessed more ICBMs than the United States. On the other hand the United States was well ahead of the Soviet Union in MIRV technology and consequently was able to attack more targets than the Soviet Union despite having fewer ICBMs. In practical terms SALT I did nothing to stop the superpowers improving the accuracy or destructive capacity of their already prodigious arsenals. In defence of SALT I, however, it has to be acknowledged that it was an interim agreement that was designed to pave the way for SALT II.

SALT II was signed by the superpowers in 1979 and, although it was not ratified, due largely to the Soviet Union's invasion of Afghanistan in December 1979, its terms were observed at least for the intended five-year duration of the treaty.[3] Under the treaty both sides agreed to limit their strategic launchers to 2,400 by the end of 1980, and thereafter to 2,250. Launchers in excess of these figures were to be dismantled by the end of 1981. The details of the treaty indicated that these agreements would require the United States to dismantle 34 launchers and the Soviet Union 254 launchers. SALT II also attempted to limit proliferation for the first time by setting sub ceilings for different categories of weapons. Both sides were limited to 1,320 MIRVed ballistic missile launchers (land-based ICBMs, SLBMs and ASBMs) and heavy bombers equipped with ALCMs. Of that subtotal, a maximum of 1,200 could be MIRVed while no more than 820 of the 1,200 could be land-based ICBMs. Both sides were also limited to the deployment of one new ICBM each; there was to be no increase in the size of silos and no conversion of light ICBMs to heavy ICBMs.

SALT II, like its predecessor, came in for considerable criticism. The most serious criticisms related to the very high ceilings set in the treaty and the concentration on launchers rather than warheads. Fewer than 300 launchers were to be dismantled and these, inevitably, were to be the older systems approaching obsolescence. Due to the high ceiling set on MIRVed missiles the United States remained able to increase its MIRVed missiles by some 15 per cent while the Soviet Union could increase theirs by approximately 60 per cent. Within the more destabilising category of land-based ICBMs the United

States retained the capacity to increase its MIRVed missiles by 50 per cent and the Soviet Union by 35 per cent.

At first sight it seems difficult to reconcile these figures with the concept of arms control. Indeed it has been calculated that, in the period immediately prior to the start of the SALT I talks, the ratio of United States to Soviet warheads was approximately 2,300 to 1,400 while in 1981, after more than a decade of arms control talks, the ratio was in the region of 13,800 to 11,000.[4] Despite these figures the treaty came under strong criticism from some sections of opinion within the United States who considered that it threatened their security. That opinion may seem ludicrous now but the treaty did seek to establish a position of approximate strategic parity whereas in the past the United States had enjoyed a position of superiority.

Of particular concern to sections of the United States population was the perception that the treaty enabled the Soviet Union to retain a significant superiority in land-based ICBMs, the most effective first-strike system. The treaty, of course, allowed each side to have the same number of land-based ICBMs. However, only 25 per cent of the United States' strategic forces were land-based compared to 75 per cent of the Soviet Union's forces. Thus if the United States wished to increase the number of its land-based systems it would need to make corresponding reductions in its airborne- and submarine-based strategic forces. Any such change would have reduced the United States' second-strike capacity and consequently contributed to a destabilisation of the strategic balance. SALT II certainly enabled the Soviet Union to retain a significant numerical superiority in land-based ICBMs but the balance of strategic forces within the terms of the treaty probably contributed to strategic stability without reducing the United States' capacity to mount a devastating second strike against the Soviet Union should the need arise.

A further limitation of the treaty was that verification was limited to national technical means. Perhaps this was not too much of a limitation in a treaty based on numbers of launchers rather than warheads and where the ceilings had, quite deliberately, been set high. To address this limitation the treaty made provision for a Standing Consultative Commission to discuss allegations of violations. Although the deliberations of the Commission remained secret, it seems reasonable to assume that its existence did much to dispel suggestions of cheating. Despite these criticisms it should be remembered that SALT II set limits that had not been set before and thus capped quantitative growth. Its major weakness was that it did not address the implications of the technology race. Its major strength, on the other hand, was that it demonstrated that, despite their adversarial positions, the superpowers were prepared to enter into serious arms control talks and to bring these to a pragmatic conclusion.

The INF treaty, signed in Washington in December 1987 and formally ratified in Moscow on 1 June 1988, was the first real disarmament treaty between the superpowers. The treaty provided for the elimination of all ground-launched missiles with a range of between 500 and 5,500 kilometres, irrespective of the nature of the warheads. The treaty defined two classes of missiles. First, intermediate-range missiles, with ranges between 1,000 and 5,500 kilometres, which had to be eliminated within three years of ratification. Second, short-range missiles, with ranges between 500 and 1,000 kilometres, which had to be eliminated within 18 months of ratification. Although the treaty made no provision for the destruction of warheads, as opposed to delivery vehicles, its detail was quite specific. A Memorandum of Understanding set out the numbers of launchers and missiles that were covered by the treaty (see Table 5.2 below) and two protocols set out the procedures for inspection and the precise methods to be used for destroying the missiles. While the INF treaty marked a substantial step forward in the arms control process, the political background to the INF agreement was of even greater significance. In the early 1960s the United States withdrew all its medium-range nuclear missiles from Europe as it was considered that they were unnecessary for the defence of NATO. In late 1979, the NATO 'dual track' decision, led vigorously by the United States, to redeploy medium-range missiles in Europe was a direct response to the Soviet Union's deployment, in 1976/77, of the new SS-20, a mobile missile with three warheads. Prior to the SS-20 deployment, the Soviet Union had maintained around 600 warheads on the medium-range SS-4 and SS-5 missiles and, although these were close to obsolescence, they were retained in service together with the ever-increasing numbers of SS-20 missiles. The intelligence community assessed that there was no practical military reason for these additional deployments and the official NATO conclusion was that their purpose was the political intimidation of Western Europe. It was this conclusion that prompted NATO's 'dual track' decision. That specified that, unless the Soviet Union was prepared to negotiate restrictions on its SS-20 deployments, the United States would deploy Pershing II ballistic missiles and GLCMs in Europe.

The first element of that decision was formally tabled in Geneva in 1981. The Soviet Union's build-up of the SS-20 system continued unabated and at the end of 1983 the United States implemented the second element of the decision by beginning to deploy 108 Pershing II missiles, with a range of 1,800 kilometres, in West Germany and 464 GLCMs, with a range of 2,500 kilometres, in the United Kingdom, West Germany, Belgium, Italy and the Netherlands. That decision led to the Soviet Union breaking off arms control negotiations and it provoked considerable public disquiet throughout Europe.

In the longer term, however, the Soviet Union not only returned to the negotiating table but accepted the United States' 'zero option' proposal on which the treaty was structured. The primary reason for the Soviet Union's change of position seems to have been the fact that, while United States' Pershing II and GLCMs could be targeted against the Soviet Union, the SS-20 missiles could only attack the United States' allies. Furthermore the United States made it clear from the outset that the price for withdrawing Pershing II and GLCMs was the elimination of all SS-20 missiles.

Table 5.2[5]

	Launchers	Missiles
US intermediate-range INF	282	689
US short-range INF	1	178
US total INF	283	867
USSR intermediate-range INF	614	910
USSR short-range INF	237	926
USSR total INF	851	1836
Treaty total INF	1134	2703

1. The US intermediate-range systems were Pershing II and GLMC and the short-range system was Pershing IA.
2. The USSR intermediate-range systems were SS-20, SS-4, SS-5 and SSC-X-4 and the short-range systems were SS-12 and SS-23.

Although the INF agreement was hailed as a political success throughout NATO Europe, there were some less publicly expressed misgivings, especially in West Germany and France. Some argued that the deployment of United States intermediate-range nuclear missiles in Europe enhanced deterrence. At a superficial level these deployments were visible evidence of the United States nuclear shield. At a more practical level it was argued that an American President would be more likely to authorise the use of intermediate-range systems to counter a conventional attack in Europe because that was less likely to trigger a Soviet strategic response against the United States homeland. In the longer term those who expressed concerns about the INF treaty also harboured misgivings about the possibility that it could represent a first step by the superpowers towards the denuclearisation of Europe which would result in it becoming increasingly vulnerable to threats from the Soviet Union. On the other hand these fears could probably best be allayed by some reduction in the political tension between the superpowers – a process likely to be facilitated more by arms control negotiations than by the deployment of nuclear weapons systems.[6]

The basic outline of a START treaty was developed between President Reagan and General Secretary Gorbachev at the 1986 Reykjavik and 1987 Washington summits. The ending of the Cold War, however, paved the way for the considerable reduction in the superpowers' strategic nuclear weapons arsenals embodied in the START treaty which was signed between George Bush and Mikhail Gorbachev in Moscow in the summer of 1991. The preliminary discussions leading up to START sought to resolve four complex issues. First, whether mobile land-based missiles should be banned and, if not, how their deployment should be limited and verified. Second, how to count ALCMs, how to distinguish between conventional and nuclear ALCMs and what range capability should be employed to define those ALCMs to be limited by the treaty. Third, whether limitations should be placed on SLCMs and, if so, how these could be verified. Fourth, what relationship there should be, if any, between reductions in strategic offensive arms and limitations on strategic defences.

START addressed the first two of these issues and made provision for the third to be addressed, albeit outside the formal confines of the treaty. Furthermore Soviet Foreign Minister Shevardnadze accepted a United States proposal to settle the fourth issue separately from the START treaty. The treaty, which had a duration of 15 years, and was renewable for successive five year periods, envisaged limitations and reductions being carried out in three phases over a seven year period. Provision was made for reductions of as much as 50 per cent in some systems and for general reductions in the region of 25 to 35 per cent. An overall limit of 6,000 'accountable' warheads for each side was established. That limit included ICBMs, SLBMs and ALCMs deployed on heavy strategic bombers and 'accountable' warheads were precisely defined. Within the overall limit the treaty set sub-ceilings. These limited the number of delivery vehicles (land- and sea-based missiles and strategic bombers) to 1,600, restricted ballistic missile warheads to 4,900 and warheads deployed on mobile ICBMs to 1,100. There was also a limit of 1,540 warheads on 154 heavy ICBMs – a limit that required the Soviet Union to reduce its SS-18 missiles by 50 per cent over a period of seven years yet had no impact on the United States as the latter possessed no heavy ICBMs. SLCMs were not constrained by the treaty, but both parties agreed to provide the other with a politically binding declaration concerning the limitation of the numbers of these weapons.

START included a wide variety of unprecedented verification measures which included 12 different types of on-site inspections, access to telemetric information, the continuous monitoring of mobile ICBM assembly facilities and the exchange of information on the size and composition of strategic forces. START required the United States and the Soviet Union to make 37 per cent and 51 per cent cuts respectively in their ballistic missile warhead holdings. In strategic nuclear delivery vehicles the United States was required to eliminate over 350 launchers and the Soviet Union over 1,000 launchers; cuts of 19 per cent and 38 per cent respectively. Furthermore the treaty required the Soviet Union to eliminate half of the Soviet Union's 308 10-war-headed SS-18 missiles, regarded as the most threatening part of their arsenal.

Despite these substantial reductions there was some disappointment that START did not go further. These views stemmed in part from the early declared position of both superpowers that their aim was a 50 per cent reduction, and in part because the ending of the Cold War had raised public expectations. Notwithstanding these reservations the real breakthrough achieved by START was not in 'bean counting' but in the adoption of intrusive verification procedures that had the potential to build confidence and to monitor compliance.[7]

The START II agreement was signed on 3 January 1993 between President Bush and General Secretary Yeltsin and while the 'bean counting' arithmetic was encouraging, the political backdrop was somewhat opaque. Essentially START II was the first post-Cold War arms reduction treaty and, perhaps not surprisingly, this brought into focus a new set of problems. The START II agreement contained six key points. First, the total number of warheads was to be set at between 3,800 and 4,250 within seven years of the treaty coming into force and by the year 2003 that figure was to reduce to between 3,000 and 3,500 – a reduction of about two-thirds over holdings in 1993. Second, by 2003 SLBM warheads were to be limited to 1,750 – a reduction that would require the United States to dismantle about half of its Trident missiles, the primary component of its second-strike deterrent. Third, by 2003 all MIRVed ICBMs were to be eliminated or, up to a maximum of 90 weapons, converted to single warhead missiles by adapting the launch pads. This provision enabled Russia to convert ninety SS-18 launch pads to take SS-25 missiles. Fourth, each country had the right to reconfigure 105 land-based multiple warhead missiles to single warhead missiles by removing a maximum of five warheads per missile. That provision enabled Russia to convert 105 of its 170 SS-19 missiles, each with six warheads, to single warhead systems. (Both this and the earlier provision reduced the cost of these proposals to Russia without affecting the overall goals of the treaty.) Fifth, the treaty made provision for the number of warheads per strategic bomber to be specified and for verification by inspection. (The START I treaty had regarded all strategic bombers as a single nuclear warhead – the only practical option without recourse to intrusive inspection techniques.) Both sides were also given the right to convert up to 100 strategic bombers to non-nuclear roles. Sixth, an appendix attached to the treaty provided details on how launch pads were to be converted in order that they could accommodate only single warhead missiles. The START II treaty represented a distinct advance on START I in the setting of overall ceilings, in the detailed definition of airborne warheads and in the increasing use of intrusive verification procedures.

The problem with START II was not what the treaty contained but whether it would be implemented. With the break-up of the Soviet Union political, and economic, responsibility for implementing the START treaties was a matter not just for Russia but also for Ukraine, Kazakhstan and Belarus. Under the terms of an agreement signed at Lisbon in May 1992 all four of these states assumed the former responsibilities of the Soviet Union in becoming parties to the START I treaty. Nevertheless it was some time before Russia, Kazakhstan and Belarus ratified the treaty; indeed START I did not come into force until 5 December 1994 when it was ratified by Ukraine. That paved the way for the ratification process for START II to begin.

Ukraine was the state responsible for the delay in START I coming into force. That position had more to do with Ukraine's political and economic relations with the international community than any specific reservations about the details of the treaty. With the break-up of the former Soviet Union, Ukraine was thrust into the position of possibly possessing the third biggest nuclear arsenal in the world. There were 176 former Soviet strategic missiles on Ukrainian territory and while 130 were the old SS-19s the remainder were the modern SS-24s, each with ten warheads. In addition two divisions of Blackjack bombers were based in the Ukraine, although their nuclear weapons remained under Russian control. Furthermore Ukraine possessed many of the factories that supported the former Soviet Union's nuclear arms industry and was judged to be the only non-Russian republic capable of becoming a nuclear power.

These strategic assets led Ukraine to conclude that it was not in its best interests to immediately renounce nuclear weapons. The Ukrainian government regarded these assets as bargaining counters in its relations with the West and sought to achieve both a more strident voice and economic aid to finance the dismantling of nuclear weapons.

The first of these demands backfired as it simply angered the international community. The second was more successful but the Ukraine's initial demand of $2.8 billion evoked a limited response from the United States. Irritated by Ukraine's failure to deliver on any of its promises, the United States was not prepared to make more than $175 million available to help the disarmament process. In theory there is no reason why the reductions quantified in the START treaties should not be made, but progress is bound to be dependent upon the political and economic stability of the Commonwealth of Independent States (CIS). In late 1996, with Yeltsin becoming an increasingly absentee president and the Chechen peace deal looking increasingly shaky with the sacking of Alexander Lebed, the prospects for stability in the states of the former Soviet Union were not encouraging.

Proliferation

The progress outlined above in nuclear arms control relates to what is termed vertical proliferation, namely the increasing size and destructive capacity of the arsenals of the nuclear weapons states, especially those of the superpowers.

Horizontal proliferation, on the other hand, refers to the spread of a nuclear weapons capacity to other states. In the 1960s there were real concerns about the potential dangers of extensive horizontal proliferation over the coming decades. While these fears have not been realised, changes in the prospects for future horizontal proliferation remain an issue of considerable strategic concern.

Since 1964, when China joined the United States, the Soviet Union, Britain and France, there have been no additions to the declared nuclear weapons states. Nevertheless much has changed since 1964. There has been a steady erosion of the technical barriers to the acquisition of a nuclear weapons capability. Today many countries have the technical ability to manufacture nuclear weapons, but access to weapons grade fissile material remains a hurdle for the majority of states. Without either plutonium or enriched uranium, nuclear warheads cannot be manufactured. Only those states with a highly developed industrial engineering infrastructure or extensive nuclear experience are likely to be able to build an enrichment plant without outside technical help. Conversely, weapons grade plutonium can be obtained by reprocessing the fuel rods from civil nuclear reactors and, although that requires the application of sophisticated technologies, it is within the capacity of those states which have developed their own nuclear research or power programmes. Thus by the mid-1980s it was estimated that Argentina possessed two metric tonnes of plutonium. Clearly, therefore, there was a link between the adoption of civil nuclear programmes and potential weapons development. That connection has been a key factor in the management of horizontal proliferation policies.

In the 1950s the United States adopted its 'Atoms for Peace' policy in order to prove its technological superiority over the Soviet Union and to generate or reinforce the political allegiance of the Third World. By 1956 it had signed bilateral civil nuclear co-operation agreements with more than 28 nations and, by 1962, it had exported over 29 research reactors. Throughout the 1960s the United States was able to use its 'Atoms for Peace' policy to control the rate and direction of civil horizontal proliferation and, as it was the sole supplier of enriched uranium for use as a nuclear fuel, it sought to make it unnecessary for other states to contemplate building expensive enrichment plants or engaging in reprocessing. Events in the 1970s, however, resulted in a fundamental questioning of the 'Atoms for Peace' policy. First, India's explosion of a nuclear device in May 1974 demonstrated that, contrary to the conventional wisdom of the period, states with civil nuclear programmes were capable of developing nuclear weapons. Second, the United States monopoly of the civil nuclear market was broken by developments in Europe. Both France and Germany, in a reaction to a downturn in orders for civil nuclear power programmes within Europe, began to compete in Third World markets previously monopolised by the United States. To ensure commercial success France and Germany offered competitive financial packages and, significantly, packages that included the transfer of sensitive technologies such as enrichment and reprocessing. The United States was consequently no longer in a position to control the spread of these technologies. These changes in commercial practice led to West Germany selling a complete civil nuclear fuel cycle, including reactors, reprocessing and enrichment technology to Brazil in 1975 and to France selling a reprocessing plant to Pakistan in 1978. Despite these controversial developments the spread of nuclear weapons states, widely anticipated in the 1970s, did not materialise. Nevertheless by the mid-1980s Argentina, Brazil, India, Israel, North Korea, Pakistan and South Africa were all regarded as 'threshold' states.

Despite the number of states that have developed the capacity to join the five nuclear weapons states the international community has demonstrated a surprising political willingness to limit the horizontal proliferation of nuclear weapons. The 1968 Nuclear Non-Proliferation Treaty (NPT), which became effective in 1970, is the cornerstone of the international community's policy on the limiting of horizontal proliferation. The treaty, to which all states were encouraged to accede, binds nuclear weapons states not to transfer nuclear weapons to non-nuclear weapons states, nor to assist them in any way to develop or acquire such weapons. Similarly each non-nuclear weapon state undertakes not to receive nor to manufacture nuclear weapons and also to accept safeguards, to be agreed with the International Atomic Energy Agency (IAEA), in order to allow verification that civil nuclear programmes are not being used to develop nuclear weapons. Furthermore all parties to the treaty undertake to pursue negotiations aimed at achieving nuclear disarmament. By the mid-1980s the treaty had been ratified by 126 non-nuclear states and signed by three others leaving only 30 non-nuclear states, including six threshold states, which were not parties to the treaty.

Despite its widespread acceptance the treaty contained a number of weaknesses. First, its concept is inherently discriminatory as it places significant constraints on the non-nuclear states yet places no constraints on vertical proliferation by the nuclear weapons states. In effect this gives *de jure* recognition to the *de facto* dominance of the nuclear weapons states in the global power hierarchy. This has led some Third World states to reject the treaty on the basis that it legitimises outdated concepts of imperialism. Furthermore that position has been exacerbated by the fact that neither of the superpowers has fully observed the spirit of the treaty. The United States has continued its bilateral partnership with Britain while China's initial development of a nuclear weapons programme was assisted by the Soviet Union. This has led many states to conclude, understandably, that the superpowers are much more concerned about their *control* of the spread of nuclear weapons than the spread of these weapons *per se*. Second, while Article VI of the treaty obliges all states to end the nuclear arms race and to move towards nuclear disarmament, the record of the nuclear weapons states, particularly the superpowers, in that respect has been far from exemplary. Third, under Article IV of the treaty, provision is made for those states that renounce nuclear weapons to receive access to civil nuclear technology. Many non-nuclear states have argued that the selective manner, and commercial basis, on which civil nuclear technology is made available by the nuclear exporting countries contravenes the spirit of the treaty – a position that is refuted by the nuclear exporting states. Fourth, and most significant, are reservations about the effectiveness of verification procedures. The IAEA was founded in 1957, but since 1968 its primary task has been to monitor the effectiveness of the treaty's safeguards. This gives the Agency powers to ensure: 'the timely detection or diversion of significant quantities of nuclear material from peaceful nuclear activities to the manufacture of nuclear weapons . . . and deterrence of such diversion by the risk of early detection'. The Agency thus has a mandate to detect and deter but not to prevent or prohibit the misuse of nuclear materials. Even the effective pursuit of its limited powers is a difficult task. Essentially the Agency's inspectors audit the nuclear accounts of those non-nuclear states that have ratified the treaty and have civil nuclear programmes to detect irregularities and provide an early warning of misuse. While that concept may have been viable in the 1970s, it has become increasingly flawed with the passage of time. The steady increase in the number of civil nuclear facilities provides the IAEA's inspectors with an ever-increasing task while, simultaneously, due to the burgeoning development of technology, it takes less and less time to develop a nuclear weapons capability from civil facilities. Thus a non-nuclear state could reach the stage of testing a nuclear weapon before any 'early warning' had been sounded by the IAEA, so even if states co-operate fully with the IAEA's inspectors there can be no guarantee that the treaty's safeguards will be effective in preventing horizontal proliferation.

Events since the treaty came into effect indicate that not all states co-operate with the IAEA. In 1981 Israel, a threshold state and non-signatory of the treaty, bombed the Tamuz research reactor in Iraq, a signatory to the treaty. Clearly Israel was not convinced that the IAEA inspectors' work was effective. More recently, events in North Korea and Iraq, both signatories to the treaty, have demonstrated the difficulties which IAEA inspectors have to face when confronted by non-cooperative régimes. A final factor affecting horizontal proliferation, but not resulting from any flaw in the treaty, has been the rapid growth of a black market in fissile material emanating from the weapons factories of the former Soviet Union. That development has raised the prospect not just of states obtaining that material from sources outside the formal controls of the Treaty but also of that material being made available to groups acting beyond the control of any state. That is a matter of very considerable concern.

The original treaty made provision for a conference to be held in 1995 to enable the international community to decide whether the treaty's terms should remain in force permanently. At the end of that conference, on 11 May 1995 in Washington, and notwithstanding the difficulties outlined above, 182 states agreed to extend the Nuclear Non-Proliferation Treaty indefinitely and unconditionally. Furthermore, while the outcome had been far from certain there was a broad consensus in support of the extension of the treaty. The nuclear weapons states have pledged to withhold civilian nuclear technology from those states that have refused to adopt the treaty's safeguards. On the other hand the non-nuclear states obtained formal, albeit non-binding, commitments from the nuclear weapons states to hasten nuclear disarmament. These commitments included setting a goal to complete negotiations for a comprehensive test ban treaty by the end of 1996 and an agreement to begin negotiating a new ban on the production of fissile materials. Clearly, despite its flaws, the Nuclear Non-Proliferation Treaty remains the international community's best instrument not only for controlling horizontal proliferation but also for achieving some progress towards nuclear disarmament. While all five of the nuclear weapons states are now signatories to the treaty three of the threshold states, India, Israel and Pakistan, have not signed it.[8] The position of North Korea and Iraq remains ambivalent but both these states are under international pressure to live up to their treaty obligations. The big challenge for the future is how the nuclear weapons states, especially the United States which campaigned vigorously for the treaty's extension, will fulfil their obligation to advance nuclear disarmament.

During 1996, in order to fulfil one of the conditions contained in the extension of the NPT, considerable effort was made to negotiate a Comprehensive Test Ban Treaty (CTBT). The draft treaty sought to ban all further nuclear tests and had almost universal support. However, in August 1996, the 61-nation Conference on Disarmament, meeting in Geneva, failed to unanimously endorse the draft. The draft was supported by the five declared nuclear-weapons states and two of the threshold states, Israel and Pakistan. India, the other threshold state, and Iran, refused to support the treaty. Significantly India was not opposed to ending nuclear tests; its objection to signing was that it felt that the terms of the treaty did not put sufficient pressure on the declared nuclear-weapons states to work towards total nuclear disarmament. India's refusal to support the draft made it procedurally impossible for the United Nations to approve the treaty at its meeting in September 1996. Despite that setback, the UN General Assembly voted overwhelmingly to open a treaty for signature banning all further nuclear tests. That move has, at least temporarily, overcome India's veto. Nevertheless, before any treaty can be effective it must have the support of all states capable of conducting nuclear tests. India's lack of support may well lead to Pakistan feeling that it has no option but to withdraw its support for a ban. A CTBT by the end of 1996 was no longer possible. Nevertheless the nuclear-weapons states have all agreed to discontinue testing and, as India is likely to come under increasing pressure to support a formal ban on testing, a CTBT may still be achievable at some stage in the future. All the indicators are that a CTBT will remain high on the international arms-control agenda.

Implications for Britain

Notwithstanding the fact that Britain has been an active participant in arms-control negotiations over several decades, so far it has not been directly affected by the outcome of that process. That position, however, is unlikely to continue. With the disintegration of the former Soviet Union, future calls for reductions in nuclear weapons are not likely to be limited to the United States and the CIS. Furthermore if, under the terms of START II, the United States and the CIS are to be limited to 1,750 SLBM warheads each by 2003, a reduction of about 50 per cent, Britain is going to find it increasingly difficult to justify the substantial qualitative and quantitative strategic increase inherent in the deployment of Trident. Thus, for both general and specific reasons, Britain is likely to be directly affected by future developments in strategic nuclear arms control.

Since the end of the Cold War, Britain has made some significant reductions in its holdings of nuclear weapons of its own volition. However, these reductions have been in tactical or sub-strategic weapons and the decisions have been prompted by the need to make savings in the defence budget rather than by an altruistic wish to provide leadership in matters related to arms reductions. Nevertheless all nuclear artillery shells and those nuclear weapons that were routinely carried on Royal Navy ships prior to 1992 have now been withdrawn. More significantly, plans to procure a nuclear armed stand-off missile for Tornado were cancelled in 1993 and stocks of the sub-strategic WE177 free-fall bombs have been halved. Those currently remaining are to be withdrawn by the end of 1998. Against that background, the 1996 White Paper on Defence states that 'by 1998 we will have 21% fewer warheads with 59% less explosive power than during the 1970s'. Doubtless that statement is true but it tells us nothing about the comparative number of strategic warheads.

Prior to November 1993 the British government envisaged replacing the four Polaris boats with four Trident boats and retaining its stock – probably some 300 to 400 – WE177 sub-strategic free-fall bombs. A Trident fleet of four boats equipped with 16 missiles, with a range in excess of 6,000 kilometres, and each capable of carrying up to 12 warheads with a yield of around 100 kt represents a 200 per cent increase in yield and a twelve-fold increase in strategic targeting capacity over the Polaris fleet. In November 1993, Defence Secretary Rifkind, at that time under considerable pressure to make cuts in defence spending, announced that the Trident boats would be limited to an (unverifiable) maximum of 96 warheads per boat. That decision to deploy boats at only half their potential capacity still ensures a 100 per cent increase in yield and a six-fold increase in targeting capacity over Polaris. Furthermore it is important to remember that Rifkind's statement was the announcement of an operational policy that, should the British government feel the circumstances warrant it, could immediately be revoked. That falls far short of an obligation to conform to the terms of an arms control treaty – a point that is not lost on the non-nuclear weapons states.

The 1995 White Paper on Defence announced that, once the second Trident boat was operational, the Trident force would have a responsibility for providing a sub-strategic nuclear capability. As an interim measure the Tornado force would continue to provide a sub-strategic capability until the WE177 free-fall bomb is withdrawn at the end of 1998 by which time it is anticipated that the third Trident boat will be operational.

That apparently illogical decision to give what has always been a strategic system a sub-strategic role raises operational questions which may, in turn, complicate the warhead arithmetic of arms control issues. A sub-strategic nuclear strike is intended to be a powerful, and probably final, demonstration of intent. To be effective it must be limited in yield, highly selective in its targeting and leave the aggressor in no doubt that if he does not make the right response he will face the prospect of a devastating strategic strike. There are inescapable operational penalties in giving that role to Trident. First, from 1996 until the end of 1998, when there are only two operational Trident boats, to avoid any possibility of a system failure, two missiles will need to be armed with single low-yield warheads thus limiting the boats' strategic payload to a maximum of 94 warheads. These could be configured as seven missiles, each fitted with 12 warheads, and one missile with ten warheads. From 1998 onwards it will be possible to deploy a second boat to fulfil the sub-strategic role, but only for limited periods. Second, if a Trident boat fires a sub-strategic strike it is immediately detectable. That could place the boat at considerable risk and, in the worst case, provoke a response on launch. In other words if the sub-strategic strike was directed at a nuclear armed state it might not wait to see if the incoming missile was low-yield (which would only be obvious on detonation) but might regard the first launch as a strategic strike and make an immediate strategic retaliation. Third, for a sub-strategic strike to be effective the aggressor should be in no doubt about the identity of the striker. While a submarine-launched ballistic missile is instantly detectable, however, the nationality of that submarine is not.

There are a number of indicators that can be postulated from the decision to give Trident a sub-strategic nuclear role. First, the British government does not envisage employing sub-strategic strikes against a nuclear armed state. To do so would inevitably put the deterrent at risk and may provoke the very exchange that a sub-strategic strike aims to avoid. Second, the British government envisages using the deterrent to coerce non-nuclear states. Logical perhaps, but likely to raise fears in many non-nuclear states, including many that the government has no wish to coerce. That implicit change of policy may well result in louder calls from the non-nuclear states to hasten total nuclear disarmament. Third, while the government wants to dispose of its stock of WE177 bombs for reasons of economy it may wish to retain, at least a nominal, sub-strategic nuclear role as a bargaining position in future arms reduction talks. For example if the government were to relinquish its sub-strategic nuclear role after 1998, when the SSNs will have the conventionally armed Tomahawk cruise missile, it might be able to claim that it had made a nuclear arms reduction concession. *De facto*, however, if the government wishes to have the ability to launcha sub-strategic strike at a non-nuclear power an SSN equipped with conventionally armed cruise missiles is a much more appropriate and acceptable system than even the lowest possible yield ballistic missile launched from a Trident boat. Trident's sub-strategic nuclear role may be no more than an hostage to future arms reduction talks.

The arithmetic apart, arms control developments may have other implications for the future of Britain's deterrent. The international community's decision to extend the NPT indefinitely has raised expectations of progress in respect of nuclear disarmament. These expectations will be greatest in the non-nuclear-weapon states but the international opprobrium attaching to the French decision to conduct nuclear tests in the Pacific in the late summer of 1995 has demonstrated the depth of feeling on that issue on an international scale. Britain may well come under increasing international pressure to reduce the size of its strategic deterrent long before Trident will be due for replacement. This could call into question the operational viability of Britain's deterrent. It would not be possible to maintain continuous operational patrols with a three-boat fleet and it seems improbable that the international community will consider Britain's self-imposed restraint on the numbers of warheads per boat as a sufficient guarantee of its commitment. International pressure to ensure progress towards a reduction in nuclear weapons holdings could also impact on Britain's special nuclear relationship with the United States. The latter will doubtless be anxious to influence the speed and direction of future arms control developments and consequently the nuclear interests of the United States may increasingly diverge from those of Britain.

It seems reasonable to conclude that while arms control had no impact on the decision to procure Trident, other than some elegant rhetoric about what the future might hold, that position might change during Trident's operational life and could be fundamentally different by the time a decision needs to made about a successor system.

NOTES

1. Extract from a background paper on comparative risks written by Professor Michael McGwire of Cambridge University for the Canberra Commission on the Elimination of Nuclear Weapons, 1996. See Field Marshal Lord Carver, 'A Nuclear (Elimination) Exchange', *RUSI Jounal* (London: RUSI, Oct. 1996) p. 52.
2. For fuller details of most of the treaties contained in this table see Windlass S. (ed.), Walker P., Shenfield S., Greenwood D. and Windsor P., *Avoiding Nuclear War: Common Security as a Strategy for the Defence of the West* (London: Brassey, 1985) Appendix II, pp. 131–46.
3. The terms of the treaty were observed until they were expressly repudiated by President Reagan in 1987. At that stage the United States had exceeded the limit of 1,320 for launchers of ballistic missiles with MIRVs and strategic bombers carrying air-launched cruise missiles.
4. See Segal G., Moreton E., Freedman L. and Baylis J., *Nuclear War and Nuclear Peace* (London: Macmillan, 1988) p. 49 (second edition).
5. For further details of the data contained in the treaty's Memorandum of Understanding see *Survival*, Vol. 30 (March/April, 1988) p. 180.
6. For a fuller assessment of details and implications of the INF treaty see *Strategic Survey 1987–1988* (London: The International Institute for Strategic Studies, 1988) pp. 21–39. As the INF was a bilateral treaty between the United States and the Soviet Union it did not limit the development of intermediate-range missiles by other states. For a good resumé of these developments see Bailey K. C., 'Can Missile Proliferation be Reversed?', *Orbis* (Winter 1991).
7. For a more detailed assessment of the START treaty see *Strategic Survey 1989–1990* (London: International Institute of Strategic Studies, 1990) pp. 194–213.
8. By the mid-1990s it was generally accepted that it was no longer appropriate to regard Argentina, Brazil and South Africa as threshold states despite their undoubted capacity to develop nuclear weapons. Only nine states now remain outside the NPT.

CHAPTER SIX

British Political Decision Making, CND and Public Opinion

Introduction

> All governments have conducted nuclear weapons policy making in the greatest secrecy . . . In this process the opinions and the facts put forward by a small group of interested scientists and other supporting staff have been given excessive weight and there has been little if any criticism or questioning of assumptions from within Whitehall . . . policy making by all governments has followed the same path and been conducted within a general consensus. In this atmosphere it has been impossible for pressure groups to exercise influence over decisions. Public opinion has rarely been thought to be important by the policy makers. In this, apart from the odd occasion, the policy makers have been backed by public opinion, content to go along with accepted policy. This obviously suits the policy makers and they devote considerable efforts to ensuring that there is not a great debate about nuclear weapons.[1]

THE KEY DECISIONS concerning the future of Britain's nuclear weapons programme have been taken by small élites and shrouded in secrecy from the outset. Nevertheless in the past there has been a remarkable consensus, by both élites and public, over the appropriateness of these decisions. This chapter reviews that position and seeks to establish what the position might be in the future. The chapter embraces three elements. First, a *résumé* is undertaken of the nuclear decision making of successive governments since 1945. Thereafter an analysis is made of the influence of the Campaign for Nuclear Disarmament (CND) and of trends in public opinion. The assessment focuses on indicators of continuity and change.

Political Decision Making

Since 1945 Britain has experienced 14 general elections, but only five of these have resulted in a change in the governing party (see Table 6.1 below). Since

1945 the Conservative party has ruled Britain for almost twice as long as Labour. Of the six post-war Labour governments, one lacked an overall majority and three possessed only marginal majorities. Furthermore the two peaks in Labour's popularity occurred as far back as 1945 and 1966 compared with the Conservative government's major electoral successes of 1959 and 1983. Nevertheless it was not until the early 1980s, when the Labour Party voted to abandon Polaris, that the political consensus on nuclear weapons began to break down.

The cohesive impact of the Second World War, during which Britain was governed by a coalition government, invariably led to senior political figures, of both the major parties, sharing common goals in respect of foreign and defence policy. That consensus was reinforced by a traditional British approach to 'high politics' that was rooted in pragmatism rather than ideology. As a consequence, as far as policy regarding the development of nuclear weapons was concerned, there were more difficulties within parties than between them and those differences that did exist were most effectively publicised by organisations independent of the main political parties, such as CND. The immediate post-war consensus is clearly illustrated by Sir Anthony Eden's comment made in the late 1940s in response to Attlee's Foreign Secretary, Ernest Bevin's, claim that: 'the (atomic) bomb must have a Union Jack on it'. Eden, the Shadow Foreign Secretary, recorded his agreement with Bevin's sentiment and added: 'I would probably have agreed with him more, if I had not been anxious to embarrass him less'.[2]

In July 1945 Labour gained its first ever substantial electoral success with an overall majority of 146 seats. Labour's victory was attributed to the success of planning and the importance of the notion of 'fair shares' during the war and to the proven ability of Labour ministers throughout the wartime coalition government. Conversely, a proportion of middle-class voters were disillusioned with the Conservative Party's pre-war record in respect of appeasement and unemployment. It was Attlee's post-war Labour government that took responsibility for initiating Britain's nuclear weapons programme.

Attlee, and some of his ministers, had been privy to the 'Tube Alloys'[3] programme during the wartime coalition government and, in view of Britain's understandable assumption of continued great power status, it was probably inevitable that these individuals would wish to see the development of a British nuclear weapon. A Cabinet Committee (GEN 75) took the critical first decision on 18 December 1945 to build an atomic pile to produce plutonium. The same Committee considered whether Britain should manufacture an atomic bomb on 25 October 1946. Both the Chancellor of the Exchequer, Hugh Dalton, and the President of the Board of Trade, Stafford Cripps, expressed doubts about the wisdom of proceeding on economic and industrial grounds and the meeting ended without a decision being taken.

Table 6.1

DATES OF ELECTIONS AND KEY STRATEGIC NUCLEAR EVENTS
SINCE 1945

Date of Election	Winning Party	Key Events
1945	Labour (Attlee)	*1947 Secret decision taken to start nuclear weapons programme* 1948 Formation of NATO 1948 Berlin crisis begins *1948 Government makes 'on the record' statement implying the existence of a nuclear weapons programme*
1950	Labour (Attlee)	1950 Korean War starts
1951	Conservative (Churchill/Eden)	*1952 Britain's first atomic bomb test* *1954 Britain decides to manufacture the H-bomb*
1955	Conservative (Eden/Macmillan)	1956 Suez Crisis *1956 V-bombers begin to enter service* *1957 Britain's first thermonuclear test (H-bomb)* *1957 Britain announces adoption of the doctrine of massive retaliation* 1957/58 CND formed
1959	Conservative (Macmillan/Home)	1961 Berlin Wall erected 1962 Cuban missile crisis *1962 Polaris purchase agreement*
1964	Labour (Wilson)	*1964 Labour decides to continue the Polaris programme* *1965 V-bomber force no longer viable* *1965 Decision not to procure fifth Polaris boat*
1966	Labour (Wilson)	*1967 Work on the Polaris improvement programme authorised (Chevaline)* *1968 First Polaris boat operational*
1970	Conservative (Heath)	*1970 Chevaline research programme continues* 1972 Britain joins the EEC
1974 (Feb.)	Labour (Wilson)	*1974 Labour authorises development of Chevaline and renounces need for Polaris replacement*
1974 (Oct.)	Labour (Wilson/Callaghan)	*1977 Labour authorises work to begin on a successor system for Polaris* 1978 Soviet Union's deployment of SS-20 missiles in Eastern Europe begins.
1979	Conservative (Thatcher)	1979 Soviet Union's invasion of Afghanistan *1980 Trident procurement decision announced* 1980 Growth of European peace movements *1981 Decision to buy Trident D-5 missiles* *1982 Chevaline enters service* *1981–2 Labour Party votes to abandon Polaris and remove United States bases from Britain* 1982 Falklands War
1983	Conservative (Thatcher)	*1983 Cruise missiles deployed in the UK in response to the deployment of Soviet SS-20s*
1987	Conservative (Thatcher/Major)	*1987 Conservative government reaffirms commitment to Trident* 1991 Gulf War
1992	Conservative (Major)	*1993 Britain announces that Trident boats will be equipped with a maximum of 96 warheads – half the potential capacity of each hull* *1994 First Trident operational patrol*

In order to circumvent that opposition, Attlee established a new Cabinet Committee (GEN 163) without Dalton and Cripps. The decision to proceed was taken by the six ministers comprising GEN 163 on 8 January 1947 and they also decided that the costs of the development should be concealed. Margaret Gowing, the official historian of Britain's atomic programme, records that the Cabinet was not involved in decisions to establish a research establishment, to build piles to produce plutonium, or gaseous diffusion plants to provide uranium-235, to develop and test an atomic bomb, or about the role of atomic weapons in British strategy.[4] The Attlee government made no formal statement that Britain was engaged in developing an atomic bomb, but the decision was placed 'on the record' in a contrived Parliamentary Question on 12 May 1948 – some 15 months after the programme had been authorised. A backbencher asked the Minister of Defence, Mr A. V. Alexander, whether he was satisfied that adequate progress was being made in 'the most modern types of weapon'. In reply the Minister gave an assurance that 'all types of modern weapons, including atomic weapons, were being developed'[5] (italics added).

Attlee's Labour administration was again successful in the March 1950 general election but with a much reduced majority of only five seats. Despite Attlee's small majority, and the outbreak of the Korean War in the summer of 1950, there were no critical parliamentary problems until mid-1951 by which time Labour had lost two ministers (Bevin and Cripps) due to death and illness and two other important figures (Bevan and Wilson) through resignation. Attlee sought a dissolution on 19 September 1951 and, at the resulting general election on 25 October, Churchill's Conservative government returned to power with a majority of 17 seats. By that time Britain's atomic weapons programme was well established and, although its existence and costs had been carefully concealed, subsequent events were to suggest that neither parliament nor the public wished to contest either the substance of that decision or the secrecy which surrounded it.

Churchill adopted a more conventional approach to nuclear decision making, possibly because he felt more certain of support from within his party, possibly because of a greater respect for the institutions of government or, alternatively, because the atomic weapons programme could not be kept secret forever. The existence of Britain's programme was acknowledged publicly by Churchill in February 1952 when he announced plans to conduct the first test of a British-made atomic bomb at the Monte Bello Islands in the autumn of 1952. The major nuclear decision of Churchill's government, however, concerned the H-bomb. It was some 15 months before the results of the United States first fusion explosion reached Churchill. He later told the House of Commons that he had been 'astounded' by the destructive capacity of the H-bomb.[6] That development led directly to Britain's decision to manufacture its own H-bomb.

The decision was taken in 1954 by a six-man Cabinet Committee (MISC 464) and endorsed by the Defence Committee. Nevertheless Churchill agreed that the practice of concealing the cost of these developments should continue. It is relevant to note that Gowing has suggested that the main reason for that secrecy was to conceal from the United States the modest scope of the British programme.[7] Churchill resigned in April 1955 and was replaced by Sir Anthony Eden who sought a dissolution. At the resulting election on 26 May 1955, the Conservative party returned to power with its majority increased to 54 seats. Following the Suez *débâcle* in 1956 Eden resigned in favour of Macmillan and in the following year Britain conducted its first thermonuclear test and shortly afterwards announced its adoption of the strategy of massive retaliation. The Conservative administrations that governed Britain in the early 1950s had taken forward the nuclear weapons programme with less secrecy than their Labour predecessors but, apart from some minority backbench Labour opposition, these developments remained uncontroversial both within parliament and with the general public.

Despite the formation of the Campaign for Nuclear Disarmament in the winter of 1957–58, and the support it subsequently received from the left wing of the Labour Party, the nuclear weapons programme was not an issue in the 1959 election. The outcome was another Conservative victory in which the party's overall majority increased to 100 seats. Macmillan's nuclear problems, however, were not assuaged by his parliamentary majority. With the imminent cancellation of the British Blue Streak missile Macmillan secured an agreement from the United States in March 1960 to purchase Skybolt. There is no evidence to suggest that, at this crucial stage in the development of Britain's nuclear weapons programme, there was any reappraisal of whether the programme should be continued. Indeed the events that took place suggest that the Macmillan government's only concern was to obtain a replacement for Blue Streak. Withdrawal from the nuclear club was simply not an option. The subsequent, and completely unexpected, cancellation of Skybolt's development in November 1962 precipitated a crisis in Whitehall. Macmillan used the newly established Defence and Overseas Policy Committee of the Cabinet to examine options that would allow Britain to remain a nuclear weapons power. Again the possibility of withdrawal from the programme was not considered. The Committee reported that the acquisition of Polaris was the only viable alternative and Macmillan travelled in person to conduct negotiations with President Kennedy. Macmillan's political future was dependent upon a speedy and successful outcome and he simply assumed full personal negotiating powers, although he did consult the Cabinet by telegram on key issues. The fact that the outcome was highly successful was due predominantly to the suitability of the Polaris system rather than to Macmillan's methodology or skills as a negotiator. Macmillan had avoided a personal disaster but the events of late 1962 marked the beginning of the end of the nuclear consensus. Labour was scathing about the Polaris deal and pledged to renegotiate it when they returned to office.

Labour's opportunity came with the election of October 1964 in which they secured a majority, albeit of only five seats. The outcome, however, was an immediate *volte-face*. It appears that Wilson consulted Patrick Gordon-Walker the Foreign Secretary and Denis Healey the Defence Secretary and then decided that the Polaris programme should go ahead although it was decided to cancel the option to purchase a fifth boat. That decision was subsequently endorsed by the Defence Committee and thereafter by the Cabinet, but there was no reappraisal of the programme, nor any attempt to renegotiate the terms of the Polaris agreement. By 1966 Labour's majority had been reduced to three but the Party's standing in the opinion polls was high and early in 1966 Wilson called another election in which his government was returned with an overall majority of 96 seats. The following year the Labour government took an even more improbable decision when it authorised the commencement of work aimed at upgrading Polaris. A secret committee, thought to consist of Wilson, Healey, George Brown the Foreign Secretary and Jim Callaghan the Chancellor, decided not to purchase the United States Poseidon missile but authorised the Aldermaston research team to start work on an improved Polaris warhead – a project that was later to be known as Chevaline. In June 1968 the first Polaris boat commenced its initial operational patrol.

The 1966 Labour government was beset by economic difficulties and in the election of June 1970, despite an improvement in economic performance and against the predictions in the polls, Heath's Conservative government secured a majority of 30 seats. The fourth Polaris boat become operational in September 1970 providing Britain with a viable second strike deterrent and the Heath government continued the Aldermaston research programme aimed at upgrading Polaris. Apart from its success in achieving Britain's entry into the Common Market Heath's government fared badly, and in the election of February 1974 Wilson returned to power, despite the fact that his government was 34 seats short of an overall majority. A further election was called for October 1974 in which Labour secured an overall majority of three seats. Despite Labour's small majority, its pledge not to build 'a new generation of nuclear weapons' and the anti-nuclear views of cabinet members Michael Foot and Barbara Castle, the Prime Minister managed to secure support for the decision to proceed with the full-scale development of the Chevaline programme. Once again the initial decision was made by a small group of five ministers (Wilson, Healey (Chancellor), Callaghan (Foreign Secretary), Mason (Defence Secretary) and Jenkins (Home Secretary)) who met informally and not as a Cabinet Committee. That group authorised development prior to the October election. Formal Cabinet endorsement was obtained on 20 November

1974 when, in keeping with Wilson's reputation as a skilful parliamentary tactician, the development programme was included as a minor item in a paper dealing with a major review of defence commitments.[8]

Callaghan succeeded Wilson in April 1976 but there was no change in the methodology of nuclear decision making. Despite the Labour party's public declaration that it did not intend to replace Polaris, ministers participated in initial work to assess the options for replacement. A formal request for this work to commence was made by the Ministry of Defence and the Foreign Office in January 1978 and work by officials began shortly afterwards. Reports on progress were not made to the Defence and Overseas Policy Committee of the Cabinet, which contained ministers with anti-nuclear views, but were restricted to the Prime Minister, Foreign Secretary (Owen), Chancellor (Healey) and Defence Secretary (Mulley). Once again that group met informally rather than as a Cabinet Committee. No decision was made prior to the 1979 election although it seems probable that the work was not inhibited by Labour's declared policy of no replacement. Labour's public position was no less tortuous than the machinations of its leadership. Despite the Party's decision not to seek a successor system to Polaris, the 1979 Manifesto deliberately kept that option open by suggesting that a future public debate might reverse the Party's official position:

> In 1974, we renounced any intention of moving towards the production of a new generation of nuclear weapons or a successor to the Polaris nuclear force; we reiterate our belief that this is the best course for Britain. But many great issues affecting our allies and the world are involved, and a new round of Strategic Arms Limitation negotiations will soon begin. We think it is essential that there must be a full and informed debate about these issues in the country before any decision is taken.[9]

Mrs Thatcher's Conservative government won the May 1979 election with a majority of 43 seats. Work on the Polaris replacement assessment continued and, although decision making remained the prerogative of a small group of ministers, they were formally constituted as a Cabinet Committee. The full Cabinet, however, was not consulted until the day on which the decision to purchase Trident was announced in July 1980 and that procedure was adopted again the following year when the Thatcher government decided to purchase the Trident D-5 rather than the original C-4 missile.

While the earlier consensus had been eroding steadily at grass roots level the early 1980s saw it collapse at the level of parliamentary élites. The Thatcher government was unequivocal in its support for Trident, it emerged successfully from the Falklands War, and was a strong supporter of the United States' 'dual track' response to the deployment of Soviet SS-20 missiles in Eastern

Europe. Labour, on the other hand, committed itself to a non-nuclear defence policy, pledged to withdraw Britain from the European Community and to renounce the use of bases in Britain by United States' forces. Indeed Labour's manifesto for the 1983 election was described by one Shadow Cabinet member as 'the longest suicide note in history'. That prediction proved correct in the election of June 1983 when Mrs Thatcher returned to power with a majority of 144 seats.

Chevaline had become operational the year before, albeit greatly over budget; the Trident programme continued as planned and cruise missile deployments, which had commenced in 1983, also continued despite an increasing wave of public protests. Notwithstanding these signs Mrs Thatcher retained a majority of 102 in the election of June 1987 and in April 1992 the Conservatives were returned for a fourth term of office, against heavy odds, with a majority of 21 seats. Despite the requirement for savings from the defence budget following the disintegration of the former Soviet Union, the Trident programme progressed as planned, on time and within budget. In November 1993 Defence Secretary Rifkind, in response to economic pressures, announced that the maximum number of warheads to be deployed on the Trident boats would be 36, half the capacity of the hull, and in December 1994 the first Trident boat left the Clyde on an operational patrol.

The Rise and Fall of CND

Since 1958 CND has sought to mobilise British public opinion against nuclear weapons. Over that period the movement's fortunes have waxed and waned and, consequently, it is instructive to assess the reasons for these fluctuations. While CND has never been a majority movement, it has enjoyed substantial support from time to time. Furthermore CND, despite the difficulties of obtaining value-free information about nuclear weapons, has, to a large extent, been an informed protest movement with a significant number of its supporters coming from the educated middle classes. Conversely it is not unreasonable to contend that a significant proportion of those who have consistently supported Britain's nuclear weapons programme (the 'silent majority' who traditionally support the *status quo*) are probably less well informed than the average CND supporter. For all these reasons CND's fortunes can be used, albeit with some care, as a barometer to detect major swings in British public opinion and to offer explanations for these changes.

The CND's origins were essentially élitist.[10] Both J. B. Priestley and Kingsley Martin, the editor of the *New Statesman*, were key figures in establishing the organisation in the winter of 1957–58 and, of the original 19 members of the Executive Committee, 13 were listed in *Who's Who*. The original members of CND's leadership, most of whom were middle-aged intellectuals, and about half of whom had been publicly associated with the Labour Party, envisaged mounting a short, sharp campaign as an élite pressure group. Consequently they were keen to disassociate themselves from any form of militant action as they felt it might damage what they perceived to be their public image of moderate and respectable dissent as opposed to militant protest. The intellectuals, however, had not grasped the breadth of public concern about nuclear weapons. The Campaign's first public meeting on 17 February 1958 attracted an audience of over 5,000 people despite the fact that it was advertised on a very restricted basis.[11] Many of those who attended that meeting espoused a much more militant approach than the leadership had envisaged and, encouraged by that support, the Executive Committee revised the Campaign's aim. The original policy statement was not unambiguously unilateralist but the revised position was unequivocal:

> We shall seek to persuade the British people that Britain must renounce unconditionally the use or production of nuclear weapons and refuse to allow their use by others in its defence.[12]

That initial change in policy was reinforced by events. In early 1958 CND absorbed the National Council for the Abolition of Nuclear Weapons Tests (NCANWT) and CND's policies were influenced by the much younger membership and more militant approach of the Direct Action Committee against Nuclear War (DAC). Thus from the outset there was a conflict within CND concerning tactics, if not strategic objectives. On the one hand there was the original, middle-aged, intellectual leadership's vision of an élite pressure group, and on the other an increasingly large number of younger, often well-educated, members anxious to demonstrate their influence as a quasi-militant mass movement aimed essentially at general protest concerning nuclear weapons rather than the achievement of influence in respect of specific policies.

In the late 1950s CND, despite its origins, rapidly developed into a mass movement. The popularity of the Aldermaston marches was seminal in that process. The first march, in 1958, was organised by the DAC and attracted over 5,000 participants and wide press coverage. The 1959 march was organised by CND and culminated in a rally of 20,000 people in Trafalgar Square, and the 1960 event was an even greater success. CND also had considerable success in attracting support from within the Labour Party and at the 1960 annual conference, to the surprise and embarrassment of the Party leadership, a motion was passed advocating that Britain should unilaterally abandon nuclear weapons. Indeed at this point CND's popularity seems to have been an accurate reflection of public opinion. In April 1960, in response to the question: 'What policy should Britain follow about nuclear weapons?' a

Gallup Poll found that 33 per cent of those polled indicated that Britain should give up nuclear weapons. This was in contrast to the usual level of support for unilateralism which runs at about 20 per cent. It is difficult to provide empirical reasons for such swings, however, a number of events in the late 1950s were probably perceived by the public to be destabilising. In 1956 the first V-bombers became operational and the following year Britain announced the adoption of the doctrine of massive retaliation and conducted its first thermonuclear test. The Soviet Union simultaneously launched Sputnik 1 and conducted its first successful launch of an ICBM. Less tangible, but perhaps more significant, in the aftermath of the Suez crisis Britain was beginning to come to terms with its new, and much less secure, position in the international community. Finally, the unusually large Conservative majority in the 1959 election seems to have raised the fears of many non-Conservative voters.

CND's spectacular initial success did not last long. The inherently incompatible origins of its early membership created internal problems while its very success created opposition from its original target – the Labour Party. The formation of the Committee of 100, committed to a strategy of organising and promoting mass civil disobedience, provided a focus for the more militant members of CND while the original leadership, in keeping with its political roots, persisted in its attempts to convert the Labour Party to unilateralism. The Labour Party leadership, however, was not persuaded by CND's arguments and successfully campaigned for the rejection of the unilateralist position at the 1961 annual conference. Thereafter the Party Leadership steadily distanced itself from CND in the lead up to the 1964 election, no doubt realising that to embrace a minority movement was to court electoral disaster. The majority of CND's supporters, however, saw themselves as participators in a moral crusade and considered efforts at political influence, whether achieved via mass militancy or élite influence, equally irrelevant.

Parkin's study of the social origins and motivation of CND members is revealing.[13] Parkin found that the campaigners were motivated by symbolic issues of a general nature rather than specific policies and that they gained at least as much from the emotional satisfaction of participation as from the achievement of successful outcomes. This led Parkin to conclude that the movement displayed the characteristics of a religious, rather than a political, movement and that consequently it was likely to have a high capacity for survival. He also found that the Campaigners were not just predominantly drawn from the educated middle classes but that they were also disproportionately from the public sector caring and teaching professions. From that analysis Parkin concluded that CND's membership was, and was likely to remain, unrepresentative of British society.

From the mid-1960s to the late 1970s CND's membership remained low and the organisation had little impact. Nevertheless it experienced a dramatic revival in the 1980s. Just as it was largely external events that had accounted for the organisation's decline so, too, was CND's resurgence influenced by external events. Significantly, however, it was predominantly policies adopted, or proposed, by the United States that rejuvenated CND (as well as the European peace movement) and these developments resulted in a wave of anti-American sentiment throughout much of Western Europe. The initial step in that process was President Carter's proposal, in 1977, to deploy the high radiation neutron bomb as a battlefield weapon for use in Europe. In response CND organised a national petition against Carter's proposal which attracted some 250,000 signatures. However, it was the American-led NATO decision in December 1979 to deploy GLCMs and Pershing II missiles in Western Europe that transformed CND's popularity; but there were other events that were also perceived as destabilising. In 1979 Mrs Thatcher's Conservative government, which was pledged to increase defence spending, replaced the Labour administration, and the Soviet Union invaded Afghanistan. In 1980 the Thatcher government announced its decision to procure Trident and the 'hawkish' Reagan succeeded Carter as President of the United States. In 1981 the United States began to stockpile neutron bombs and announced its decision to build 100 MX ICBMs while, in 1983, Reagan made his 'Star Wars' speech which undermined support for a freeze in the arms race. In the same year cruise missiles were first deployed in Britain and the global 'nuclear winter' hypothesis was first espoused.

Against that background CND's membership grew from just a few thousand in the late 1970s to some 100,000 nationally recruited members and 250,000 locally recruited members by 1984. The burgeoning arithmetic apart, the new CND displayed one unsurprising similarity with the original movement and one interesting change. The major continuity was in the social composition of the campaign's membership while the change was in the motivation of its members. The original CND was essentially a moral crusade but 20 years later the movement's common motivator was fear. A rational analysis of comparative strategic security would not lead to the conclusion that Britain was any less secure in the early 1980s than it had been in the late 1950s. Rational analysis, however, is not the key determinant of public perception.

Nevertheless there were a number of factors that led the British public to feel less secure in the early 1980s. The Soviet Union's well-publicised military build-up coupled with the deployment of SS-20 missiles and the invasion of Afghanistan was clearly of concern. Conversely the British public was well aware of the country's reduced status in the international community and people were even more aware of Britain's comparative economic weakness. These events appear to have contributed to a national psychology in which perceived increasing weakness had given rise to a sense of relative helplessness which, in its more extreme form, manifested itself in a fear of nuclear war.

Gallup poll findings support this hypothesis. In January 1980 Gallup found that 57 per cent of those polled felt that there was 'much danger' of a world war compared with only 15 per cent in 1975. These concerns, however, were not reflected by support for unilateralism as, in 1980, only 21 per cent supported that position although, probably influenced by CND's publicity, that proportion had grown to 33 per cent by the following year. At the same time the Labour Party voted to abandon Polaris and remove United States bases in Britain. Nevertheless, by the end of the 1983 election campaign, support for unilateralism had fallen back to about 17 per cent and in the election itself Labour secured only 28 per cent of the votes cast. Clearly, in 1983 at least, unilateralism was not a vote winner. CND's fortunes continued to fluctuate in the late 1980s. While the use of British bases by the USAF to mount a strike against Libya and the Chernobyl disaster in 1986 promoted the movement's fortunes, the end of the Cold War and the subsequent disintegration of the former Soviet Union resulted in yet another fall in membership.

Public Opinion

It is relatively easy to assess the public's opinion about a specific event or issue at a particular time but it is much less easy to draw meaningful comparisons about the public's attitude to similar events and issues over time. Changes in the wording of opinion polls are an obvious problem. Furthermore changes in opinions may be due, at least in part, to reactions to specific events and they would therefore be of limited use in drawing long-term comparisons. It is also important to note that it is not unusual for researchers to find that responses to multiple choice questions are frequently illogical.[14] One must also remember that, even when a poll suggests that public opinion has changed little over a period of years, that does not mean that very many individuals may not have changed their own views. Some understanding of which segments of a sample espouse certain views may be more illuminating than the global level of support for a specific policy. Indeed, when attempting to draw comparisons from opinion poll findings over a period of time it is appropriate to remember the adage that 'no man can cross the same river twice: both the man and the river are constantly changing'. Despite all these caveats, this section seeks to give some pointers towards apparent trends in public opinion in relation to certain key nuclear issues in the past and to suggest the principal lines of continuity and change.[15]

In some respects public opinion has been remarkably consistent although on some, perhaps more peripheral, issues it has demonstrated interesting changes. It is instructive to draw comparisons between the views expressed in the 1950s and early 1960s, when the Cold War was at its height, with those which came to prevail in the 1980s and 1990s, when assessed security risks were lower. The first survey of support for the British deterrent was conducted by Gallup in 1952 and it revealed a 3:1 majority in favour of the development of the atomic bomb.[16] That position was fairly representative of the early period when the majority of surveys indicated that some two-thirds of the electorate supported Britain's possession of nuclear weapons. Conversely there has always been a substantial minority that has opposed Britain's nuclear weapons programme and the evidence suggests that the quantity and intensity of that opposition has been much more dynamic than the level of support. As with CND's fortunes, the indications are that the 'opposers'' views were conditioned by events. Thus while in May 1954 Gallup found that 24 per cent of respondents were broadly unilateralist, a year later, following Britain's announcement of the decision to develop and deploy the H-bomb, unilateralist support ranged from 31 to 48 per cent.[17]

The need to conduct testing also swayed the public away from support for Britain's nuclear policies. Thus in the spring of 1957, when Britain was about to conduct its first thermonuclear test, those opposed to testing amounted to over 50 per cent and soon after the formation of CND in the following winter support for unilateralism reached 30 per cent.[18] In the early 1960s the position was more stable with unequivocal support for a British deterrent ranging from 31 to 39 per cent and unequivocal support for unilateralism ranging from 20 to 26 per cent. The signing of the Limited Test Ban Treaty in 1963, just a year after the Cuban missile crisis, seems to have been a watershed. During the period from 1960 to 1963 the unilateralist position had the backing of between 20 to 25 per cent of poll samples while from 1963 to 1970, a period which saw the signing of several arms control treaties, most notably the NPT, and the initial talks between the superpowers on strategic arms limitation, support fell to around 15 per cent. During the same period support for Britain retaining its independent deterrent fell from 40 to 26 per cent while support for the retention of British nuclear weapons as part of a Western defence system rose from 42 to 50 per cent.[19]

The underlying reason for the difference between the earlier period and opinions expressed in the 1980s lay in perceptions of nuclear war. McInnes has recorded just how divided and disillusioned public opinion had become and how public support for Britain's nuclear weapons policy was no more than marginal:

> A Marplan opinion poll published in the Guardian, 22 April 1981, showed 53% of these were against buying Trident and only 23% in favour (compared to 37% and 44% respectively in the previous year). 56% of those interviewed, however, believed that the deterrent should

be maintained, and 47% believed that defence spending should be kept at the same level (with 28% wanting an increase and 20% a decrease.) Indicative of the pessimistic mood of the country at the time was the 65% who believed the prospects for world peace had deteriorated over the past year. The poll clearly displayed a growing belief that the world situation was deteriorating, and a disaffection with nuclear weapons.[20]

Over the 20 years from 1963 to 1983 Professor Ivor Crewe noted an increase from 16 to 49 per cent in the sample that considered nuclear war to be likely while those who thought nuclear war was unlikely decreased from 59 to 36 per cent.[21] An increasing number of people, but still a minority, clearly felt that Britain's possession of a nuclear deterrent did nothing to reduce that risk as the proportion favouring unilateralism grew to 33 per cent in the early 1980s.[22]

A survey by MORI in 1981 was particularly illuminating. It found that almost 70 per cent of voters favoured the retention of a nuclear deterrent. On the other hand only 52 per cent supported Britain retaining a deterrent independent of the United States, with much of the opposition coming from those below the age of 25 and from Labour voters. Finally 59 per cent thought that United States nuclear weapons should not be based in Britain, a position that found substantially more support from Labour than Conservative voters. The indications are that in the early 1980s the public harboured substantial reservations about the decision to deploy United States GLCMs in Britain and, as a consequence, there was increasing cynicism about the appropriateness of the United States nuclear policies and a marked drop in support for President Reagan. Against that background it is not surprising that support for unilateralism appeared to move back to around the 33 per cent level with a more or less corresponding decrease in those continuing to support the retention of Britain's deterrent.

In general there have been few major swings in public opinion regarding the central issues of nuclear defence in the post-war period. There have, however, been some changes in the views expressed by specific sections of the electorate. In the 1960s, while Conservative voters were more likely to support the retention of the deterrent, the similarities between Conservative and Labour voters were more noteworthy than the differences. As a broad generalisation a little fewer than half of Conservative voters supported Britain's nuclear weapons policies but they were joined by approximately one-third of Labour and Liberal voters.[23] That broad consensus seems to have remained valid until about 1980 when Gallup found that while 81 per cent of Conservative voters supported the retention of nuclear weapons for defence that view was also shared by 61 per cent of Labour voters.[24] In the 1980s opinions became more closely identifiable with voting patterns, with some 75 per cent of Labour voters opposing both Trident and the deployment of GLCMs while about 66 per cent of Conservative voters supported these policies. More recent work undertaken by Jones and Reece in the late 1980s has largely confirmed the findings of earlier surveys.[25] A majority of the electorate continues to express support for the retention of the deterrent while only a narrow majority of Labour voters supported that party's position in favour of unilateralism. Significantly, however, there was overwhelming support, across party political lines, for the idea of a nuclear freeze – proliferation was seen as a major problem – and consequently multilateralism was widely supported. There was also considerable evidence to suggest that much of the electorate was not clear about what purpose was served by the possession of nuclear weapons. Despite these reservations most voters believed in the effectiveness of deterrence but many also believed that a nuclear war might come about as a consequence of an accident or an irrational act.

In general, Conservative voters were more optimistic about the future than Labour voters. There were also some variations attributable to gender and age with women tending to be between 5 and 10 per cent more supportive of unilateralist policies than men and younger age groups tending to express more concerns about their future security than older age groups. While these differences were not particularly significant in a statistical sense their political significance may be of greater importance.

Finally it is worth noting that while the massive, and unnecessary, increase in Trident's firepower was not a public issue in the late 1980s or early 1990s, this was almost certainly because the public was unaware of the position. It seems certain that there would be little public support for a massive increase in the British deterrent's capability when some 85 per cent of the electorate favoured multilateralist policies and expressed substantial support for further arms control initiatives.

Findings and Indicators

The above assessment provides a number of findings and some indicators for the future. First, no post-war government has ever formally questioned the wisdom of retaining a strategic nuclear deterrent. Second, the early consensus between the two main political parties on nuclear weapons policies no longer exists. Significantly, however, there has been a much greater degree of consensus between political élites than between backbenchers and party members – although that, too, has eroded over time. Third, Conservative governments have always been strong supporters of a British strategic nuclear deterrent and they have enjoyed the undisputed support of their Party and a majority of the electorate in the pursuit of that policy. Fourth, despite the fact that successive post-war Labour governments have consistently sought to maintain and upgrade Britain's deterrent, that policy has not enjoyed the full support of some ministers and many backbenchers and, on occasions, the actions of the leadership have been contrary to the policies of the Labour Party. On the other hand there is no evidence to suggest that a majority of Labour voters favoured a policy of unilateralism, whether or not that was the official policy of the Labour Party. Furthermore decisions by Labour administrations have frequently been taken by a small group of ministers acting outside the formally constituted mechanisms of parliamentary government. Against that background it is difficult to predict what the views of a future Labour government might be on the deterrent other than to suggest that while Labour would probably retain Trident, (because, unlike in 1987, there is no longer any financial windfall to be gained from decommissioning the boats), it is probably less likely to seek a successor system than a Conservative administration. Fifth, while all the early key decisions regarding the nuclear weapons programme were taken in considerable secrecy, especially by Labour governments, decisions made more recently by Conservative governments have been more open and it would seem probable that future governments would wish, or feel it necessary, to pursue more open decision-making procedures regarding the future of Britain's deterrent.

The picture of CND that emerges is one of a movement that is greatly influenced by events yet is largely unable to exert any direct influence over long-term policies. Nevertheless it would be wrong to be dismissive of CND's influence. CND's fortunes may have risen and fallen but the movement itself has survived and it has demonstrated that, even when external events do not swell its membership, there remains a core of support for the adoption of a unilateralist position and the infrastructure to capitalise on events that popularise the Campaign's aims. It is also significant that CND is no longer a moral crusade but that its members link unilateralism with economic materialism and security. If, in the future, the public perceives there to be a reduction in the threat to Britain's security there may be greater public support for the renunciation of British nuclear weapons, not for reasons of morality or safety but rather for reasons of practical economics. Conversely all the available evidence suggests that unilateralism is unlikely to be able to attract a majority level of support from the British electorate. If, however, CND was to renounce unilateralism in favour of a vigorous but pragmatic multilateralist stance it might well attract support from a majority of the electorate. Indeed that transformation might enable the movement to achieve the position that its original leadership envisaged, namely that of an influential political pressure group.

The overall picture that emerges from surveys of public opinion is one of an electorate that has favoured the *status quo*, with a somewhat static majority supporting the retention of the strategic deterrent, but that majority being always opposed by a significant minority in favour of unilateralism. It is, however, probably reasonable to suggest that a fair proportion of the 'supporters' have passively accepted successive governments' policies in respect of the deterrent throughout the duration of the Cold War. As memories of the Cold War recede, however, so might that traditional base of support erode.

While the overall picture has been remarkably consistent over the last four decades there are other indicators that suggest that perceptions might be different in the future. First, there is now a clearer split along party political lines with Labour voters tending to support unilateralism and Conservative voters remaining in favour of the deterrent. Second, while external events have given periodic boosts to the 'opposers' they have also had an adverse impact, albeit a modest one, on the 'supporters'. These fluctuations suggest that while a majority might continue to support the retention of Trident, a proportion of those 'supporters' might not wish, unthinkingly, to carry forward that support for a successor system. Indeed support for a successor system might well be increasingly conditioned by international developments in arms control reflecting increasing public support for multilateral disarmament. Third, a substantial number of voters from across the political spectrum are not clear on what purpose is achieved by the possession of Britain's deterrent and, as threat perceptions become more opaque, the proportion of doubters is likely to increase. Furthermore if doubts about the continuing need for a deterrent rise these are likely to be accompanied by a more rigorous questioning of the deterrent's costs. These could challenge the conclusion drawn in Chapter 4 that Trident provides a cost-effective insurance policy in respect of the country's security on the straightforward basis that, although the threat has diminished, the costs of the deterrent are not adjustable to compensate for that change. Finally, women and young voters tend to be rather less supportive of the deterrent than men and older voters and that 'voice' might become a more strident one once the replacement of Trident is on the government's agenda. In that respect the lessons that emanated from the opposition by women to the deployment of cruise missiles should not be forgotten. Women's votes are likely to be more volatile than men's as women tend to be more responsive to 'issues' than policies. The protest at Greenham Common may not have been successful in preventing the deployment of cruise missiles but it was very effective in raising public awareness of the implications of the 'dual track' decision and there is no doubt that it caused the government of the day considerable concern. Most governments wish to avoid confrontation over issues of that nature – especially when they appear to have a large level of support from women from across party political lines. At the end of 1996, in the lead up to the next general election, public opinion is playing a bigger part in the formulation of policy than ever before. Public revulsion against the Dunblane tragedy looks set to ensure swingeing changes in British gun laws. That position is not confined to Britain. In October 1996 huge crowds protesting about the Belgian authorities handling of an investigation into an international paedophile ring brought Brussels to a standstill. Recognising the consequences of these and other similar changes David Omand, Deputy Under Secretary of State (Policy) at the Ministry of Defence, in an address to the Royal United Services Institute for Defence Studies in the summer of 1996 stated: 'That people's fears about nuclear weapons should now be setting the agenda is in many ways understandable'.[26]

The overall conclusion that emerges from this chapter is that while there is nothing to suggest that the present majority in favour of Trident will change, it would be imprudent to assume that a successor system will attract a similar level of support. That assumption rests on three key reasons. With the end of the Cold War the threat to Britain's security is likely to become more complex and, in the future, a strategic nuclear deterrent may not be the best means of safeguarding Britain's strategic national interests. Recent developments in arms control, especially the indefinite extension of the NPT in the summer of 1995, and the almost unanimous support for the CTBT in 1996, mean that all nuclear weapons states will be under increasing international pressure to reduce their weapons holdings. Britain has given a formal, albeit non-binding, undertaking to pursue that policy and the British political élite of the day may well come under pressure from its own electorate as well as from the international community to fulfil that commitment. Multilateral disarmament may be a major issue in the early twenty-first century. For both the above reasons the British electorate may increasingly wish to question the future costs of a strategic deterrent. While the economic issue alone is unlikely to sway a decision about a Trident successor system it may, in conjunction with a diminishing threat and heightened arms control aspirations, have some influence on the outcome.

NOTES

1. Marsh C. and Fraser C. (eds), *Public Opinion and Nuclear Weapons* (London: Macmillan, 1989) p. 190.
2. Eden A., *Full Circle* (London: Cassell, 1960) p. 5.
3. 'Tube Alloys' was the cover name for the Manhattan Project.
4. See Gowing M., *Independence and Deterrence: Britain and Atomic Energy 1945–52* (London: Macmillan, 1974) p. 20.
5. See Pierre A. J., *Nuclear Politics: The British Experience with an Independent Strategic Force 1939–1970* (London: Oxford University Press, 1972) p. 78.
6. See ibid. p. 90.
7. See Gowing M., p. 406.
8. Barbara Castle recorded that there was only token opposition from herself and Michael Foot and makes it clear that Wilson was looking for the Cabinet to endorse a decision that, in effect, had already been taken. There was no debate and only few questions. See Castle B., *The Castle Diaries 1974–1976* (London: Weidenfeld & Nicolson, 1980) p .228.

9. The Labour Party Manifesto, 1979, pp. 37–8.
10. For a fuller treatment of the origins and development of CND see Driver C., *The Disarmers: A Study in Protest* (London: Hodder and Stoughton, 1964) and Taylor R. and Pritchard C., *The Protest Makers: the British Nuclear Disarmament Movement of 1958–1965 Twenty Years On* (Oxford: Pergamon, 1980).
11. The only notification of the meeting that appeared in the press was restricted to small advertisements in the *New Statesman* and *Peace News*.
12. Taylor R. and Pritchard C., p. 7.
13. See Parkin F., *Middle Class Radicalism: the Social Bases of the British Campaign for Nuclear Disarmament* (Manchester and Melbourne University Presses, 1968).
14. For example Dunleavy and Husbands, when conducting surveys about nuclear disarmament, found that nearly a third of their sample gave logically inconsistent answers to questions. See Dunleavy P. and Husbands C., *British Democracy at the Crossroads* (London: Allen & Unwin, 1985) pp. 178–80.
15. For a much more detailed assessment of these issues see Marsh M. and Fraser C., (eds); see also Jones P. M. and Reece G., *British Public Attitudes to Nuclear Defence* (London: Macmillan, 1990).
16. *Gallup International Public Opinion Polls (GIPOP): Great Britain 1937–1975*, Vol. I (New York: Random House, March 1952) p. 263.
17. See *GIPOP*, Vol. I (February 1955) p. 345 and (March 1955) p. 346.
18. See *GIPOP*, Vol. I (May 1957) p. 411 (October 1957) p. 429, (April 1958) p. 461 and (September 1958) p. 476.
19. See Butler D. and Strokes D., *Political Change in Britain* (London: Macmillan, Second Edition, 1974) p. 465.
20. McInnes C., *Trident: The Only Option?* (London: Brassey's, 1986) p. 22.
21. Crewe I., 'Britain: Two and a Half Cheers for the Atlantic Alliance', in Flynn G. and Rattinger H. (eds), *The Public and Atlantic Defence* (London: Croom Helm, 1984).
22. *Gallup Political Index, (255)* (November 1981) and *(267)* (November 1982).
23. *Sunday Telegraph*, 26 July 1964.
24. *New Society*, 25 September 1980.
25. See Jones P. M. and Reece G., pp. 87–91.
26. See Omand D., 'Nuclear deterrence in a changing world: the view from a UK perspective', *RUSI Journal*, June 1996, p. 15.

CHAPTER SEVEN

The French Experience:
a Comparison

France's nuclear policy has been remarkably consistent over the course of four decades, despite changes in regimes. The policy pursued by successive French governments, in spite of political hostility and technical difficulties, has been based on the predicament of an enduring trans-Atlantic defence Alliance, while their twin foreign-policy objectives have been to maximise both French independence and influence.[1]

THIS CHAPTER SEEKS to highlight the similarities and differences between the British and French governments' experience with a strategic nuclear deterrent. It begins by addressing the underlying reasons for, and the origins of, France's quest for nuclear weapons. It then assesses the development of strategic theory, targeting policy and weapons systems. The chapter ends with an appraisal of the prospects for Anglo–French nuclear co-operation.

While French scientists, under the leadership of Professor Joliot, contributed significantly to the pre-war discovery of nuclear fission, that early involvement came to an abrupt end when the German Army occupied France and members of Joliot's team fled to Britain. By 1945 the development of nuclear weapons had become essentially a United States initiative, albeit with some British participation. Not surprisingly, there were fundamental differences between Britain and France in the immediate post-war period. The French military had been discredited by a humiliating defeat and the nation had been shaken by the trauma of occupation. Furthermore a large part of the armed forces, especially the navy, had been seriously tarnished by its association with the Vichy régime. It took several years to rebuild homogeneous armed forces from the diverse elements of de Gaulle's Free French forces, the communist-dominated resistance and the former Vichy forces. Against that background the primary political goal of all post-war French governments had to be the re-establishment of France as a major power within a secure Europe.

While the formation of NATO was welcomed as an aid to security there were, from the outset, deep-rooted doubts in the minds of France's leaders about the validity of Anglo-Saxon military guarantees to the mainland of Europe. France's doubts had both a military and a political focus. On the military level France found it hard to believe that the United States would commit itself unreservedly and timeously to the defence of Europe. France's experience in two world wars made its scepticism understandable. No less important was France's unwillingness to acknowledge, on the political level, that the key actor in Europe's future security was the United States. Seen through French eyes the leadership of Europe would rightly revert to Paris now that Berlin was no longer in contention for that role. The presence of the United States in Europe, while necessary, was regrettable. It was, however, only a temporary arrangement. Once France had rebuilt its military strength there would, once again, be a Eurocentric world with Paris at its heart.

There emerged, at the same time, a body of military opinion that regarded nuclear weapons as an essential part of the nation's armoury. Nevertheless, although successive governments examined the question of producing nuclear weapons, decisions were always postponed. Despite this formal position, French nuclear research was well advanced by 1956. Indeed Yost has indicated that the research programme had progressed well beyond the authorised level of political approval.[2] As with Britain, the Suez crisis was the turning point. On 6 November 1956 President Eisenhower delivered an ultimatum to Prime Minister Eden requiring the British to halt the progress of their forces down the Suez Canal within 12 hours or to face financial pressure on the pound. Britain immediately yielded to the United States' demands. Significantly Eisenhower made no similar demand on Guy Mollet, the French Prime Minister. Nor did Eden consult his French ally before acquiescing to Washington's threat. The inescapable conclusion was that both the United States and Britain regarded France as a lesser power. This was not lost on the French and the reaction in Paris was bitter. While the Suez *débâcle* was fatal for conservative Eden's political future, French public opinion rallied behind the, in French eyes betrayed, socialist Mollet. Britain sacrificed the capacity to act independently in the international arena in favour of retaining the 'special relationship'. France, however, adopted the opposite course. The *entente cordiale* between Britain and France which had existed, albeit less than solidly, for half a century was shattered at a stroke and has remained so ever since. The Suez experience reinforced mistrust of Anglo-Saxon politicians and it was no coincidence that Prime Minister Mollet gave formal approval to develop nuclear weapons on 6 December 1956, exactly one month after the collapse of the Anglo-French Suez venture.

Thus the French decided to enter the nuclear community almost a full decade later than Britain but, in contrast to Britain, in circumstances that had, and indeed were to retain, substantial all-party support for an independent nuclear capability. French perceptions of British acquiescence to United

States hegemony, together with France's search for major power status, proved to be both the catalyst and, later, the continuing justification for the development of an independent French nuclear capability. Significantly France's motivation was derived more from a wish to demonstrate its independence both at home and abroad and a requirement to be able to compete, in terms of political influence, with allies, than to strengthen its defence against potential enemies. An early, continuing and significant difference between French and British declared policy has been the public emphasis that successive French governments have placed on the political significance of nuclear weapons.

Despite these origins it was loosely assumed during the Fourth Republic that French nuclear weapons would have a role, albeit an independent one, within the NATO alliance. The emergence of de Gaulle changed this. De Gaulle's initial position seemed to be ambivalent. In July 1958 he questioned Dulles on the possibility of France sharing Britain's special treatment on nuclear matters. That approach was decisively rejected. Despite this, in September 1958, de Gaulle sent a memorandum to Washington and London proposing the creation of a tripartite nuclear directorate to co-ordinate Western nuclear development.[3] Not surprisingly this was also rejected. De Gaulle's aim, however, was not to join the Anglo–American club. His real purpose was to establish an independent position within NATO and to take a stance against what he perceived as the Anglo-Saxon domination of the Alliance.[4] This was to remain a tenet of French policy for many years and was one that attracted, and was to continue to attract, considerable domestic support across the entire French political spectrum. Again the contrast with the British position is both substantial and significant.

Notwithstanding these differences, some tentative moves towards co-operation were taken in the early 1960s. The delicate relationship between Anglo-French nuclear co-operation and Britain's unsuccessful application to join the EEC, which began in the summer of 1961 and ended abruptly after Nassau, was central to these discussions.[5] The Nassau Conference, in December 1962, confirmed French suspicions and ended any possible prospect of French co-operation with Britain or America. Not only did Nassau demonstrate the advantages to Britain of the Anglo-Saxon relationship it also, somewhat clumsily, exacerbated French susceptibilities:

> In terms of tactics, American diplomacy had been unusually maladroit. The Nassau agreement was a plan for revising the organisation of the Atlantic Alliance's nuclear defences, yet it had been drawn up at a bilateral Anglo–American meeting. This served only to underline the kind of Anglo–American domination of the Alliance which de Gaulle had for so long deplored. The general had neither been invited to

Nassau, nor consulted beforehand about the new NATO multinational or multilateral nuclear formulas. To make matters worse, the post-Nassau offer to France was made publicly; de Gaulle probably read about it first in the newspapers. This was not the way to treat a man so sensitive to protocol and status as the general. At the very least the Nassau communiqué could have left the Polaris offers to Britain and France in vague terms, to allow for consultation and further negotiations privately through diplomatic channels.[6]

Against that background it is not surprising that, on 14 January 1963, only a month after Nassau, de Gaulle held a press conference at which he simultaneously rejected Kennedy's offer of Polaris missiles and his proposals for the MLF, proclaimed unalterable attachment to full nuclear independence and vetoed Britain's application for membership of the EEC.

Under de Gaulle the French nuclear programme became a key instrument in the attainment of his twin policy aims of reasserting France's independence of superpower hegemony and demonstrating France's distinctive national identity. De Gaulle saw the possession of nuclear weapons as fundamental to the realisation of his political goals: 'A great state which does not have them, [nuclear weapons] while others have them, does not command its own destiny'.[7] Although France began to develop nuclear weapons much later than Britain, French strategic thought did not suffer from any similar delay. Indeed the concepts of retired generals Pierre Gallois and André Beaufre were more-or-less contemporaneous with the work of Slessor and as influential in the context of the Fourth Republic. Gallois was an early proponent of the potential of nuclear weapons for both political influence and military power. He was adamant that conventional defence was futile and, therefore, the use of nuclear weapons was unavoidable. As a result of these beliefs he argued that it was important to embrace openly the early use of nuclear weapons. That position rested on the basis that, if an opponent was in no doubt from the outset what the level of response would be, the likelihood of deterrence being successful was enhanced:

> In principle, a determined policy of deterrence could solve all Western military problems. If the potential assailant believed that even on the occasion of a conflict of secondary importance to himself, the opposing side would not hesitate, rather than surrender, to use its nuclear arsenal, he would have to abandon force as a means of persuasion.[8]

Gallois' greatest contribution to French strategic thinking was his articulation of the concept of proportional deterrence.[9] The theory underlying Gallois' thesis was that the perceived value of France's ability to respond to a threat with nuclear weapons was proportionate to the risk involved. Thus, rather

than nuclear weapons having an absolute value of their own, the crucial determinant of the outcome was some form of cost-benefit calculation. That
concept, however, was embedded in the notion of the nation state. While
that posed no problems for Gallois nor, later, de Gaulle, it was largely incompatible with the notion of a NATO Alliance where the majority of the member
states had their security underwritten by two nuclear powers, both of whom
were relatively distant, in geographical terms, from the likely geopolitical
flashpoints.[10] Beaufre's strategic thinking was essentially more pragmatic than
that of Gallois and focused on the need to maximise France's deterrent capacity rather than Gallois' emphasis on an assured nuclear response.[11] Beaufre
favoured multilateral deterrence and the concept of multiple decision centres
as these would induce greater caution in a potential enemy. The central thesis
of Beaufre's work was that the strategic arena should not be predictable.[12]
Beaufre's views were very much at variance with thinking in the United States
and especially with McNamara's drive for a controlled policy of step-by-step
escalation. Furthermore, much of the discussion in the 1960s on the role of
French nuclear forces saw them as the detonator of the United States arsenal.
Indeed Raymond Aron went so far as to state that: 'The threat, though not
explicit, of using the French atomic force as a detonator is its sole conceivable
deterrence function within the framework of the present Atlantic Alliance.'[13]
Thus both Gallois' and Beaufre's ideas, for different reasons, found no favour
in the United States and consequently made little impression on thinking
in Britain or among the other European NATO allies. Conversely, French
strategic thinking served to reinforce France's drive for independence and that
did much to make these theories, and subsequently the consequences of the
resultant policies, acceptable to the French electorate. That position was
markedly different from the historically pragmatic British approach. Slessor,
rather than seeking independence for his strategic vision sought to persuade
his United States colleagues to embrace his views. Post-war British political
and military thinking has centred on retaining the Atlantic Alliance and ensur-
ing the United States' commitment to that Alliance, a policy that lies at the
other end of the foreign policy spectrum from the French position.

Although de Gaulle made no contribution to nuclear strategy *per se*, the
utility of nuclear weapons was central to his *modus operandi* within the international community. As a consequence of this approach, four important
political principles relating to the use of nuclear weapons became explicit
during the Fifth Republic. First, the French consistently refused to allow
United States nuclear weapons to be deployed on French territory. Second,
France would not consider integrating its nuclear targeting policy with allies.
Third, France was consistently reluctant to make an unambiguous threat to
use its strategic nuclear weapons other than in the direct defence of its own
territory. Finally, France maintained a declared policy of threatening the

first use of nuclear weapons in response to a conventional attack on French territory.

General Charles Aillert's concept of *tous azimuts* provided a strategic rationale that was complimentary to de Gaulle's vision of a Eurocentric world with Paris as its nodal point.[14] Aillert's thesis took as its point of departure the view that the post-war international system was so uncertain that it was impossible to formulate strategic plans on the assumption of potential enemies, or indeed allies. That led Alliert to believe that France needed to embrace a concept of total strategic flexibility. Although Aillert's theory was never unequivocally endorsed by any French government it was clearly a concept that was attractive to de Gaulle. France, however, failed to develop a global nuclear capability. Furthermore the concept was generally viewed as incredible on the basis that the French nuclear force had limited range, remained vulnerable and lacked a practical solution to the question of warning time. Despite de Gaulle's and Aillert's visions, France's nuclear capacity confirmed its position as a regional, rather than a global power. Moreover, France's position as a reluctant partner in the major political and military alliance of its region served only to marginalise its influence even further.[15]

Over the last two decades France has gradually come to accept its diminished international role. This has led it back towards an acceptance of the aims and policies of NATO and more specifically to a new, closer and pragmatic relationship with Germany. Yost drew two illuminating, and rather different, conclusions from his assessment of French nuclear policy:

> . . . the French discuss more candidly than the British – the options their strategic forces may offer in an uncertain future. Increased US unreliability, the end of the Atlantic alliance, its restructuring, or other events (eg, fundamental political changes in Germany) may give the independent strategic nuclear forces more credible missions in changed international contexts . . . For example Raymond Tourrain argues that 'we must develop our nuclear forces to render *technically possible* the defense of Western Europe when it will be *politically* feasible'. Prime Minister Mauroy has added that Europeans should reflect on 'the perspective of [Western Europe] as a political whole maintaining an autonomous defense,' in view of US unreliability.[16]

Notwithstanding the above, Yost sees France's policy as essentially realistic:

> Such rhetoric is readily exaggerated into an extreme view that claims for France a 'politico-strategic insularity', allowing it to assure its security 'without anyone's help'. In practice, however, French behaviour suggests full awareness that France's security depends mainly on the state of East-West military balances and political relations, inside as well

as outside Europe. France's continued membership in the Atlantic alliance and its security diplomacy regarding the maintenance of the US presence in Western Europe and in West Germany in particular illustrate France's prudence and realism.[17]

It is in the field of weapon systems that the French differ most markedly from Britain. Following de Gaulle's rejection of Kennedy's offer of Polaris missiles in 1963 the French committed themselves to a lengthy, and expensive, production programme designed to provide them with a triad of strategic nuclear forces.[18] From 1964 to 1971 the French had to rely exclusively on the Mirage IV bomber. From 1971 onwards, however, the French began to catch up with the British capability with the introduction into operational service of the first of their six missile-launching submarines and their first land-based strategic missiles. While there remained questions about the vulnerability of French air-launched and ground-based systems, the French programme sent a clear signal to the international community. France, despite potential technical difficulties and economic consequences, was determined to deploy truly independent strategic nuclear forces to underwrite French political policy. What France may have lacked in hardware she certainly made up for in terms of political will. De Gaulle was quite explicit about the French quest for nuclear weapons. In 1958, shortly after coming to power, he enunciated his position to United States Secretary of State John Foster Dulles. De Gaulle made it clear that France intended to pursue an independent defence and foreign policy and that French nuclear weapons were essential to underpin these policies.[19] De Gaulle was no less forthright at his press conference in July 1964 when he announced a doctrine that has remained central to France's strategic policy ever since. Furthermore de Gaulle's adoption of proportional deterrence, together with the operational deployment of the Mirage bombers, provided the justification for France's withdrawal from NATO's military structure in March 1965.[20] Sixty-two Mirage IV bombers were delivered to the French air force between 1964 and 1968 and 34 remained in service as strategic bombers until 1985. These aircraft had a speed of Mach 2.2 and were capable of carrying a single 70 kt gravity bomb. With a maximum range of only 3,200 kilometres they could only reach the Soviet Union with the aid of in-flight refuelling and therefore the force was dependent upon the availability of eleven KC-135 tanker aircraft, supplied by the United States. Eighteen advanced Mirage IVs were fitted with the ASMP (*air-sol moyenne portée*) medium-range air-to-ground missile in the mid-1980s in an effort to extend the aircrafts' operational life into the mid-1990s. The ASMP provided a stand-off capability with a range in excess of 100 kilometres and a missile speed of Mach 2.5. It carried a warhead in the 100 to 300 kt range. There were clearly major questions about the survivability of these aircraft. Both the bombers and the tankers were vulnerable on the ground and the Mirage's ability to penetrate sophisticated defensive systems became increasingly questionable. Indeed, by the late 1970s Ian Smart had expressed the view that the Mirage IV had: 'only a small chance of penetrating the large and elaborate defences of the Soviet Union'.[21] That opinion was supported by official French sources in 1978 when it was acknowledged that, of the three elements of the triad, the Mirage IVs were:

> obviously the most vulnerable; their destruction at their bases theoretically offers little difficulty as soon as their bases are identified; their destruction in flight today is more problematic, for these planes fly at low altitudes, below radar detection zones; but technology is progressing rapidly in this area and, in a few years, planes flying at low altitudes will be detected and destroyed as readily as those flying at high altitudes today.[22]

The Mirage force was never capable of providing a credible nuclear deterrent, nor even of making a significant contribution to the other elements of the triad. The force probably had its greatest potential around the mid-1970s. However, of the 36 aircraft in the three operational squadrons it was considered that only a handful were likely to survive a Soviet first strike. The airborne element of France's second strike at this time was limited, at launch, to five or six aircraft, each carrying a single 70 kt bomb. By the time the advanced Mirage, equipped with the ASMP, became operational the penetrability of manned aircraft was no longer credible. Yost has attributed four major arguments for maintaining strategic aircraft to air force officers and Gaullist politicians, despite mounting evidence about their vulnerability:

> diversification, since technological breakthroughs could suddenly endanger the SSBN and IRBM; penetrability, since a piloted aircraft might have special advantages in overcoming defences; adaptability, since the aircraft could also be used in conventional and tactical missions within or outside Europe; and controllability, since bombers are 'slow to take offence' and could therefore help in managing crises by demonstrating French resolve without the need for irrevocable employment decisions.[23]

When France decided to deploy land-based IRBMs in 1964 it was envisaged that 54 silos would be constructed. By 1971–72 when the weapons became operational 18 silos had been built at launch sites on the *Plateau d'Albion* in *Haute Provence*. Plans to provide additional silos were dropped in the mid-1970s. Each silo housed one S-2 missile with a range of 3,000 km and a 150 kt warhead. During 1980–82 the missiles were replaced with the S-3 with a range of 3,500 kilometres and a 1 mt warhead. As with manned bombers the survivability of the IRBM force has frequently been questioned. French sources have not denied their vulnerability but have sought to make a virtue of this weakness. The official French position has been that because the IRBM force existed, an aggressor had no option but to attack it thus supplying unequivocal evidence of his hostile intentions. That, it is argued, would enable the French to unleash their second strike capability without having any doubts about the identity of the aggressor. That scenario has to be compared with the possibility of an anonymous attack on the SSBN force. The argument was, and remains, fatally flawed. It is simply incredible that an aggressor that had the capacity to locate and destroy the SSBN force, overtly or covertly, would not have the capacity, and the wit, to deal similarly with the IRBM force.[24] Like the airborne element of the triad, the IRBM has never had the capacity to make any credible contribution to the French deterrent largely because of its small size. From the time French IRBMs became operational the Soviet Union has had the strategic capacity to destroy them in a first strike without losing the ability to inflict unacceptable damage on the United States.[25]

The real power of the French nuclear deterrent lies in the SSBN force.[26] Six SSBN entered service between 1971 and 1985. The first two boats, *Le Redoutable* and *Le Terrible*, became operational in 1971 and 1973 respectively and were each equipped with 16 M-1 ballistic missiles with a range of 2,500 km and a single 500 kt warhead. The third boat, *Le Foudroyant*, became operational in 1974 with 16 M-2 ballistic missiles containing the same warhead but with the range increased to 3,000 km. With the entry of *Le Foudroyant* into operational service France gained the capability of maintaining at least one boat on operational patrol at all times. That was not possible earlier because *Le Redoutable's* reactor 'went critical' in May 1969, some 30 months before the boat became operational. As the fuel elements of the propulsion reactors were designed to last three years before requiring replacement this meant that *Le Redoutable* was due for a major refit as soon as *Le Terrible* became operational. The fourth boat, *L'Indomptable*, became operational in 1977 with 16 M-20 ballistic missiles, which each had the capacity to carry a single 1 mt warhead over the same range as the M-2 missile. Between 1977 and 1980 the first three boats were all retrofitted with the M-20 missile and by the time this process had been completed the fifth boat, *Le Tonnant*, had entered service. The five boats had a combined capacity to launch 80 1 mt missiles. The entry of the sixth boat, *L'Inflexible*, to operational service in 1985 marked a major increase in operational capability. The new boat was equipped with 16 M-4 SLBMs, each of which carried six independently targetable 150 kt warheads with a range in excess of 5,000 kilometres. Thus the sixth boat was capable of launching 16 more warheads than the combined resources of the first five boats. By 1993 the first boat to enter operational service had been decommissioned and the next four boats had all been retrofitted with the M-4 missile. By 1993, therefore, the French force had the

Table 7.1

THE GROWTH OF THE FRENCH SSBN FORCE

This table shows the increase in destructive capacity of the force calculated in megaton equivalents (MTE) as opposed to total megatonage. Equivalent megatonage counts the yield of the weapons, but adjusts for the relative waste of explosive energy in larger weapons through overconcentration near the target. Thus the relative destructive capacity of low yield weapons is greater than high yield weapons. The MTE is calculated by using the formula $MTE = NY2/3$ where N equals the number of warheads and Y the yield per warhead.

1971
Le Redoutable	(16 × M-1)	16 × 500 kt	=	10.0 mte

1973
Le Redoutable	(16 × M-1)			
Le Terrible	(16 × M-1)	32 × 500 kt	=	20.1 mte

1974
Le Redoutable	(16 × M-1)			
Le Terrible	(16 × M-1)			
Le Foudroyant	(16 × M-2)	48 × 500 kt	=	30.2 mte

1977
Le Redoutable	(16 × M-1)			
Le Terrible	(16 × M-1)			
Le Foudroyant	(16 × M-2)	48 × 500 kt		
L' Indomptable	(16 × M-20)	16 × 1 mt	=	46.2 mte

1980
Le Redoutable	(16 × M-20)			
Le Terrible	(16 × M-20)			
Le Foudroyant	(16 × M-20)			
L' Indomptable	(16 × M-20)			
Le Tonnant	(16 × M-20)	80 × 1 mt	=	80.0 mte

1985
Le Redoutable	(16 × M-20)			
Le Terrible	(16 × M-20)			
Le Foudroyant	(16 × M-20)			
L' Indomptable	(16 × M-20)			
Le Tonnant	(16 × M-20)	80 × 1 mt		
L' Inflexible	(16 × M-4)	96 × 150 kt	=	106.9 mte

1993
Le Redoutable	(decommissioned in 1991)			
Le Terrible	(16 × M-4)			
Le Foudroyant	(16 × M-4)			
L' Indomptable	(16 × M-4)			
Le Tonnant	(16 × M-4)			
L' Inflexible	(16 × M-4)	480 × 150 kt	=	134.4 mte

The relative values for the British force are 65.7 mte for Polaris: 441.2 mte for Trident C-4 and 1121.3 mte for Trident D-5.

theoretical capacity to launch 480 independently targetable warheads each with a yield of 150 kt (see Table 7.1 opposite). Since 1983, three SSBNs have been on patrol at all times. (Prior to 1983 the third boat was available only 150 to 200 days per year.) Thus the force was permanently capable of launching 288 warheads and, in a crisis, it has been estimated that a fourth boat might be made operational in as little as 72 hours, raising the warheads available at sea to 384.[27]

From Table 7.1 it can be seen that, from 1973 until 1977, France had the capability of maintaining one boat, equipped with 16 missiles with 500 kt warheads, on firing station at all times. That capacity, however, did not match Kemp's assured destruction criteria in terms of equivalent megatonage.[28] Nevertheless it clearly had the ability to inflict very substantial damage on the top 10 cities in the Soviet Union which, between them, house around 25 per cent of the population and roughly the same proportion of its industrial capacity.[29] While the arithmetical rigour of Kemp's 'assured destruction' model is impeccable it is, nevertheless, based on a subjective assessment of the force required to *destroy* the Soviet Union. It can, however, be argued that a much smaller force may be sufficient to *deter*. Kemp himself acknowledges this position and indeed cites McGeorge Bundy's concept of a 'minimum deterrence' theory:

> There is an enormous gulf between what political leaders think about nuclear weapons and what is assumed in complex calculations of relative 'advantage' in simulated strategic warfare. Think-tank analysts can set levels of 'acceptable' damage well up in the tens of millions of lives. They can assume that the loss of dozens of great cities is somehow a real choice for sane men. They are in an unreal world. In the real world of real political thinkers – whether here or in the Soviet Union – a decision that would bring even one hydrogen bomb on one city of one's own country would be recognised in advance as a catastrophic blunder: ten bombs on ten cities would be a disaster beyond history: and a hundred bombs on a hundred cities are unthinkable.[30]

If one sets the capacity of the French SSBN force between 1973–77 in the context of the Soviet Union having to retain the ability either to attack the United States or to be able to deter a United States first strike while simultaneously being able to counter a French threat then it would seem that a single boat would be sufficient to be credible. Furthermore, from 1977 that capability more than doubled and from 1985 it considerably more than trebled.

Early in 1996 the French decided to scrap their land-based missiles but plans were made to continue with the manned bomber force. It appears that the French, in contrast to the British, feel that there are advantages in retaining an aircraft delivering sub-strategic nuclear capability. The present air component,

18 ageing Mirage IVP equipped with the ASPM, will be replaced by 60 Mirage 2000N bombers by 2000. Plans have been in place for some time to ensure that the SSBN force remains viable. Four new submarines, not dissimilar to the Trident boats in capability, will replace the existing force by around 2005, despite the massive cuts in French defence spending announced in 1996. The first boat of the new class, *Le Triomphant*, commenced sea trials in July 1993 and is due to enter service in late 1996. The second boat, *Le Téméraire*, is under construction and is expected to start sea trials in 1997 and become operational in 1999. It is planned that the two remaining boats will enter service in 2002 and about 2005 respectively. These boats will be equipped with an upgraded version of the M-4 missile, the M-45, but there are plans to replace this with an M-51 SLBM by 2010. This missile will have a range in excess of 6,000 km and will carry six MIRVed warheads, probably with yields in excess of 150 kt. Thus by the year 2010 the French force should possess 384 SLBM warheads (the same number of warheads that Britain has chosen to limit itself to), half of which should always be available in extremis for launch at sea.[31]

As is clear from the above, the saga of the lack of Anglo–French co-operation on nuclear matters has been as fraught as the issue has been persistent. Nailor, while acknowledging the lack of progress achieved, records that: 'There is a persistent, resilient and largely instinctive feeling that the two states ought to be more aligned, in security matters, than recent history has led them to be.'[32] This is the dichotomy that lies at the heart of this issue. In the past detailed assessments of the lack of Anglo–French co-operation on strategic nuclear matters have tended to conclude that, while improvements in the situation would be logical, and should lead to some limited, practical advantages, there has been little to suggest that this was about to happen. Notwithstanding these somewhat ambivalent conclusions about the foreseeable future there is also a view that improved co-operation may be the inevitable outcome in the long term.[33] Despite these apparent ambiguities the matter deserves some consideration, partly because it is important to understand the reasons for the situation, and partly because the conditions and constraints that have moulded the present position are not absolutes, despite their persistence over the last 40 years.

At first sight it seems extraordinary that both Britain and France have been unable to benefit from some technical, economic or operational advantages that one might expect would accrue from some degree of co-operation. On the other hand a closer scrutiny of these issues indicates that there are practical differences that would make co-operation difficult even if the political will existed to foster greater collaboration. The practical difficulties should not be understated. Close British co-operation with the United States over many years has resulted in a situation which Smart has described as: 'an alloy which it would be almost beyond the wit of man to re-divide.'[34] The reality is that

Britain's special nuclear relationship with the United States has precluded it from co-operating to any meaningful extent with any other country. Furthermore, even if full operational co-operation were possible between France and Britain it may not lead to any significant increase in boats on station at any one time due to the need for retrofit and refitting operations to be carried out in national shipyards.[35] In the early 1980s the French floated the idea of a Franco–British joint deterrent force in trusteeship for Europe.[36] The difficulties that would have to be overcome before that concept could become viable were made explicit in the 1987 Statement on the Defence Estimates:

> If one were considering a fully integrated, jointly controlled Anglo-French nuclear deterrent, significant problems would arise. Our two countries would need to agree on the criteria the force would have to meet, the targets that would be put at risk, the details of complementary refits and patrol cycles and, by no means least, the process of consultation leading to the launch of a nuclear weapon and the authority for the actual firing of a weapon. And if a jointly controlled force were contemplated, which country would change its defence philosophy? For certainly there would have to be a change. British nuclear forces are committed to NATO, and the Alliance would unquestionably be weakened in military and political terms if they were removed. France, on the other hand, although a member of the Alliance, is not part of the NATO military structure, and its forces are therefore independent of the Alliance.[37]

A detailed study of the past does not always provide the best insight into the future. Both Nailor and Davidson, writing in 1989, indicated that radical change in the international arena could be the catalyst for co-operation in years ahead.[38] While it would be premature to suggest that this level of change is imminent it is important to note that France has recently reviewed its role in the world. One outcome of that process was the publication in 1994 of a new White Paper on Defence – the first since 1972.[39] That document gives a different focus for French defence which, in the aftermath of the Cold War, seeks to integrate French military policy more closely with that of its allies. Significantly, while nuclear deterrence remains a central pillar of French defence policy the proportion of defence spending on the *force de frappe* is due to decrease for the first time since the 1960s, reflecting a perceived need for better equipped conventional forces in the future and an unstated recognition of the reduced significance of strategic nuclear weapons following the disintegration of the former Soviet Union. Quite apart from the general trends towards closer European co-operation implicit in the White Paper there has been one other important development:

A joint (Anglo-French) commission on nuclear co-operation has been meeting monthly, without publicity, since 1992 to produce working papers on nuclear doctrines. British officials now talk of the 'high degree of agreement' with the French on this highly sensitive question. This represents a quiet revolution.[40]

At the Franco-British summit in October 1995 Prime Minister Major and President Chirac announced that the two countries intended to deepen their co-operation on nuclear policy. That position was reiterated in the 1996 White Paper which talked of: 'Greater bilateral co-operation with France . . . to enhance overall deterrence in Europe which we continue to see being provided by NATO'.[41] That position was subsequently made more explicit by a senior Ministry of Defence official:

> It is clearly important that the UK and France, as the two west European powers who are also members of the Alliance, co-ordinate their thinking of matters of nuclear policy and doctrine both in relation to the traditional roles of the Alliance and to the new risks and challenges that the Alliance may face over the years ahead.[42]

It seems clear that there may be much closer Anglo-French nuclear co-operation in the future. Such a development could result in an Anglo-French strategic nuclear force making a contribution to a European defence policy. That might alleviate arms control constraints, assuage public opinion and, in the long term, reduce costs. It could also provide a forum in which Britain might be able to continue to be a nuclear weapons state without being dependent upon the United States, either because the United States was no longer willing – or able – to sustain that relationship, or because Britain chose to integrate itself more fully with its European allies. Clearly that scenario is far from imminent but it is worthy of consideration. To borrow Davidson's terminology it is not inconceivable that, in the future, Anglo-French strategic nuclear co-operation may become *necessary*.

NOTES

1. Debouzy O., *Anglo-French Nuclear Co-operation: Perspectives and Problems*, Whitehall Papers (London: Royal United Services Institute for Defence Studies, 1991) p. 21.
2. See Yost D. S., 'France's Deterrent Posture and *Security in Europe. Part I:* Capabilities and Doctrine', *Adelphi Papers*, No. 194 (London: The International Institute for Strategic Studies, Winter 1984/5) p. 4.
3. For the text of de Gaulle's improbable and propagandist memorandum see Grosser A., *The Western Alliance: European–American Relations since 1945* (London: Macmillan, 1980) p. 187.
4. See Kohl W. L., *French Nuclear Diplomacy* (Princeton, NJ: Princeton University Press, 1971) p. 16.
5. This episode is well covered by Kohl pp. 320–35.

6. Ibid., p. 233.
7. Quoted in ibid., p. 129.
8. Gallois P., *The Balance of Terror: Strategy for the Nuclear Age*, translated by Howard R. (Boston: Houghton Mifflin, 1961) p. 93.
9. See ibid., p. 22.
10. For a fuller exposition of Gallois theories see Freedman L., *The Evolution of Nuclear Strategy* (London: Macmillan, 1981) pp. 314–18.
11. Beaufre's ideas were originally published as *'Dissuasion et Stratégie'* (Paris: Colin, 1964). The English version was published by Faber & Faber, London, 1965.
12. See Beaufre A., 'The Sharing of Nuclear Responsibilities: A Problem in Need of a Solution', *International Affairs*, Vol. XXXI (July 1965) p. 416. Quoted in Freedman L., p. 319.
13. Aron R., *The Great Debate* (New York: Doubleday, 1965) p. 142.
14. For further details of this concept see Freedman L., pp. 321–4.
15. For a good *résumé* of the implications of French policy not to collaborate with its allies in nuclear matters see Yost D. S., 'French Nuclear Targeting' in Ball D. and Richelson J. (eds), *Strategic Nuclear Targeting* (Ithaca and London: Cornell University Press, 1986) pp. 144–8.
16. Ibid., p. 154.
17. Ibid., p. 155.
18. The French six-year military equipment plan for 1977–82 envisaged expenditure on nuclear forces amounting to 15–17 per cent of defence expenditure. See Smart I., *The Future of the British Nuclear Deterrent: Technical, Economic and Strategic Issues* (London: Royal Institute of International Affairs, 1977) Appendix IX. Writing in 1991 Debouzy claimed that there was evidence to suggest that the nuclear programme had consumed 40 per cent of the defence budget between 1958 and 1968. See Debouzy O., p. 30.
19. See de Gaulle C., *Memoirs of Hope: Renewal and Endeavour* (New York: Simon and Shuster, 1971) p. 202.
20. See Yost D. S. in Ball D. and Richelson J. (eds) p. 129.
21. Smart I., 'Strategic Nuclear Deterrence in Western Europe: From 1980 to the Future', *RUSI and Brassey's Defence Yearbook 1980* (London: Brassey's, 1980) pp. 108–9.
22. See Yost D. S., pp. 18–19 and Note 56 to Chapter 1 on p. 66.
23. Ibid., p. 19.
24. See ibid., p. 20 and Smart I., 'Future Conditional: The Prospect for Anglo–French Nuclear Co-operation', *Adelphi Papers*, No. 78 (London: The International Institute for Strategic Studies, August 1971) p. 5, Note 7.
25. See Smart I., p. 5 and Note 6.
26. Useful sources for detailed information on the French SSBN force are: Smart I. (1977), Appendix IX, pp. 77–82: Yost D. S., pp. 21–6 and Palmer D. A. R., pp. 6–8 and 58.
27. See Yost D. S., p. 22.
28. For a good assessment of France's limited strategic capabilities see ibid., *passim*, but particularly pp. 135–6.
29. See Kemp G., 'Nuclear Forces for Medium Powers: Part I: Targets and Weapon Systems', *Adelphi Papers*, No. 106 (London: The International Institute for Strategic Studies, Autumn 1974) p. 27 and Figure 2 on p. 28.
30. McGeorge Bundy, 'To Cap the Volcano', *Foreign Affairs* (October 1969). Quoted in Kemp G., p. 28. Reprinted by permission of Foreign Affairs by the Council on Foreign Relations Inc.
31. See Palmer D. A. R., p. 58 and *Maritime Defence* (October 1994) p. 210. It is interesting to note that even before the Trident fleet is operational, Britain has chosen to limit its number of warheads to the same number as the French force has been able to launch *in extremis* since 1993, and will continue to possess once the French deterrent is upgraded. As both nations have declared their allegiance to a 'mimimum deterrence' posture the implication has to be that Britain made a mistake.
32. Nailor P., 'The Difficulties of Nuclear Co-operation', in Boyer Y., Lellouche P. and Roper J., *Franco-British Defence Co-operation* (London: Routledge, 1989) p. 32.
33. This is an underlying theme of three detailed assessment of this issue. See Smart I. (1971); Boyer Y., Lellouche P. and Roper J.; and Debouzy O.
34. Smart I. (1971), p. 34.
35. See Grove E., 'An Anglo-French Minimum Deterrent – A New Approach', *The Council for Arms Control Bulletin* (January 1987).
36. See Debouzy O., p. 59.

37. Cmd 101–1, *'Why not an Alternative?'*, *Statement on the Defence Estimates 1987*, Vol. 1 (London: HMSO, 1987) pp. 41–2.
38. See Boyer Y., Lellouche P. and Roper J., Chapters 3 and 13.
39. Details of the French White Paper and its implications were given by Admiral Jacques Lanxade, Chief of the French Defence Staff, in a presentation to the Royal Institute for Defence Studies on 3 March 1994. See *RUSI Journal* (April 1994) pp. 17–21. For a more detailed assessment of France's new defence policy see Menon A., 'From Independence to Co-operation: France, NATO and European Security', *International Affairs*, No. 71, Vol. 1 (London: Chatham House, 1995) pp. 19–34.
40. *Foreign Report* (1 December 1994) p. 4.
41. Cm 3223, Statement on the Defence Estimates 1996 (London: HMSO, 1996) paragraph 155.
42. Oman D. 'Nuclear deterrence in a changing world: the view from a UK perspective', *RUSI Journal*, June 1996, p. 18.

CHAPTER EIGHT

Tomorrow's World:
The Post-Cold War Arena

> We have seen extraordinary changes in the past seven years. . . .
> The end of the Cold War and the collapse of communism
> in Europe have presented us with serious challenges. But also
> wonderful opportunities. Across Europe many more people live
> in democratic countries than at any time in history. This is the
> fundamental change since the Cold War.[1]

P RIOR TO CONCLUDING this work it is appropriate to provide a *résumé* of
the current post-Cold War scene; the arena in which Britain's new nuclear
deterrent has started to operate and against which decisions affecting its future
will be taken. In the concluding chapter this assessment will be used as a backdrop to review the contemporary validity of Britain's strategic nuclear deterrent and to evaluate the issues underlying that analysis.

Since the summer of 1989, the Western world's international security arena
has been undergoing a period of rapid, fundamental and intoxicating transformation. As a consequence old power structures have disappeared and new
associations, based on dynamic and complex webs of interdependence, have
arisen. The demise of the Brezhnev doctrine was marked by Hungary's rejection of the Iron Curtain in its move towards political pluralism, and in Poland
by the installation of a non-communist democratic government. Within the
Soviet Union the Gorbachev revolution gathered pace with growing appeals
for better living standards and greater democracy leading, inexorably, to
widespread criticism of the existing regime and increasing expressions of
nationalism. Dramatic breakthroughs in disarmament talks on conventional
forces in Europe and strategic arms limitation were achieved following years
of relative stalemate. The breaching of the Berlin Wall at the end of 1989
spectacularly marked the simultaneous failure of communism as a viable
political creed in Eastern Europe and the concomitant reunification of
Germany. Radical change followed quickly in both Czechoslovakia and
Bulgaria bringing these countries into line with earlier developments in
Hungary and Poland.

In the space of a few months the West's security system, based as it had been
for the previous 40 years on superpower confrontation embodied in the Cold

War, no longer possessed a *raison d'être*. This posed fundamental questions about the foreign policy of the Atlantic Alliance, both as a collectivity and as a group of individual nation states. More specifically it called into question the continuation of the role of the United States *vis à vis* Europe and the future viability of NATO. Change was not confined to the East. The collapse of communist political hegemony in Eastern Europe and of the Warsaw Pact as a military alliance has been matched by less dramatic, although nevertheless substantial, developments in the West. The European Community is on the point of emerging as a major force in its own right, in political as well as economic terms. The WEU has been rejuvenated and France has re-emerged as an active contributor to European security. The new pan-European situation undoubtedly poses challenges. More importantly, however, it also offers unprecedented opportunities for the future of Europe's place and role in the world.

Significantly the dynamics of change, in both East and West, have demonstrated a social perspective as well as a political one. Throughout the 1980s, non-state actors played an increasing part in the achievement of change, often as pressure groups against political élites that have been anxious to maintain the *status quo*. Religious bodies, environmentalists, peace movements, ethnic groups, refugees, protesters and consumers, all variously aided by the media, have influenced the international agenda.

The most dramatic, and profound, demonstration of that phenomenon has been the advent of German unity. Reunification was achieved because very substantial numbers of people demonstrated that they wanted reform. They achieved their aim against a particularly repressive regime which ultimately, although fundamentally opposed to their wishes, was unable to hold out against a massively popular peaceful movement. Collectively a range of non-state actors brought the Cold War to an end, despite the governments of Eastern Europe. While Gorbachev deserves the credit for placing change on the Soviet bloc agenda it is unquestionable that the initiative ultimately rested with the people rather than their leaders. Nor should we forget that Western leaders and their officials were little more than passive spectators of the East European revolution. These events call into question established positions regarding political credibility, and therefore legitimacy, in both Eastern and Western Europe. The new order, whatever its ultimate structure, will ignore these developments at its peril. The choices of élites have been constrained and the expectations of citizens raised. Managing the future will be more difficult.[2]

This brief overview needs to be expanded to enable answers to be offered to three key questions that have been thrown into focus by these changes. First, what are the contemporary security requirements of the East European states and how can the West best accommodate them? Second, with the end of superpower confrontation will the United States continue to play a role in the future of Europe? Third, how do these changes affect British foreign policy; what role should Britain play in the security of the new Europe and, more specifically, how might these changes affect the future validity of Britain's strategic deterrent?

In the post-Cold War period British public interest has focused on the problems of security emanating from the Balkans and the states of the former Soviet Union. These are real enough.

They should not, however, be allowed to overshadow the equally important and positive, albeit less televisual, developments that have been taking place in Eastern Europe. Howard Frost, in an article in *Orbis* in late 1992, provided a valuable and comprehensive summary of the security needs of the Eastern European states.[3] Frost made it clear that there was a strong wish, articulated most actively by Czechoslovakia, Poland and Hungary, but shared by other states, for intra-European co-operation on security. That movement was given stimulus by the successes of the CSCE and led these states to seek closer ties with NATO and the EU. Jefferey Simon, writing in the same journal, spelt out the military details of the security vacuum as perceived from Eastern Europe and argued that, while NATO's response had been remarkable, in that so many initiatives had been undertaken in such a short period of time, it had, nevertheless, been insufficient in relation to the speed of change, and therefore East European expectations. Interestingly Simon claimed that the importance of NATO as a means of guaranteeing security, rather than the CSCE or the WEU, stemmed from its perceived potential to keep the United States directly engaged in European security.[4] Despite the fact that full membership of NATO was not an option for the East European states at that time, it remained clear that it was widely perceived in the East that NATO was the only institution capable of guaranteeing the security of these countries. Vaclav Havel, the former President of Czechoslovakia, articulated these views forcefully in the early 1990s. He argued that the ideals of freedom and democracy were common to East and West European countries; that Czechoslovakia and her neighbours had great hopes in the future of CSCE and in the ideal of a united Europe.[5] The security concerns of Eastern Europe were well demonstrated by the fact that in the two years between August 1990 and July 1992 no less than 38 bilateral and 34 multilateral Co-operation Agreements had been completed, or were in the process of being negotiated, between the former East European states of the Warsaw Pact and other European states or organisations. Both the volume and diversity of these agreements are remarkable and they provide ample evidence of the energy and vision of East European leaders in the field of security policy.

It is perhaps unsurprising that the former Warsaw Pact states felt that they were operating in a security vacuum. Their new independence inevitably brought with it a sense of vulnerability. Nevertheless it can be argued that the reality of the security situation in Eastern Europe was rather more stable than its new leaders might initially have perceived. An embryonic interdependence already exists, both between informal groupings of East European states and between them and the West European states and the states of the former Soviet Union. Consequently there is a general, but not total, willingness to create an international framework for the peaceful resolution of regional conflicts that did not, and could not, exist either during the Cold War or during the balance of power arena that characterised pre-1939 Europe. (It is illuminating that the one area in which security has collapsed is the former Yugoslavia which was neither a member of NATO nor of the Warsaw Pact and was therefore outwith the former political framework for the containment of conflict. Furthermore it can be argued that there is conflict in the former Yugoslavia because there is no commitment to a lasting peace in that area and that situation itself is due to the lack of any compelling external influence.) The challenge for the West is to understand the perceptions of, and developments in, Eastern Europe and to react to them positively and with vision.

In practical terms this means continuing and broadening the initiatives undertaken initially through the North Atlantic Co-operation Council (NACC) and, since January 1994, through NATO's Partnership for Peace (PFP) policy under which former members of the Warsaw Pact and European neutrals can become candidate members of NATO. States joining the PFP process have to commit themselves to five objectives: the democratic control of their armed forces; transparent defence budgets; the capacity and willingness to contribute to NATO operations authorised by the UN or the CSCE; joint planning and training with NATO members to prepare for these operations; and the long-term development of military forces that can operate side by side with NATO members.[6]

When PFP was set up, many observers felt it was no more than a device to enable NATO to postpone decision making about its future composition. However, within two years of its formation, it was clear that the PFP initiative had been remarkably successful, despite the fact that no timetable had been set as a target for candidate states nor had any security guarantees been given to these states. By April 1996, 27 of the eligible states had joined the PFP initiative, including Russia. The 1996 partnership programme contained 700 specific activities including 17 major exercises. More significantly, 14 partner states contributed 10,000 of the 50,000 troops to make up the NATO led Peace Implementation Force (IFOR) in Bosnia. These states include Bulgaria, the Czech Republic, Estonia, Hungary, Latvia, Lithuania, Poland, Romania and Slovakia who are all Associate Partners in the WEU. Without doubt one of the primary reasons for the success of PFP has been the establishment of IFOR which has given 'partnership' a practical focus.

There have been some interesting developments arising out of that success.

First, Austria, Sweden and Finland are now members of PFP. Clearly the first two of these states have no wish to forego their traditional neutrality by seeking membership of NATO and consequently they see membership of PFP having a security value in its own right. That is a significant, and most welcome, political step and, as a bonus, both Austria and Sweden will bring useful peacekeeping experience to the PFP. Second, a meeting of NATO's foreign ministers in Berlin in June 1996 approved a significant variation in the Alliance's command structure. In future, should a number of European NATO members wish to participate in peacekeeping operations, the political control of that operation can be vested in the WEU. To enable that change to be effective a combined joint task force headquarters is being set up to manage future operations. That is an important political development. In particular it will enable those PFP states who are unlikely to qualify for early NATO membership to participate in a WEU led security community which would allow them, as in Bosnia, to operate alongside NATO forces. Thus PFP seems likely to continue as an organisation in its own right rather than being solely a step towards NATO membership. Taken together these changes are quite significant. Already there is a new European security forum potentially capable of operating under the leadership of the WEU, albeit only with the approval of an American led NATO. Unsurprisingly against that background, it is widely expected that, in early 1997, NATO will open negotiations for membership with Poland, Hungary and the Czech Republic. Those three states might be joined by Slovenia and Romania who have strong backing from Germany and France respectively.

However, only part of the problem is currently being addressed. By admitting some countries to membership NATO may provoke a countervailing reaction in the East. There are risks inherent in any expansion of NATO and much will depend on how expansion is conducted. Significantly a RAND Corporation pro-expansion study group has stated that: 'depending upon how it is handled, expansion could stabilise a new European security order or contribute to the unravelling of the alliance or a new Cold War with Russia'.[7] The central problem is that candidate states have different and, in some cases, irreconcilable aims. Poland, for example, seeks enhanced security from Russia. Conversely Russia fears an expanded NATO on its borders.[8] Russia's position as a member of PFP is clearly anomalous. Russia does not aspire to NATO membership, nevertheless it feels, at least at present, that it is better to contribute to the development of the PFP process than to be driven into isolation. Indeed, there is a strong case for arguing that there is more to be gained regarding the future security of Europe by avoiding driving Russia into isolation than by admitting former Warsaw Pact states to membership of NATO – particularly at a time when Russia poses no threat to these states. On the other hand there is no doubt that Germany favours the eastward expansion of NATO, for political and economic reasons, as well as security considerations. That expansion seems set to go ahead, albeit slowly.[9] To make that development acceptable to Russia there may need to be a parallel diplomatic effort to negotiate a friendship treaty between Russia and NATO that helps to allay the former's fears. Certainly something has to be done to avoid another dangerous division within Europe.[10]

There are also potential problems of a more domestic nature for both existing and potential NATO states. Are the electorates of NATO's 16 nations ready to expand the territorial limits of the Alliance's collective defence? Possibly not. Are the citizens of the candidate states ready to accept the stationing of foreign troops on their soil should that be appropriate? Probably not. Are any states prepared, or able, to take on the financial commitments implicit in an enlarged NATO? Probably not.[11] Notwithstanding these reservations, PFP has emerged as the most politically expedient interim solution to the issue of security in Central and Eastern Europe. At present it provides a forum that excludes no one and, most significantly, one that enables Russia to participate in the development of a new European security process. How that process develops will depend largely on Russia's reactions to NATO's plans for expansion. Nevertheless, the present arrangement avoids the obvious danger of contributing to the isolation of Russia. PFP also has the potential to promote internal reform in the East and, because it promotes the concept of collective security, it also enhances the prospect of internal investment. These steps may be relatively intangible but they are critical to long-term success.[12]

Partnership for Peace, however, should be regarded as no more than an initial step towards fundamental change. The long-term aim should be the establishment of a pan-European security network, managed initially by a NATO that continues to evolve progressively and sensitively, in order to respond to the new political situation in Europe. The timing of that evolutionary security process must depend upon political progress and it must be sufficiently flexible to accommodate changing roles for both the United States and Russia. The East European states must prove their candidature through the establishment of legitimate representative democracies and stable market economies. The West must, at the same time, actively encourage that process in order to foster political cohesion. On this basis a new Europe can be constructed on the twin pillars of increased political union and mutual security. The future of Europe's security, however, can only be assured if the West responds intelligently to the East's needs and accepts the opportunity to lead the process of change by building on the successes of NATO, the CSCE and the EC to create a new pan-European security structure. The present, when European security faces no external threat, presents an opportunity that Europe cannot afford to squander.

While there can be no doubt that there is a move within Europe towards closer integration, questions are being raised about the role the United States may wish, or be able, to play in the Europe of the future. A trio of academics from the Graduate School of Public and International Affairs at the University of Pittsburgh has made an assessment of the probable relationship between the United States and Western Europe in the future.[13] They identified three competing pressures: the calculus of United States interests, the psychological desire for leadership and the salience and complexity of the domestic problems facing the Clinton administration. They used these to construct three possible policy options for the United States. The first option envisaged that the United States would seek to continue to exert influence in Europe through NATO in its existing role as Alliance leader. While it was felt that this might, at least initially, be the preferred option of the United States' establishment it was considered unlikely that it would prove to be attractive either to the American electorate or to the states of Western Europe. The second option envisaged the United States relinquishing its traditional position in favour of a more modest supporting role within NATO, leaving the Europeans to shoulder more responsibility for their own security. That option was considered to offer most benefit to both the United States and Europe. It was felt, however, that its attainment was beyond the capacity of United States statecraft in the absence of a clear and compelling political goal. The third option foresaw the disengagement of the United States from Europe as a consequence of the growing influence of domestic issues leading, ultimately, to confrontational political and economic introversion. This, although the least desirable outcome for both parties, was felt to be the most likely. In another, albeit more subjective, assessment Christopher Coker argues forcefully that the United States is poorly equipped, poorly placed and poorly motivated to play a leading role in what President Bush described as the 'New World Order'. Coker concluded that America has neither the will, the military resources nor the financial strength to build a new security order.[14] The United States was thrust into world leadership in 1945 not because it sought such a position, nor because it was seen as the political champion of the West, but rather because it emerged from the war with its armed forces intact and its national wealth doubled. A persistent feature of the Cold War period was the inability of Congress, and the American people, to understand the complex web of interstate issues that lay at the heart of European politics. United States leadership existed because it was militarily necessary. In political terms it was accepted rather than sought. That problem has been exacerbated by recent events, particularly in the Balkans, while there is simultaneously an increasing weight of informed opinion suggesting that the motivation of the American people to continue to be involved in Europe is diminishing. The United States' vigorous claims in the early 1990s that it intended to retain its world leadership role have not been matched by events.[15] There is a general consensus amongst analysts that George Bush's 'New World Order' and Bill Clinton's doctrine of 'enlargement' have both failed to win domestic support or to demonstrate their effectiveness abroad.[16]

The demise of the former Soviet Union has created two major challenges that the United States is probably unable to overcome. First, the West now has less need of the United States' security guarantee and, consequently, is increasingly unlikely to accept the United States' undisputed right to be Alliance leader. Second, the collapse of the Soviet Bloc has robbed the United States of the domestic cohesion that emanates as a countervailing response to an external threat. There are, therefore, powerful internal and external forces that are likely to challenge the United States' leadership of the Western world to a degree unknown since the 1940s. As evidence of these developments the 'declinist theory', postulating a return to isolationism, was much in vogue in Washington before the Gulf War.

The lessons of the East European revolution indicate that it would be prudent to give due cognisance to the factors at work within American society as these may well compel changes in Washington's foreign policy despite the wishes of the establishment. There are three trends that are of particular importance. First, the ethnic cocktail of American society is becoming progressively less European. Of the two million legal and illegal annual immigrants fewer than ten per cent are European. Consequently, by 2005, one-third of all Americans will be non-white. That situation has led David Rieff to suggest that America is no longer an extension of Europe but rather a non-white country adrift in a non-white world.[17] Second, there is growing support, in both élite and popular circles, for the concept of 'America first' based on an awareness of a domestic imperative that can no longer be ignored. President Clinton is trying to grapple with a major budget deficit and to seek ways in which his country's economic competitiveness can be restored. The scale and urgency of that problem is demonstrated by the fact that he faces a major crisis in the provision of health care and education and a deepening social crisis in which over 30 million Americans live below the poverty line. Peter Peterson, a former Secretary of Commerce, and James Sebenius have claimed that:

> After four decades of the Cold War, failure to make progress on a 'domestic agenda' now threatens American long-term security more than the external military threats that have traditionally preoccupied security and foreign policy . . . failure to invest in productive capacity, research and development, and infrastructure; the crisis in American education; the exploding underclass, and other domestic problems may have greater direct impact on American institutions and values than the threats from abroad which have traditionally preoccupied the national security community.[18]

Third, there is evidence to suggest that the United States is increasingly becoming a 'Pacific' rather than an 'Atlantic' state. Until the 1980s European markets were more important for American exporters than those in Asia. That is no longer the case. East Asian markets are now of more significance to the United States and Japan has become the United States' most important economic contact. A Japanese research report has claimed that East Asia:

> is fast becoming the growth centre of the world . . . If they can maintain a seven per cent growth rate until the 21st century they are certain to rival the economic scale of even a 'Super EC' incorporating the European Free Trade Association and Eastern Europe.[19]

In the recent past there has been a dramatic shift of population within the United States away from the white pro-European north-east towards the predominantly Hispanic, black and Asian south-west. Already presidential elections are won or lost in California and Texas rather than in Massachusetts and Pennsylvania. Increasingly the focus for domestic politics, economic interests and security concerns will be decided in the south and west of the United States. In its external relations the United States will be further developing a sphere of influence that extends south to Mexico and the Caribbean and west across the Pacific. That development may prove to be irreconcilable with the United States' position as leader of the Western Alliance. It is not implausible that the establishment will reluctantly relinquish its European role on the basis that it will become too difficult to sustain: a situation that might be perceived to be to the mutual satisfaction of the majority of the United States electorate and the European leadership.

A brief scrutiny of opinions being expressed by a range of commentators from late 1994 to late 1996 provides a disturbing picture of a United States that has lost its *raison d'être*. The central theme of Harvey Sicherman's article 'Winning the Peace' published in *Orbis* in the autumn of 1994 is that the problem at the heart of American post-Cold War foreign policy is America itself. Sicherman claims that Americans have lost their way largely because the collapse of international communism has not led to an increase in the acceptance of democracy and free markets and consequently they are having to question the validity of the ideology that sustained them throughout the Cold War. Sicherman urges the United States to adopt a foreign policy model based on co-existence rather than one that emphasises cultural and institutional conformity and urges Americans to disabuse themselves of the illusion that 'what we call democracy and free markets are *not* ascendant in the world, and most nations are *not* remaking themselves voluntarily in our image'.[20] Wallace J. Thies's article 'Rethinking the New World Order' in the same edition of *Orbis* and an article dated 27 May 1995 in *The Economist* by Raymond Seitz, America's ambassador to Britain in 1991–94, are both critical of recent failures in American foreign policy. They subscribe these failures to an inability to balance foreign and domestic policies on the basis that in the past America has either been isolationist or an Alliance leader and that it cannot yet visualise itself in a role that lies between these extremes. Both writers expound the belief that the United States still has much to offer the world but that it must find a new role that balances the electorate's economic needs with the country's international aspirations. Both writers suggest that contemporary America lacks a vision of its new role and believe that situation will result in failure, growing disillusion and ultimately increasing isolation.

Ronald Steele, Professor of International Relations at the University of Southern California, writing in the *International Herald Tribune* in June 1995, developed that theme. He argued that America should embrace internationalism but only as a complement to nationalism as that pragmatic compromise will ensure domestic support for a new foreign policy. Implicit within his theme, however, is the concept that the American electorate will not support an idealistic foreign policy, only a realistic one that, when necessary, protects American citizens from economic competition.[21] There is some interesting evidence to suggest that there is a growing gulf between the views of the American electorate and its leaders on foreign policy issues. Every four years since 1974 the Chicago Council on Foreign Relations has commissioned an opinion poll on the views of leaders and the public concerning America's foreign policy. The results of the last poll were published in the spring of 1995. Leaders rated foreign relations tenth in their top ten areas of concern. The public's top concerns were crime, unemployment and health care/health insurance – foreign relations did not feature in their list. Sixty-five per cent of leaders but only 29 per cent of the public felt that the United States should 'take an active part in world affairs'. There was a similar division over the use of military force. The balance swung the other way in respect of the perceived utility of international organisations. Over 50 per cent of the public wanted the UN strengthened, a prospect supported by only one-third of the leaders and, while the public retained its majority support for NATO, the leadership, strong supporters 20 years ago, were strongly negative about the Alliance's future. These changes were highlighted by Michael Howard in an address to the French Institute of International Relations which focused on the split between American policy makers and the electorate. His remarks were reported in the *International Herald Tribune* on 24 June 1995 in the following terms:

> the close alliance of Europe with America now 'will be difficult to sustain'. He (Howard) said that the American people's primary interest in the European countries was as allies in the Cold War. 'Now that is gone. There is no longer any overriding issue to unite the Americans

behind a single foreign policy, and there are many to divide them. Their internal problems are quite literally terrifying. Their elites may continue to urge on them the responsibilities of world leadership, but they themselves are divided over the direction in which to lead, and their electorates show no enthusiasm about following.[22]

The neo-isolationist case continues to be argued forcefully in the United States. That position was pushed further into the arena of serious policy debate by the publication of a new book by the widely-respected political-science professor Eric Nordlinger of Brown University in 1995.[23] Nordlinger advocated cutting the United States defence budget in half, terminating security alliances, withdrawing troops from overseas bases and confining United States' security perimeter to North America and the Caribbean. Nordlinger's case rests on a number of assumptions – many of which are probably attractive to much of the American electorate. First, he argues that the United States is 'strategically immune' from external danger. Second, he states that American military commitments overseas have allowed allies to avoid making adequate political and economic provision for their own security. Third, he reasons that, as the United States cannot deduce the intentions of possible adversaries, it is both impractical and costly to make contingency plans to deal with such adversaries. Finally, he asserts that because of the United States' strategic position and overwhelming military power it will always have the ability to successfully defend its national interests. If the United States wished to change its ideological stance *vis-à-vis* the international community then Nordlinger's arguments provide a powerful intellectual backdrop for that revision. There is no evidence that the United States' leadership wishes to embrace these changes at present but, equally, it would be unwise to imagine that the neo-isolationalist argument will be easily laid to rest.

The evidence presented above indicates that a new world order is beginning to take shape. Against that background Britain must reassess its foreign policy aims and adjust its security policy. Throughout the Cold War period, during which the United States retained the role of undisputed Alliance leader, Britain enjoyed a special position as the 'link' between the United States and the European allies. Although the 'special relationship' became less special with time, Britain benefited from a level of access to security intelligence and nuclear technology denied to the other European states. Clearly if the United States is to embark upon a policy of relative introversion this will, to some extent, eclipse Britain's position within Europe. The Cold War provided an arena in which the diplomacy of managed confrontation flourished and consequently provided Britain with a stage on which it could act with experience and confidence, thus providing status for the state and its ministers and officials, notwithstanding Britain's declining economic position. The post-Cold War scenario requires that priority be given to the diplomacy of political and economic integration, an arena in which Britain's track record is at best dubious. Britain must recognise the significance of that position. Britain's enhanced status, due to its unique relationship *vis à vis* the United States, could dissipate as a source of strategic influence, just as its economic leadership of the industrial world did in the late nineteenth century and just as, in the second half of this century, its influence has declined as a former member of 'The Big Three'

There are other considerations. Significantly the location of Britain's core security interest, Central Europe, has not changed. What has changed is the focal point for Britain's political influence. While the reduction of United States influence in Europe will reduce Britain's standing the opposite is the case in respect of Germany. One of the key reasons why the United States' position in Europe was never seriously challenged was that, for most European states, the alternative – Germany – was worse. The contemporary reality, however, is that Germany is the only European country that has the political *entrée* to the former Warsaw Pact European states and the economic strength to lead the new Europe. Germany has already bridged the gap between East and West; it has established formal co-operation agreements with all the former Warsaw Pact states of Eastern Europe (in this respect it is well ahead of its West European partners) and in December 1991 it demonstrated its political interest in the Balkans by insisting that the EC recognise the independence of Croatia and Slovenia. Significantly the EC gave way to Germany's demands. The indications are that the focus of German interest has shifted to the East. The future may no longer be constrained by American hegemony, nor by the machinations of French diplomacy. There are new opportunities in Central Europe, the Baltic, the Balkans and the Ukraine – and few external restraints: Germany is best placed to benefit from these developments.[24]

The indications are that, while the domestic power base within the United States is moving steadily westwards, the focus for international power in the north Atlantic/European theatre is becoming increasingly Eurocentric – with Berlin as its probable future hub. As Britain's core security needs will remain in Central Europe, it will have to decide whether to remain on the periphery of Europe or to commit itself, wholeheartedly, to the new Europe. Logic dictates that the first priority for Britain's future foreign policy should be to contribute to the construction of a stable Europe. In theory it should not be difficult for Britain to take that step. In the past Britain played a significant role in the balance of power politics of pre-1914 Europe. In 1914 it entered the First World War following a crisis in Serbia; in 1939 it entered the Second World War following the failure of its efforts to maintain Czechoslovakia's independence and its determination to honour its guarantee to Poland. During the post-war period it has maintained a large proportion of its army and air force in

West Germany to help maintain the security of Central Europe. Simultaneously, albeit somewhat reluctantly, it has increasingly participated in the economic and political integration of Europe. During that process Germany has progressively replaced the United States as Britain's most important economic partner and is now potentially Britain's most important political contact.

France's post-war foreign policy is, on the other hand, in tatters. France has been waiting in the wings to assume the mantle of European leadership once the United States relinquished that role. What it had not bargained for was that Germany would be reunified before the United States' influence waned. France's policy was to be the driving force in the EC, and its aspirations to control a sphere of influence were based on Western Europe. France has no claims to special status between East and West, nor can it compete in economic terms with a unified Germany. Indeed the burgeoning Deutschmark is currently destroying France's goal of early European economic union as a precursor to political union. The EMF is moribund and the costs of trying to maintain a strong Franc for more than a decade have been a 12 per cent overall unemployment rate with 20 per cent among the country's youth. The three major assumptions underlying French foreign policy throughout the Cold War are now fatally flawed. France's interests are no longer synonymous with those of the EU; France can no longer masquerade as the EU leader to woo Germany in an effort to maintain the fiction that both countries are equals; France can no longer claim to occupy a middle position within the Atlantic Alliance – the middle has moved too far to the east. None of these developments will lead to a dramatic change in Franco-British relations overnight. Nevertheless there could be a viable political and security role for such a partnership *within* the new Europe. If Britain does commit itself to Europe's future a new *entente cordiale* could replace the 'special relationship' with the United States. Thus the twenty-first century could begin, as the twentieth did, with France and Britain having to seek common strategic ground in an effort to present a countervailing force against a burgeoning Germany that increasingly sees its future in a greater *Mitteleuropa*. The critical difference, however, is that the opportunity exists today for Britain and France to fulfil that role as Germany's political partners rather than as adversaries.

NOTES

1. Portillo, M., 'Cooperation and Partership for Peace: A Contribution to Euro-Atlantic Security into the 21st Century', *RUSI Whitehall Paper No 37*, (London, 1996), p. 2.
2. For other *résumés* of the post-Cold War scenario see Booth K. (ed.), *New Thinking About Strategy and International Security* (London: Harper Collins, 1991) pp. 11–13; RUSI International Security Review 1993, *Peace and War in Transition* (London: Royal United Services Institute for Defence

Studies) pp. 7–15 and Williams M. C., 'Neo-Realism and the Future of Strategy', *Review of International Studies* (April 1993) pp. 103–21.

3. See Frost H. E., 'Europe's Past, Europe's Future: Eastern Europe's Search for Security', *Orbis* (Winter 1993) pp. 37–53. Howard E. Frost is a Washington-based security affairs analyst and was a visiting scholar at the Federal Institute for Soviet and International Studies, Cologne, from October 1990 to October 1991.

4. See Simon J., 'Does Eastern Europe belong in NATO?', *Orbis* (Winter 1993) pp. 21–35. Jeffrey Simon is a senior fellow at the Institute for National Strategic Studies of the National Defense University in Washington, DC.

5. See Frost H. E., p. 41.

6. These objectives were set out in the invitation and PFP framework document, both issued at the North Atlantic summit in January 1994. They are summarised in Moltke G. von, *NATO Review* (June 1994).

7. For a good *resumé* of the problems inherent in expansion see Atkeson E. B., 'NATO Expansion', *Army*, (June 1996), pp. 32–40.

8. Russia's fears have been clearly articulated by Academician Oleg T. Bogomolov, Director, Institute of International Affairs, Political Studies, Moscow. See Bogomolov O. T., 'Russia and Europe's Security', *RUSI Whitehall Paper No 37*, (London, 1996), pp. 17–24.

9. Expansion is not necessarily inevitable. Proposals need to be ratified by national parliaments. For fifteen states that needs a simple majority. In the United States, however, consent requires a two-thirds vote in the notoriously independent Senate.

10. Some of the possible consequences of NATO expansion are set out in 'The Future Shape of Europe', *Foreign Report*, (4 July 1996), pp. 3–4.

11. In mid-1996 a report in *The Economist* claimed that while a majority of Czechs, Hungarians and Poles favoured joining NATO it was only in Poland that a majority of people favoured sending troops to defend another country and having NATO troops based in their country. No where was there majority support for regular in-country NATO exercises or regular NATO over flights. Most significantly only 23 per cent of Poles favoured spending more money on defence and that position was shared by only nine per cent of Hungarians and eight per cent of Czechs. See 'NATO Enlargement – Take Three', *The Economist*, (London, 29 June 1996), p.45. For a good insight on the possible costs of admitting the Czech Republic, Poland, Hungary and Slovakia see *The Economist*, (London, 3 August 1996), p.36. The most probable military configuration arising from membership is assessed at $42 billion.

12. For a more detailed analysis of the advantages and disadvantages of the PFP see Lepgold J., 'The Next Steps Towards a More Secure Europe', *Journal of Strategic Studies*, Vol. 17 (December 1994) pp. 7–26.

13. See Brenner M., Hammond P. and Williams P., 'Atlantis lost, Paradise regained? The United States and Europe after the Cold War', *International Affairs*, No. 69, Vol. 1 (London: Chatham House, 1993) pp. 1–17.

14. See Coker C., 'Britain and the New World Order: the Special Relationship in the 1990s', *International Affairs*, No. 68, Vol. 3 (London: Chatham House, 1992) p. 411.

15. The United States has been at pains to expound its continuing commitment to world leadership. The New World Order as a concept was first set out by President Bush in an address to the UN General Assembly, New York, 1 October 1990. See *The UN: World Parliament for Peace*, Current Policy, No 1303, US Department of State, Bureau of Public Affairs, Washington DC, 1991. Deputy National Security Adviser, Robert Gates, in a speech on 7 May 1991 to the American Newspaper Publishers Association claimed that 'In all the usual measures of national power – economic, military, cultural, political, even philosophical – we have no challengers.' See *American Leadership and a New World Order* (Washington, DC: Department of State, Bureau of Public Affairs, 1991).

16. For a detailed analysis of these issues see Sicherman H., 'Winning the Peace', *Orbis* (Fall 1994) pp. 523–44.

17. See Rieff D., *Los Angeles, Capital of the Third World* (London: Cape, 1991) p. 189.

18. See Peterson P. G. and Sebenius J. K., 'The Primacy of the Domestic Agenda', in Allison G. and Treverton G. F. (eds), *Rethinking America's Security* (New York: Norton, 1992) p. 59. Reprinted by permission of W W Norton & Company, Inc.

19. Hoshino S., *Japan in the Post-Cold War Era: an Economic Superpower in Transition* (Tokyo: National Institute for Research Advancement, 1992) p. 4. The *Financial Times* provided substantial

collateral for this assertion when on 7 April 1992 it reported that the growth rate of Guangdong province in southern China had been over 20 per cent in 1990–91.

20. Sicherman H., p. 537. Emphasis in the original.
21. See Steel R., 'Internationalism as a Complement to Nationalism', *International Herald Tribune* (8 June 1995).
22. Pfaff W., 'A Critical New View of the United States Is Turning Allies Off', *International Herald Tribune* (24 June 1995).
23. See Nordlinger E. A., 'Isolationism Reconfigured: American Foreign Policy for a New Century', (Princeton, NJ: Princeton University Press, 1995).
24. See Treverton G. F., 'Europe's Past, Europe's Future: Finding an Analogy for Tomorrow', *Orbis* (Winter 1993) pp. 1–20.

CHAPTER NINE

The Past as Prologue: From the V–Bomber to Beyond Trident?

There is presently a sense of change in international politics which is as profound as any this century.[1]

THIS CONCLUDING CHAPTER summarises the main themes of the book and seeks to provide answers to the two following questions. First, does the analysis of the political, operational and economic factors indicate that Britain was 'right' to procure and deploy the V-bomber force and subsequently to replace it with Polaris and thereafter with Trident? Second, what factors are likely to influence Britain's decision to procure a successor system to Trident?

Britain's decision to develop nuclear weapons was made in January 1947 and, more-or-less simultaneously, specifications for the V-bombers were issued. At the time these decisions were made Britain considered itself to be one of 'The Big Three' and this perception was widely held both at home and abroad. Furthermore Britain had played a seminal role in the initial development of nuclear weapons during the war. Against that background it is not surprising that Britain's political leaders felt that Britain must possess the 'capital' weapon of the period: such attributes were *de rigueur* for a major power. This position had the support of the political élites of both the major parties and a substantial majority of the public. The decision of the United States administration to pass the McMahon Act in the summer of 1946 simply reinforced Britain's justification for pursuing its own nuclear programme.

If an operational justification was necessary to support that stance, and there is nothing to suggest that one was sought, there was no lack of available evidence. While the Red Army remained in Europe, the Americans were rapidly returning home. There was no NATO. The communists seized power in Hungary in 1947, Czechoslovakia followed in 1948. The Berlin blockade began in March 1948 and the Korean War in June 1950. The Soviet Union conducted its first nuclear test in August 1949 and by 1954 it possessed a fleet of nuclear armed strategic bombers capable of reaching Britain. In operational terms it would be difficult to refute the argument that Britain needed to possess the most modern weapon systems available. Less realistically it was assumed at the time that Britain possessed the economic capacity and the technological base to pursue its own nuclear programme. Prior to the early 1950s the economic assumption was probably tenable, however, the economic consequences of the Korean War were profound. Defence expenditure rose to 8.7 per cent of GDP, inflation to 12 per cent, industrial production collapsed and a balance of payments surplus of £300 million in 1950 became a deficit of £400 million in 1951. These economic and industrial reverses, together with some political indecision by Attlee's Labour government, impacted adversely on the V-bomber production programme which took 13 years to complete. The Valiants were delivered to the RAF in 1956 but the deployment of the longer range Victors and Vulcans was not completed until 1961. Thus while from 1954 onwards the Soviet Union posed a threat to Britain which could only be deterred by the possession of a credible nuclear deterrent, Britain was unable to deploy such a force until the late 1950s. Britain's initial nuclear capability reached its peak in 1962 but it declined rapidly thereafter due to the withdrawal of the vulnerable, dual-operated, Thor IRBMs and the increasing inability of the V-bombers to penetrate Soviet air defences.

In summary, Britain's decision to procure and deploy the V-bomber force was politically and operationally justified and, at the time the decision was made, there was no reason for the government to doubt its affordability. Nevertheless, Britain's first strategic deterrent became operational two years later than that of the Soviet Union and, of much greater concern, its delivery system remained viable for only a few years, leaving Britain without a credible deterrent from 1965 to 1969. Economic pressures were partly responsible for that position but the future would reveal Britain's technological and economic weakness. Britain's leaders, supported by a substantial majority of its public, believed that nuclear weapons were necessary but this perception was based on an assumption, rather than any rational appraisal. Notwithstanding the lack of any formal decision-making methodology, and given the historical background, Britain's perception of its future role in the world and the absence of robust financial information, the decision to develop nuclear weapons was politically, operationally and economically correct. Furthermore, at that time the manned bomber was the only viable delivery system, and the V-bomber was the most sophisticated strategic bomber of the 1950s. In these circumstances the evidence also suggests that Britain chose the correct system to deliver its nuclear bombs.

Work on a successor system had begun before the V-bomber fleet was operational and, in recognition of doubts about the future viability of manned bombers, it included work on the Blue Streak missile system as well as a new strategic bomber. Technological and economic constraints were to force the cancellation of both projects.

There were two key developments in weapons technology that impacted critically on operational requirements. When the V-bomber force was conceived it was not envisaged that the threat of pre-emptive strikes would make it necessary for aircraft to move from dispersed bases on a four-minute alert. That requirement greatly increased the operating costs of the force and development work on a replacement for the V-bomber was cancelled in 1957, due in part to increasing costs and in part to the increasing vulnerability of manned bombers. Thereafter Britain was committed to developing a missile-borne strategic deterrent. However, when work began on Blue Streak it was not foreseen that developments in missile accuracy would render missiles vulnerable unless they were fired from hardened silos. As Blue Streak was a liquid fuel missile which required some 10 to 15 minutes preparation time immediately before launch it was not possible to guard against vulnerability even if funds could be made available for the construction of silos. Blue Streak was cancelled in April 1960, but only after the Conservative government had received an assurance that, once development was complete, it would be able to purchase the United States Skybolt missile system. A sum of £65 million had been spent on Blue Streak's development and it was estimated that to continue the project would cost between £500 and £600 million. Furthermore while Blue Streak had been portrayed as a British deterrent its rocket motor and inertial guidance system were based on the United States Atlas missile and were being made in Britain under licence. This fact was not made public until after the decision had been made to cancel further development. Thus, even if Blue Streak had been a viable system, it would have resulted in Britain procuring an interdependent deterrent because it lacked the technical capacity to develop an independent system. The Skybolt project was cancelled, without warning, by the United States administration in November 1962 and Macmillan, in an act of political desperation, secured the Polaris purchase agreement the following month.

As with the decision to procure and deploy a nuclear armed V-bomber force there was no rational appraisal during the late 1950s and early 1960s to support Britain's policy to seek a successor system. The Macmillan government clearly felt that Britain needed to remain a member of the nuclear club if it were to remain a first-rank power. This perception was heightened by France's decision, in December 1956, to embark upon its own nuclear weapons programme. It was inconceivable to most Conservative politicians that Britain could renounce its nuclear birthright and leave France as the only nuclear armed power in Western Europe. That position had the support of a majority of the electorate but, unlike the position a decade earlier there were influential politicians, mainly but not exclusively from the Labour benches, who felt that Britain should not seek a successor system on the basis that it was not affordable.[2]

It is certainly arguable that politicians of vision should have concluded in the aftermath of the Suez débâcle that Britain was no longer a first-rank power and that its political and economic future would be best assured if it acknowledged the reality of that situation. It was, however, to be another decade before Britain's leaders would come to terms with Britain's new position in the international community. On the other hand, it was not difficult to argue from the operational perspective, at least up until the early 1960s, that Britain had a continuing need for nuclear weapons. The first Soviet ICBMs became operational in 1959; the 'Missile Gap' crisis was reverberating around the United States in 1960; the Berlin Wall was erected in the summer of 1961; the United States, in recognition of the state of nuclear parity between the superpowers, announced its adoption of flexible response in June 1962 and the Cuban missile crisis occurred in October 1962. The viability of Britain's deterrent was increasingly questionable. From the time the first Soviet ICBM became operational the V-bomber fleet was vulnerable to attack on the ground and it was becoming increasingly obvious that the fleet's ability to penetrate Soviet air defence systems was decreasing. The prospects for geopolitical stability were far from encouraging and, although tensions waned during the 1960s, these developments occurred after the decision to procure Polaris had been taken. There is nothing to suggest that any form of financial appraisal was carried out either to support the development work on Blue Streak or to support the decision to purchase Skybolt and later Polaris. Indeed the clear implication is that Macmillan, with the support of his Cabinet, considered it essential that Britain remain a nuclear power and that the economic consequences were to remain firmly subordinate to the government's political goal.

The evidence suggests that it would have been politically more astute for Britain's leaders to have decided not to seek a successor for the V-bomber force and therefore, from the political perspective, Britain was 'wrong' to proceed as it did. Conversely, if one accepts, as many did at the time, that the adoption of flexible response by the United States marked a diminution of that state's commitment to Europe, then a clear case can be made for the procurement of a credible strategic deterrent. From the operational perspective, therefore, the decision to seek a successor system was correct. Prior to the last minute crisis decision at Nassau in December 1962 Britain was 'wrong' to seek a successor system from the economic perspective: Blue Streak had failed on economic and technological grounds and the unproven Skybolt project was also a high-risk strategy. On the other hand it has to be acknowledged that Polaris, by accident rather than design, proved to be a cost-effective deterrent that retained its operational credibility for some 25 years. Despite the total lack of rigour in the government's decision-making process Polaris proved not just to be the 'right' deterrent but, in operational and economic terms, it was the 'best' deterrent to meet Britain's needs. These attributes served to conceal the underlying weakness of the political justification for the decision.

The British government announced its decision to replace Polaris with Trident in 1980. By that time the political consensus on nuclear weapons had broken down. Nevertheless the evidence suggests that a majority of the electorate and a number of senior Labour ministers favoured replacement. As with the decision to deploy Polaris, the government made much of the threat posed by the Soviet Union as the underlying reason for its decision. In that regard the government could point to the Soviet Union's decision to deploy SS-20 missiles in Eastern Europe in 1978 and its invasion of Afghanistan in 1979 as illustrations of its concern. There were, however, some marked differences between the scenarios pertaining to these two procurement decisions. In the late 1970s the Soviet Union undoubtedly possessed the military capacity to critically damage Britain's national interests. Nevertheless there was a substantial consensus in support of the view that, despite the Soviet Union's capability, its political intentions were less bellicose than they had been at the time the Polaris procurement decision was taken in December 1962.

There were two other illuminating differences in declared British policy. Much was made of the continuation factor in arguing for a replacement for Polaris and considerably more emphasis was put on the contribution that Trident would make to the NATO Alliance. Both these arguments suggested that, proportionally, Britain needed Trident more for its political influence than for the operational needs of the policy of defence by deterrence. Certainly by the late 1970s Britain's political position within the international community, vis à vis allies as well as potential opponents, was less influential than it had been 20 years earlier. This was markedly different from any change in Britain's security position where, if there was movement, it was towards increased stability. Thus while it would be foolish not to give due credence to the threat posed by the Soviet Union's nuclear arsenal, the indicators suggest that a nuclear exchange was less likely at the time the Trident decision was made. Furthermore, by 1980, the United States' commitment to the defence of NATO Europe was well proven and that commitment was backed with more than adequate nuclear resources. If Britain needed Trident, this need had more to do with a combination of historical precedence and political influence than operational necessity.

In operational terms, provided there was a threat that justified a requirement for a nuclear deterrent, the decision to choose Trident was justifiable as a total system, although flawed in respect of the weapons fit within that system. All the operational arguments favoured the retention of a deterrent force that combined a nuclear powered submarine launch platform with a ballistic missile delivery system. That combination provided the most efficient second strike capability. Such a capability is best configured on a minimum capacity basis. Indeed, a system that clearly possesses a destructive capacity well above that requirement risks being perceived as something other than solely a second strike deterrent, and consequently weakens its own credibility. Trident, even as configured after November 1993, manifestly is not a minimum capacity deterrent and thus its operational rationale remains significantly flawed.

In contrast to the Polaris decision, the decision to procure Trident was subject to detailed analysis and as a result of that process the government concluded that Trident was operationally and politically necessary and affordable. The assessment conducted here suggests that despite the fact that Trident was expected to cost twice as much as Polaris it remained economically viable – in short it was the 'right' decision from the economic perspective. The political and operational arguments are less clear-cut. If there was a continuing need for a strategic deterrent all the arguments support the choice of a submarine launch platform linked to a minimum capacity ballistic missile delivery system. What is obvious from this analysis, however, is that there was less political and operational justification for Trident than there was for Polaris. Conversely it seems clear that Britain has benefited, in terms of political influence, from its possession of a nuclear deterrent even if Britain's security did not need the addition of a 'British' deterrent to the all-embracing United States nuclear guarantee to NATO Europe. On balance Britain's decision to procure Trident was probably only marginally 'right' from the political perspective but, on the basis that a British Trident was an unnecessary addition to the United States deterrent, it was probably 'wrong' from the operational perspective.

Looking back at all three decisions it is possible to identify some interesting trends. First, Britain has only been able to afford a viable deterrent as a consequence of its special nuclear relationship with the United States. Despite that relationship, however, the costs of the deterrent are rising. Second, while there was a clear operational rationale for a nuclear armed V-bomber force, the operational justification for a British deterrent became suspect once the United States' nuclear guarantee to Europe was perceived as being credible. It is more difficult to evaluate the political justification for Britain's deterrent. The initial decision to develop nuclear weapons and the V-bomber fleet sought to maintain Britain's global position as a major power and that decision was seen to be legitimate at home and abroad. However, Britain failed to develop an effective deterrent and the Suez crisis brutally demonstrated that Britain was no longer a major power. On the other hand Britain has used its nuclear status since the 1960s to heighten its political standing. That position has enabled it to play a link role between the United States and the European members of the NATO Alliance. Whether that position will be tenable in the future depends upon the developing relationship between the United States and Europe. If the interests of these two parties diverge Britain is likely to lose its special position as the 'link' state and its nuclear status might become politically irrelevant. Conversely Britain might seek to develop a new special nuclear relationship with another state or group of states.

A brief comparison with the French position is illuminating. From the outset France made it clear, both at home and abroad, that its decision to procure a nuclear deterrent had at least as much relevance to France's political status as it had to its need for national defence. That position was entirely commensurate with France's independent role within the NATO Alliance and at the same time fundamentally different from Britain's. Again, in stark contrast with Britain, France's nuclear policy has had the continuous support of the country's leaders and citizens. France, however, has had to pay a high price for its independence – at least twice as much as Britain and, as in Britain, that level of expenditure is coming under increasing scrutiny. France's experience in the operational field has been very similar to Britain's. The French decision to retain a strategic bomber force can only be judged as seriously flawed in operational and economic terms and, at best, politically dubious. The rationale for France's land-based IRBMs was equally suspect. The French experience in both these fields suggests that Britain was right to cease its development of similar systems in the late 1950s. Conversely France overcame the disadvantage of a late start in the field of SLBM systems to achieve a respectable capability by 1980. Furthermore French current forward plans suggest that France will possess a formidable second strike capability well into the twenty-first century. Clearly over the last few decades French and British operational and economic experience have been converging. Indeed in recent years there has been a remarkable level of dialogue on the development of future cooperation although that, at least at present, is limited to talks between officials. In the operational field Britain retains its special nuclear relationship with the USA while France remains strongly independent.

What, then, are the future prospects for Britain's deterrent? Had the Cold War not ended in 1990 it seems probable that this analysis could have concluded that Trident would probably remain in operational service until about 2025 and thereafter be replaced by the purchase of a new United States system. But the world has changed and while these changes may make little material difference to Trident's deployment they might have an altogether different impact upon the decision about a successor system. With the end of the Cold War the traditional threat scenario is no longer valid. The fact that the deterrent's missiles are no longer targeted on the Soviet Union, that the number of warheads per boat has been reduced to 96 and that Trident has recently been given a 'sub strategic' role is ample evidence of just how much the Cold War threat has dissipated.[3] As a consequence of that change the influence of arms control developments, domestic budgetary pressures and public opinion is likely be of increasing significance. Furthermore, the political justification and operational need for a replacement strategic nuclear deterrent will need to be established against a new set of geopolitical factors. This work concludes with a consideration of these issues.

Chapter 5 showed that, while developments in arms control have not had any direct impact on Britain's deterrent in the past, the position in the future is likely to be different. That assertion is based on two major developments. First, once the reductions in the nuclear arsenals of the United States and the CIS agreed in the START II agreement have been implemented Britain will no longer be able to maintain that its deterrent is statistically insignificant. Indeed if the 50 per cent reductions called for under START II are achieved, and current progress is reasonably promising despite political and economic difficulties, Britain is likely to come under increasing pressure to limit Trident's nuclear capacity in a manner that meets the international community's verification procedures.[4] Second, Britain, in common with the other nuclear states, will come under increasing pressure from the international community to fulfil its obligations under the NPT. Britain has given an undertaking that it will work towards a goal of nuclear disarmament and she will need to live up to that commitment. Clearly that obligation will be called into question should the international community consider that Britain intends to seek a successor system to Trident. The United States is under the same obligation and, as that state put a very high level of diplomatic effort into securing the indefinite extension of the NPT, it seems probable that it will wish to take a lead in pressing for nuclear disarmament. This position might well put Britain's special nuclear relationship with the United States at risk, which could mean that a Trident successor system might not be available from the United States.

Now that the operational justification for Britain's deterrent is more opaque it seems probable that its costs will come under increasing scrutiny. It was originally estimated that Trident would cost no more than six per cent of the defence budget. Although that was twice as much as Polaris it could still reasonably be asserted that Trident displayed the potential to be a cost-effective system – provided always that it was both politically and operationally necessary. Apart from one specific area Trident is presently proving to be an exemplary programme. The 1996 Defence Estimates claim that the Trident programme is on time and that there is a real cost budget underspend of £3,430 million on the original estimate made in 1982.[5] That, however, is not the whole truth. It seems likely that the Ministry of Defence has only purchased half the number of missiles covered by the original estimate and therefore presumably intends to manufacture only half the original number of warheads. That change in procurement policy should represent something like a reduction of about one-fifth over the programme budget. In other words a substantial underspend is what one would expect from a policy change of that magnitude. Furthermore that overall healthy economic assessment would have been 25 per cent better if there had not been an overspend of £800 million on the infrastructure programmes at the Faslane and Coulport bases on the Clyde.[6] Nevertheless, changes in defence spending since the end of the Cold War have had a dramatic effect on the comparative costs of the Trident programme. In 1985, the year Gorbachev came to power, the United Kingdom spent 4.6 per cent of its GDP on defence. In the ten years up to 1995 the real change in Britain's defence spending was a reduction of 29.6 per cent. Defence spending in 1991–92 amounted to £24,438 million and represented 4.2 per cent of GDP while the planned expenditure for 1996–97 is £21,425 million – around 2.8 per cent of GDP. Because the overall defence budget is decreasing while the expenditure on Trident remains more-or-less constant the relative costs of the strategic deterrent have risen considerably over the original forecast.[7]

Public expenditure forecasts are invariably optimistic about longer-term prospects and as the year in which expenditure will be incurred approaches, forecasts tend to be revised downwards. Furthermore future expenditure assumes continuing low inflation and also assumes that the savings identified in the Defence Costs Study will be realisable. It is anticipated that these will amount to £750 million in 1996–97, rising to £1 billion by 1998–99 and £1.1 billion by 1999–2000.[8] These are considerable sums of money and it remains to be seen whether savings of that size can be achieved. Finally, there are the pressures of domestic politics. There are few votes in defence and as the next election approaches the government may alter its spending priorities to enhance its prospects for a further term of office. Conversely if Labour win the next election they are likely to alter the pattern of defence expenditure. All these pressures indicate that the proportion of the defence budget allocated to the strategic deterrent is likely to rise. That is unlikely to have any material effect on the future of the Trident programme as the expenditure is already committed but it may well influence opinions about the affordability of a successor system.

There is evidence to suggest that public opinion is becoming increasingly influential, especially in issues concerning the environment and nuclear weapons. Two occurrences in the summer of 1995 demonstrate this development. First, the outcry throughout Western Europe against Shell's decision to dump the Brent Spar platform in the Atlantic forced that company to abort their plan notwithstanding the fact that it had the full support of the British government. Second, the international outcry against French nuclear tests in the Pacific was far greater than expected and, probably as a direct consequence of that dissent, many governments felt it appropriate to protest against

France's actions. Public opinion will have more impact on future decisions about nuclear weapons than it has in the past and economic and arms control considerations are both likely to inform public opinion to a significantly greater extent in the future. At present the evidence indicates that a majority of the electorate support the retention of Britain's deterrent. Nevertheless a substantial minority opposes that position and the assessment of public opinion conducted in Chapter 6 demonstrates that external events can cause the numbers of 'opposers' to rise.

As we have now entered a dynamic period of geopolitical change it would be imprudent to assume that public opinion will remain a constant. In that regard it is significant to remember that there is a considerable majority of support for multilateral disarmament. The extension of the NPT will give hope to all those in Britain and abroad who support that goal and it is important to remember that Britain, in common with most of the international community, has declared its support for that goal since the NPT was signed in 1968. Unless there is an obvious threat to Britain's national interests in the future it seems probable that it will be more difficult for governments to secure support for a continuing role for the strategic deterrent than has been the case in the past.

The critical variable regarding the scenario within which Britain will determine whether or not to seek a successor to Trident will be the prevailing geopolitical strategic situation at the time that decision has to be made. It is possible, although perhaps unlikely, that NATO, at least in its present form, will continue to be the forum that best serves Britain's security needs. It seems more likely that, in addition to a nuclear-armed China, the early twenty-first century will see the emergence of three not necessarily adversarial but probably politically and economically competitive power blocs all of which will inherit a nuclear weapons capability. As has been argued in Chapter 8, the United States may disengage from Europe as a consequence of the pressures of, *inter alia*, its 'domestic agenda' and adopt a 'Pacific' focus for its evolving economic and security interests. Russia might emerge as the leader of a new alliance embracing most of the Western states of the CIS while the future European security and economic grouping seems set to embrace at least some of the former states of the old Warsaw Pact. Over time this could lead to the adoption of less harmonious political and economic policies between Europe and the regions under the hegemony of the United States and Russia. The power vacuum within Europe that would arise as a consequence of the United States' withdrawal is most likely to be filled by Germany. That, despite the probability that Germany would do all in its power to avoid it, would inevitably give rise to new pressures within Europe. A new Eurocentric power bloc could have Berlin at its axis and, significantly, Berlin is closer, in miles and culture, to Warsaw, Prague and Budapest than it is to Paris, London or

Moscow. While, until recently, Europe has suffered an imposed and artificial division through its centre, in future it may consist of a more cohesive core and a rather more apprehensive periphery.

Within that strategic setting the need for Britain to possess a strategic nuclear deterrent, either as a national system on the periphery of Europe or as part of a new European alliance, may be quite different from the scenario that has existed in the past. The strategic logic of the evolving scenario suggests that Germany should become a nuclear military power. That development could provide Germany with a capacity to deter any potential threat posed by a Russia that remains outwith the new Europe.

The political logic, however, is different. An inescapable fact that arises from a scenario in which Germany replaces the United States as the political leader within Europe is the degree of apprehension that it would give rise to from the Atlantic to the Urals. All the political logic points to Germany remaining a non-nuclear state. Nevertheless if the new Europe believes it might be faced with a strategic nuclear threat at some stage in the future then it is likely to feel a need for a strategic nuclear capacity to deter that threat. Such a force could be based on a development of the current British and French nuclear deterrents as part of a European force in which Germany has a major role in operational decision-making, and in which the funding is a European commitment. That scenario might meet not just new security considerations but it might also assuage economic pressures and the constraints of inter-national arms control agreements. Furthermore Trident would be more appro-priate in that scenario than it would be in a Europe in which a nuclear armed United States remained the dominant power.

A strained and dangerous period in modern history has come to an end, mercifully with a lack of violence that probably no one would have dared to predict. The bipolarity that marked the Cold War is being replaced by new international power structures. What these structures will be is not yet clear but they are likely to be more dynamic than those that existed throughout the Cold War and they will embrace complex patterns of interdependence. Such a scenario will not be easy to manage and it will call for all the skills and under-standing that the new Europe can muster if it is to be successful. Military force will have its role to play within that process, although there is good reason to believe that, if it has to be used, it will be limited by clear political objectives. The threat of nuclear devastation in central Europe has substantially reduced and the indicators are that this position will continue. Nevertheless there is nothing to suggest that the United States, Britain, France, Russia or China will renounce their nuclear weapons. It would be comforting to be able to believe that the United States will continue to contribute to a remodelled NATO in a manner that would let the European states take progressively more control over their own destiny. Within that framework strategic arms reduction initiatives are most likely to continue and progressively Britain, in common with other states, might have less need for its deterrent.

It seems more probable, however, that Europe will be increasingly left to manage its own future. That responsibility is likely to fall increasingly on Germany which will need all the help it can get. Britain, possibly in partnership with France, could play a major role in building stability within a new Europe and contributing to the external security of that structure. Both countries would enhance their political position by adopting such a stance. Furthermore if Britain adopts that role there could be a continuing need for a British nuclear deterrent, possibly operating jointly with a French deterrent as part of a European system. In the longer term Germany, France and Britain might jointly develop and operate new strategic deterrent systems deployed in the defence of a new Europe.

On recent evidence, however, Britain's commitment to Europe has to be questioned.[9] Psychologically Britain is likely to continue to cling to a history that is different from that of continental Europe. If Britain does remain on the periphery of Europe it may well continue to suffer continuing political and economic decline. To throw Britain wholeheartedly into Europe would require statesmanship of Churchillian stature. Perhaps it could be done but history suggests that it will be otherwise. In 1962 *The Economist*, in respect of British foreign and defence policy, declared that, 'the psychology of the declining power is not to choose but to wait upon events'.[10] That position does not appear to have changed over the last 35 years. The stakes, however, have risen exponentially. The challenges and opportunities that the new Europe will present are likely to be crucial to the future security of the northern hemisphere. Britain, given the political will, could and should be a major contributor to that process.

NOTES

1. Booth K. (ed.), *New Thinking About Strategy and International Security* (London: Harper Collins Academic, 1991) p. ix.
2. See Pierre A. J., *Nuclear Politics: The British Experience with an Independent Nuclear Force 1939–1970* (London: Oxford University Press, 1972) pp. 217–219
3. For the Ministry of Defence's view on the deterrent's post-Cold War role see Henderson D., 'Shaping the United Kingdom's Minimum Nuclear Deterrent for the Turn of the Century', *Royal United Services Journal*, Vol. 140, No. 3 (June 1995) pp. 43–6. See also Omand D., 'Nuclear Deterrence in a Changing World: The View from a UK Perspective', RUSI Journal, (London: RUSI, June 1996).
4. For a good resumé of progress being made by the CIS towards START II targets see Lockwood D., 'New Data on the Strategic Arsenals of the Former Soviet Union', *Jane's Intelligence Review*, Vol. 7, No. 6 (June 1995) pp. 246–9.
5. Statement on the Defence Estimates 1996, para. 405, p.56.
6. See Kemp I., 'Higher Costs and Longer Delays', *Jane's Defence Weekly* (10 June 1995) p. 80 and *Statement on the Defence Estimates* (1995) 'Stable Forces in a Strong Britain', Cm 2800 (London:

HMSO, 1995) para. 406 p. 63.
7. See Statement on the Defence Estimates 1993, *Defending Our Future*, Cm 2270 (London: HMSO, 1993) Table 4, p. 23.
8. See Statement on the Defence Estimates 1996, para. 603, p. 88.
9. See Sampson A., *The Essential Anatomy of Britain: Democracy in Crisis* (Aylesbury: Hodder and Stoughton, 1992) pp. 157–62.
10. *The Economist* (24 February 1962). Quoted in Chichester M. and Wilkinson J., *The Uncertain Ally: British Defence Policy 1960–1990* (Aldershot: Gower, 1982) p. 5.

Chronology

Date	Event
1938	
Dec. 1938	Discovery of nuclear fission
1939	
1 Sep. 1939	Bohr–Wheeler theory of fission published
3 Sep. 1939	Second World War starts
1941	
Jul. 1941	MAUD Report shows bomb possible
6 Dec. 1941	USA enters war
1942	
2 Dec. 1942	First nuclear reactor works
1943	
28 Aug. 1943	Quebec Agreement on Anglo-US co-operation
1944	
30 Sep. 1944	Churchill–Roosevelt 'Agreement'
1945	
4 May 1945	Capitulation of German Forces
Jun. 1945	United Nations established
16 Jul. 1945	First nuclear explosion – 20 Kt
26 Jul. 1945	Call on Japan to surrender
6 Aug. 1945	13 kt U-235 (untested) bomb dropped on Hiroshima
9 Aug. 1945	19 kt Pu (tested) bomb dropped on Nagasaki
14 Aug. 1945	Japan surrenders
1946	
24 Jan. 1946	UN Atomic Energy Commission formed
Mar. 1946	Churchill's 'Iron Curtain' speech
Mar. 1946	USAF Strategic Air Command formed
22 Jun. 1946	US McMahon Act forbids nuclear co-operation
Nov. 1946	US Atomic Energy Agency formed

1947

Jan. 1947   UK decides to develop nuclear weapons
Feb. 1947   Truman Doctrine announced
Jun. 1947   Marshall Plan announced

1948

Mar. 1948   Brussels Treaty
30 Mar. 1948   Berlin Blockade begins
12 May 1948   UK's decision to make bomb announced

1949

4 Apr. 1949   North Atlantic Treaty signed
12 May 1949   Berlin Blockade ends
29 Aug. 1949   USSR's first nuclear test

1950

31 Jan. 1950   US decides to develop H-bomb
Jun. 1950   Korean War starts
mid-1950   USAF bombers based in UK equipped with nuclear bombs
Dec. 1950   First SACEUR appointed

1951

May 1951   First US fusion explosion at Eniwetok Atoll

1952

11 Jan. 1952   UN Atomic Commission disbanded; UN Disarmament Commission
                   set up
Oct. 1952   First UK atomic bomb test at Monte Bello
1 Nov. 1952   First operational H-bomb test 10 Mt yield (US)
1952   UK's Global Strategy Paper

1953

Jul. 1953   Korean War ends
12 Aug. 1953   First USSR fusion explosion
1953   USA announces 'New Look' strategy

1954

12 Jan. 1954   Massive Retaliation enunciated by Dulles
1 Mar. 1954   Bikini 15 Mt H-bomb test, fission-fusion-fission
30 Aug. 1954   US Atomic Energy Act – some exchange of data
Oct. 1954   Paris Treaty – allows West German rearmament – UK agrees to
                   station four Divisions and a Tactical Air Force in West Germany
1954   UK helps to establish SEATO

1955

5 May 1955	West Germany joins NATO
14 May 1955	Warsaw Pact established
1955	USA starts to develop ICBMs
1955	UK helps to establish CENTO

1956

early 1956 USSR's strategic bombers capable of reaching the US for the first time

early 1956 First RAF squadron becomes operational with Blue Danube – Britain's first fission weapon.

31 Oct. 1956 Anglo-French Suez expedition begins

6 Nov. 1956 Anglo-French Suez expedition ends

6 Dec. 1956 Prime Minister Mollet authorises the development of French nuclear weapons

late 1956 V-bombers begin to enter operational service

1957

May 1957 First UK H-bomb (thermonuclear) test

Oct. 1957 USSR launches Sputnik

1957 UK announces adoption of massive retaliation in annual Defence White Paper

1957 USSR launches its first successful ICBM

1958

31 Jan. 1958 First US satellites

Feb. 1958 CND formed in UK

May 1958 De Gaulle becomes Premier of France

3 Jul. 1958 US–UK nuclear co-operation agreement

17 Sep. 1958 De Gaulle proposes tripartite nuclear directorate – rejected by USA

1959

20 Feb. 1959 First military satellite – US Discoverer

1959 First USSR ICBM operational

1 Dec. 1959 Antarctic Treaty

1960

13 Feb. 1960 First French nuclear test

24 Mar. 1960 Camp David agreement – Skybolt/Polaris base

Apr. 1960 UK cancels Blue Streak development

Nov. 1960 Kennedy elected US President

1960 US Atlas ICBM operational

1960 USN tests first SLBM – Polaris

| 1960 | US first SIOP to integrate targeting |
| 1960 | Sino–Soviet 'split' begins |

1961

13 Aug. 1961	Berlin Wall erected
1961	McNamara's Flexible Response doctrine formulated
Summer 1961	UK initiates application for membership of EEC
20 Nov. 1961	McCloy–Zorin disarmament principles

1962

16 Jun. 1962	McNamara announces Flexible Response in his Ann Arbor speech
Oct. 1962	Cuban missile crisis
7 Nov. 1962	US cancels Skybolt
Dec. 1962	Nassau Agreement to buy Polaris from US
1962	UK annual Defence White Paper acknowledges a state of mutual assured destruction

1963

14 Jan. 1963	De Gaulle proclaims policy of full nuclear independence and vetoes UK membership of EEC
20 Jun. 1963	USA–USSR hot-line agreement
5 Aug. 1963	Limited Test Ban Treaty signed
22 Nov. 1963	Kennedy assassinated
1963	Minuteman I operational

1964

16 Oct. 1964	First Chinese nuclear test
1964	New Labour government decides to continue the Polaris programme
1964	Valiants grounded due to metal fatigue
1964	French Mirage IV bombers enter service

1965

early 1965	V-bomber force no longer able to penetrate USSR's air defences
1965	US military units sent to Vietnam
1965	UK decides not to procure fifth Polaris boat
19 Mar. 1965	France withdraws from NATO's military command

1967

| Feb. 1967 | President Johnson offers USSR talks on strategic arms limitation |
| Dec. 1967 | NATO adopts doctrine of flexible response |

1968

| 1 Jul. 1968 | Nuclear Non-Proliferation Treaty |
| Aug. 1968 | Brezhnev Doctrine |

20 Aug. 1968	USSR suppresses 'Prague Spring'
1968	First UK Polaris submarine operational
1968	McNamara develops 'assured destruction' criteria

1969

Jun. 1969	French *force de frappe* operational
21 Oct. 1969	Brandt becomes West German chancellor – start of *Ostpolitik*

1970

11 Feb. 1971	First US MIRVed ICBM in service
30 Sep. 1971	Sea Bed Arms Control Treaty
1971	USA–USSR agreement on measures to reduce risk of nuclear war French land-based strategic missiles become operational as does its first SSBN

1972

26 May 1972	SALT I ABM Treaty limits deployment of ABM systems
26 May 1972	SALT I Interim Agreement (5 years) freezes number of ICBMs and SLBMs at current levels
1972	UK joins EEC

1973

1973	UK starts Chevaline programme
Sep. 1973	Geneva conference on security and co-operation in Europe opens in Helsinki

1974

1974	USSR develops MIRV – first test late 1972, operational 1975
10 Jan. 1974	Schlesinger doctrine – use of nuclear weapons for limited war or counter-force purposes
18 May 1974	First Indian test explosion
3 Jul. 1974	Threshold Test Ban Treaty – underground tests limited to 150 Kt (observed but not ratified)
1974	Labour government announces adherence to Chevaline but renounces replacement

1975

1 Aug. 1975	Helsinki Conference (Final Act)
1975	War in Vietnam ends with a nationalist victory

1976

28 May 1976	Treaty on Underground Nuclear Explosions for Peaceful Purposes (observed but not ratified)

1978

Jan. 1978	USSR deploys SS-20 missiles in Europe
Apr. 1978	Afghan government overthrown
1 Jul. 1978	First UN special session on disarmament

1979

18 Jun. 1979	SALT II Agreement puts ceilings on strategic weapons (observed but not ratified)
12 Dec. 1979	NATO Council agreement to deploy IRBMs and cruise missiles in Europe
27 Dec. 1979	Soviet invasion of Afghanistan
1979	Trident deployed on operational service in the USN

1980

15 Jul. 1980	UK Trident decision announced – four boats to be procured; a decision on the fifth boat to be deferred until 1982 or 1983
Jul. 1980	PD 59 – US nuclear targeting policy
1980	Growth of European peace movements

1981

7 Jun. 1981	Israel bombs Iraqi reactor
8 Aug. 1981	USA to stockpile neutron bombs
2 Oct. 1981	USA to procure 100 MX ICBMs
30 Nov. 1981	INF negotiations begin in Geneva
1981	UK government decides to purchase the D-5 Trident missile

1982

7 Jun. 1982	UN second special session on disarmament opens – results inconclusive
29 Jun. 1982	START talks begin
1982	Chevaline enters service

1983

23 Mar. 1983	Reagan's 'Star Wars' speech
23 Nov. 1983	INF talks suspended
31 Oct. 1983	Global 'nuclear winter' hypothesis
Dec. 1983	Cruise missiles deployed in UK
8 Dec. 1983	START talks suspended
1983	French SSBN force capable of maintaining three SSBN on patrol at all times

1985

1985	Sixth French SSBN enters service

1986

Jan. 1986	USSR seeks rapprochement with China
15 Jan. 1986	Gorbachev announces three-stage plan for nuclear-free world by 2000
Sep. 1986	UK Gallop pole shows 44 per cent in favour of unilateral disarmament
22 Sep. 1986	Stockholm conference on European Security concludes with troop inspection agreement
Nov. 1986	France announces development of neutron bomb
28 Nov. 1986	131st US cruise missile carrying B-52 enters service – breaks SALT II limit
Dec. 1986	USSR launches 2 SSBNs – breaks SALT limit
22 Dec. 1986	First ten MX operational – first new US ICBM since Minuteman – Mk III deployed 1970

1987

1 Mar. 1987	Report claims Pakistan has nuclear weapon
Mar. 1987	USSR successfully tests modified SS-18
11 Jun. 1987	Conservative government re-elected – Trident programme to proceed

1989

1989	First boat in new class of French SSBNs laid down – due to become operational in 1994
1989	Installation of democratic, non-communist government in Poland
1989	Dismantling of Iron Curtain in Hungary
1989	End of Brezhnev Doctrine
1989	Perceptible progress in disarmament talks at CFE
1989	Expectation of deep cuts in START
Nov 1989	Breaching of Berlin Wall

1990

Jul. 1990	Options for Change announced
3 Oct. 1990	Reunification of Germany

1991

Aug. 1991	Moscow coup
19 Sep. 1991	USSR begins to disintegrate
Nov. 1991	NACC established

1992

7 Feb. 1992	Formal signature in Maastricht of Treaty on European Union

1993

1 Jan. 1993	EC single integrated market established
3 Jan. 1993	START II Treaty signed

14 Aug. 1993	Vanguard handed over to the Royal Navy
Nov. 1993	Defence Secretary announces that Trident will be deployed with no more than 96 warheads per boat

1994

Jan. 1994	NATO's Partnership for Peace policy announced
Mar. 1994	French Defence White Paper published
Dec. 1994	First operational patrol by Trident boat (*HMS Vanguard*)

1995

May 1995	NPT extended indefinitely
Sep. 1995	French nuclear tests in the Pacific
Oct. 1995	Third Trident boat (*Vigilant*) launched
Dec. 1995	Second Trident boat (*HMS Victorious*) enters service

1996

1996	Last Polaris boat (*HMS Repulse*) withdrawn from service
May 1996	Defence White Paper announces that the Trident force will have a sub-strategic role and that Anglo-French talks on cooperation on nuclear policy will continue
Sep. 1996	India blocks progress on a CTBT at the UN General Assembly

Select Bibliography

Public Documents

Command papers

Cmd 6743, *Statement Relating to Defence: 1946* (London: HMSO, 1946).

Cmd 9074, *Statement on Defence: 1954,* (London: HMSO, 1954).

Cmd 9391, *Statement on Defence: 1955* (London: HMSO, 1955).

Cmnd 124, *Defence: Outline of Future Policy: 1957* (London: HMSO, 1957).

Cmnd 952, *Statement on Defence: 1960* (London: HMSO, 1960).

Cmnd 1288, *Statement on Defence: 1961* (London: HMSO, 1961).

Cmnd 1639, *Statement on Defence: 1962: The Next Five Years* (London: HMSO, 1962).

Cmnd 1936, *Statement on Defence: 1963* (London: HMSO, 1963).

Cmnd 2724, *The National Plan* (London: HMSO, 1965).

Cmnd 5976, *Statement on Defence Estimates: 1975* (London: HMSO, 1975).

Cmnd 7826-I, *Defence in the 1980s* (London: HMSO, 1980).

Cmd 101-1, '*Why Not an Alternative?*', *Statement on the Defence Estimates 1987* (London: HMSO, 1987).

Cm 2270, '*Defending Our Future*', *Statement on the Defence Estimates 1993* (London: HMSO, 1993).

Cm 2800, '*Stable Forces in a Secure Britain*', *Statement on the Defence Estimates 1995* (London: HMSO, 1995).

Cm 3223, Statement on the Defence Estimates 1996 (London: HMSO, 1996).

Other government publications – Britain

Pym F., *Britain's Strategic Nuclear Force: The Choice of a System to Succeed Polaris*, Defence Open Document 80/23 (London: Ministry of Defence, July 1980).

Nott J., *The United Kingdom Trident Programme*, Defence Open Government Document 82/1 (London: Ministry of Defence, March 1982).

Other government publications – United States

Dulles J. F., 'The Evolution of Foreign Policy', *Department of State Bulletin*,

Vol. XXX (25 January 1954).

McNamara R. S., 'Defence Arrangements of the North Atlantic Community', *State Department Bulletin*, No. 49 (9 July 1962).

McNamara R. S., 'The Dynamics of Nuclear Strategy', *Department of State Bulletin*, LVII (9 October 1967).

NSC-162/2, The Garvel Edition, *Pentagon Papers*, Vol. 1 (Boston: Beacon Press, 1971).

Books

Aron R., *The Great Debate* (New York: Doubleday, 1965).

Ball D. and Richelson J. (eds) *Strategic Nuclear Targeting* (Ithaca: Cornell University Press, 1986).

Bartlett C. J., *The Long Retreat: A Short History of British Defence Policy 1945–1970* (London: Macmillan, 1972).

Baylis J. (ed.) *British Defence Policy in a Changing World* (London: Croom Helm, 1977).

Baylis J., Booth K., Garnett J. and Williams P., *Contemporary Strategy Vol. I Theories and Concepts* and *Vol. II The Nuclear Powers* (New York and London: Holmes and Meier, 1987).

Bellini J. and Pattie G., *A New World Role for the Medium Power: The British Opportunity* (London: Royal United Services Institute for Defence Studies, 1977).

Booth K., *Strategy and Ethnocentrism* (London: Croom Helm, 1979).

Booth K (ed.), *New Thinking about Strategy and International Security* (London: HarperCollins, 1991).

Boyer Y., Lellouche P. and Roper J., *Franco-British Defence Co-operation* (London: Routledge, 1989.

Brodie B., *Strategy in the Missile Age* (Princeton, NJ: Princeton University Press, 1959).

Chalmers M., *Paying for Defence* (Pluto Press, 1985).

Chichester M. and Wilkinson J., *The Uncertain Ally: British Defence Policy 1960–1990* (Aldershot: Gower, 1982).

Clark I. and Wheeler N. J., *The British Origins of Nuclear Strategy 1945–1955* (Oxford: Oxford University Press, 1989).

Darby P., *British Defence Policy East of Suez 1946–1968* (London: Oxford University Press, 1973).

Dilks D. (ed.), *Retreat from Power, Vol. 2* (London: Macmillan, 1981).

Dow J. C. R., *The Management of the British Economy 1945–1960* (London: Cambridge University Press, 1964).

Freedman L., *Britain and Nuclear Weapons* (London: Macmillan, 1980).

Freedman L., *The Evolution of Nuclear Strategy*, 2nd Edition (London:

Macmillan, 1989).

Garden T., *Can Deterrence Last?* (London: Royal United Services Institute for Defence Studies, 1984).

Gowing M., *Britain and Atomic Energy 1939–1945* (London: Macmillan, 1964).

Gowing M., *Independence and Deterrence: Britain and Atomic Energy 1945–1952, Vol. 1 Policy Making* (London: Macmillan, 1974).

Groom A. J. R., *British Thinking About Nuclear Weapons* (London: Frances Pinter, 1974).

Jones P. M. and Recce G., *British Public Attitudes to Nuclear Defence* (London: Macmillan, 1990).

King-Hall S., *Power Politics in the Nuclear Age* (London: Gollancz, 1962).

Kissinger H. A. (ed.), *Problems of National Strategy* (New York: Praeger, 1965).

Kohl W. L., *French Nuclear Diplomacy* (Princeton, NJ: Princeton University Press, 1971).

Marsh C. and Fraser C. (eds) *Public Opinion and Nuclear Weapons* (London: Macmillan, 1989).

McInnes C., *Trident: The Only Option?* (London: Brassey's, 1986).

Navias M. S., *Nuclear Weapons and British Strategic Planning 1955–58* (Oxford: Clarendon Press, 1991).

Northedge F. S., *Descent from Power: British Foreign Policy 1945–73* (London: Allen & Unwin, 1974).

Pierre A. J., *Nuclear Politics: The British Experience with an Independent Strategic Force 1939–70* (London: Oxford University Press, 1972).

Rosecrance R. N., *Defence of the Realm: British Strategy in the Nuclear Epoch* (New York: Columbia University Press, 1968).

Schelling T. C., *Arms and Influence* (New Haven and London: Yale University Press, 1966).

Schwartz D. N., *NATO's Nuclear Dilemmas* (Washington, DC: The Brookings Institute, 1963).

Segal G., Moreton E., Freedman L. and Baylis J., *Nuclear War and Nuclear Peace* (London: Macmillan, 1988) second edition.

Smith K., *The British Economic Crisis* (London: Penguin, 1984).

Snyder W. P., *The Politics of British Defence Policy 1945–62* (Columbus, OH: Ohio State University Press, 1964).

Windlass S. (ed.), Walker P., Shenfield S., Greenwood D. and Windsor P., *Avoiding Nuclear War: Common Security as a Strategy for the Defence of the West* (London: Brassey's, 1985).

Articles and Periodicals

Brenner M., Hammond P. and Williams P., 'Atlantis Lost, Paradise Regained? The United States after the Cold War', *International Affairs*, No. 69, Vol. 1 (London: Chatham House, 1993).

Buchan A., 'The Multilateral Force: An Historical Perspective', *Adelphi Papers*, No. 13 (London: Institute for Strategic Studies, October 1964).

Carver M., 'A Nuclear Elimination Exchange', RUSI Journal (London: RUSI, Oct. 1996).

Coker C., 'Britain and the New World Order: the Special Relationship in the 1990s', *International Affairs*, No. 63, Vol. 3 (London: Chatham House, 1992).

Debouzy O., 'Anglo-French Nuclear Co-operation: Perspectives and Problems', *Whitehall Papers* (London: Royal United Services Institute for Defence Studies, 1991).

Frost H. E., 'Europe's Past Europe's Future: Eastern Europe's Search for Security', *Orbis* (Winter 1993).

Garnett J. C., 'The Defence Debate', *International Relations*, Vol. II, No. 12 (October 1965).

Greenwood D. and Hazel D., *The Evolution of Britain's Defence Priorities 1956–76*, Aberdeen Studies in Defence Economics, No. 9, Centre for Defence Studies, University of Aberdeen (1978).

Greenwood D., *The Polaris Successor System: At What Cost?*, Aberdeen Studies in Defence Economics, No. 16, Centre for Defence Studies, University of Aberdeen, Spring (1980).

Greenwood D., *Reshaping Britain's Defences*, Aberdeen Studies in Defence Economics, No. 19, Centre for Defence Studies, University of Aberdeen (1981).

Grove E., *An Anglo-French Minimum Deterrent – A New Approach* (London: The Council for Arms Control Bulletin, 1987).

Kaiser K., Leber G., Mertes A. and Schultze F.-J., 'Nuclear Weapons and the Preservation of Peace', *Foreign Affairs*, Vol. 60, No. 5 (Summer 1982).

Kemp G., *Nuclear Forces for Medium Powers, Part I: Targets and Weapon Systems*, Adelphi Papers, No. 106 (London: The International Institute for Strategic Studies, 1974).

Kemp G., *Nuclear Forces for Medium Powers, Parts II and III: Strategic Requirements and Options*, Adelphi Papers, No. 107 (London: The International Institute for Strategic Studies, 1974).

Martin L., 'The Market for Strategic Ideas in Britain: The Sandys Era', *American Political Science Review*, 56, No. 1 (1962).

Martin L., *Force in Modern Societies: Its Place in International Politics*, Adelphi

Papers, No. 102 (London: International Institute for Strategic Studies, 1973).

Nailor P. and Alford. J., *The Future of Britain's Deterrent Force*, Adelphi Papers, No. 156 (London: The Institute for Strategic Studies, 1980).

Omand D., 'Nuclear Deterrence in a Changing World: The View from a UK Perspective', *RUSI Journal*, (London: RUSI, June 1996).

Palmer D. A. R., *French Strategic Options in the 1990s*, Adelphi Papers, No. 260 (London: The International Institute for Strategic Studies, Summer 1991).

Simon J., 'Does Eastern Europe belong in NATO?' *Orbis* (Winter 1993).

Slessor J., 'British Defence Policy', *Foreign Affairs*, 35, No. 4 (1957).

Smart I., *Advanced Strategic Missiles: A Short Guide*, Adelphi Papers, No. 63 (London: The Institute for Strategic Studies, 1969).

Smart I., *Future Conditional: The Prospect for Anglo-French Nuclear Co-operation*, Adelphi Papers, No. 78 (London: The International Institute for Strategic Studies, August 1971).

Smart I., *The Future of the British Nuclear Deterrent: Technical, Economic and Strategic Issues* (London: Royal Institute of International Affairs, 1977).

Smart I., 'British Foreign Policy to 1985. I: Beyond Polaris' *International Affairs*, Vol. 53, No. 4 (London: Chatham House, October 1977).

Smart I., 'Strategic Nuclear Deterrence in Western Europe: From 1980 to the Future', *RUSI and Brassey's Defence Yearbook 1980* (London: Brassey's, 1981).

Treverton G. F., 'Europe's Past, Europe's Future: Finding an Anology for Tomorrow', *Orbis* (Winter 1993).

Wallace W., 'British Foreign Policy after the Cold War', *International Affairs*, Vol. 68, No. 3 (London: Chatham House, 1992).

Williams M. C., 'Neo-Realism and the Future of Strategy', *Review of International Studies* (London: April 1993).

Wheeler N. J., *The Roles Played by the British Chiefs of Staff Committee in the Development of British Nuclear Weapons Planning and Policy Making 1945–55*, PhD Thesis, Department of Politics, University of Southampton (1988).

Yost D. S., *France's Deterrent Posture and Security in Europe. Part I: Capabilities and Doctrine*, Adelphi Papers, No. 194 (London: The International Institute for Strategic Studies, Winter 1984/5).

Index

ABM defence systems, 40, 79
ABM system, Moscow, 45–6, 74
ABM Treaty, 65, 99, 101
Advisory Committee on Uranium (US), 4
ALCM, 40, 75, 78, 83, 101, 105
Aldermaston marches, 124
America first, concept of, 158
Anglo-American Agreement for Co-operation on the Use of Atomic Energy for Mutual Defence Purposes, 11, 38
Anglo-French nuclear co-operation, 62, 68, 135, 137, 146–8, 163, 172
Antarctic Treaty, 100
arms control, 2, 13, 65, 95–9, 102–4, 112–15, 130, 132–3, 148, 173, 175–6
arms race, 25, 96, 98, 110, 126
ASPM, 141–2, 146
assured destruction criteria, 25, 145
Atlantic Nuclear Force, 24
atomic bomb, 4–6, 14–15, 17, 41, 117, 119, 128
Atomic Energy Act (US), 11
Atoms for Peace Policy, 108
Attlee, Prime Minister, 6–7, 15–16, 117, 119, 167

balance of payments, 16, 47–8, 50
BAOR, establishment of, 32
Beaufre, André, 138–9
Berlin blockade/crisis, 7–10, 15–16, 38, 166
bombers: B-1, 75; B-1B, 39; B-29, 8, 11, 18; B-52, 18; Blackjack, 107; Canberra, 11, 44; F-111, 51; Mirage, 141–2, 146; TSR-2, 23; TU-16 Badger, 44; V-bombers, 11, 22–3, 39, 41–6, 51–3, 56–7, 125, 166–9; Valiant, 44–5, 167; Victor, 43, 45, 167; Vulcan, 43, 167
Brandt, West German Chancellor, 38, 65
Brezhnev Doctrine, 38, 151
Brussels Treaty, signing of, 7
Bulgaria, post-Cold War, 151
Bush, President, 104, 106, 157

C^3I, 40
capital weapons, 7, 14, 53, 55, 89–90, 166
Carter, President, 1, 70, 126
CENTO, 32
Chevaline, 29, 45–6, 55, 65, 68, 70, 73–4, 121, 123

Churchill, Prime Minister, 5–6, 16, 49, 119–29
Circular Error Probability (CEP), 39
CIS, 107, 112, 173, 175
Clinton, President, 157–8
CND, 2, 116–17, 120, 123–8, 131
Cold War, 7, 10, 31, 128, 132, 151–2, 154, 157, 159, 161, 172, 176
CSCE, 65, 153–4, 156
Comprehensive Test Ban Treaty (CTBT), 111–12, 133
consensus, British political, 1, 68, 116–17, 121–2, 129, 170
Conservative government/party, 16, 34–5, 37, 45, 50, 68, 70, 74, 81, 117–23, 125–6, 131, 168
counterforce strategy/targets, 22, 24, 42, 45, 65, 77
countervalue strategy/targets, 21, 42, 46, 63, 73–4, 77
Cuban missile crisis, 38, 44, 62, 99, 128, 169
Czechoslovakia, post-Cold War, 151, 153–5; post-war, 7, 10, 166

Defence Costs Study, 174
defence expenditure/spending, 16, 24, 31, 45, 48–55, 57, 81–2, 87–8, 91–2, 112–13, 123, 126, 129
Defence White Papers: 1946, 16, 31; 1954, 19; 1955, 19, 42; 1956, 43; 1957, 19–20, 23, 29, 34–7, 49–50; 1958, 23; 1960, 23; 1961, 23; 1962, 23; 1963, 23; 1966, 24; 1987, 147; 1994, 147; 1995, 115; 1996, 112, 148, 173
de Gaulle, President, 135, 137, 139–41
delivery vehicle/system, 11, 39–41, 75–7, 80, 91, 105, 171
deterrence, 13–14, 16–20, 22–3, 32, 35, 37, 95–6, 104, 138, 145; by punishment, 18; extended, 9; 98; graduated, 23; intra-war, 22; multilateral, 139; proportional, 138, 141
dual track decision, 103, 132
Dulles, US Secretary of State, 18, 141

Eisenhower, President, 11, 18, 20–1, 136
Eisenhower, SACEUR, 9
EMT, 41
Eniwetok Atoll, 15
European Community, 63, 66, 68, 123, 137–8, 152, 156, 162–3

first strike/pre-emptive strike, 17–18, 20, 24, 40–2, 45, 97, 102, 140, 142–3, 145, 168
first use, concept of, 17, 25, 138
flexible response, 13–14, 21–2, 24–5, 29, 169
France, post-Cold War role, 163
French nuclear independence, 135, 137–9, 141
French White Paper on Defence, 147

Gallois, Pierre, 24, 138–9
GDP comparisons, 47–51, 57
Germany, post-Cold War role, 162
Global Strategy Paper (1952), 16, 35
Gorbachev, General Secretary, 104, 151–2, 174

H-bomb, 19, 34, 119, 128
Havel, Vaclav, President, 153
Healy, Denis, Defence Minister, 50, 54, 121–2
heavy water, 5
Helsinki, 65
Hiroshima, 1, 6, 73
Hot-Line Agreement (US–USSR), 38, 100
Hungary: post-Cold War, 151, 153, 155; post-war, 7, 166

IFOR see UN Peace Implementation Force
Independent Atomic Energy Agency (IAEA), 109–10
INF Treaty, 100, 102–4

Johnston, President, 25
Joint Strategic Planning Staff (JSTPS), 21

Kennedy, President, 21, 24, 43, 52, 62, 120, 138, 141
Korean War, 7–10, 16, 18, 31, 48, 53, 119, 166–7

Labour government/party, 16, 23–4, 29, 49, 51, 54–5, 68–70, 74, 81, 117–21, 123–7, 130–1, 167, 174
Labour's National Plan (1965), 50, 54
launch platform, 39–40, 75–8, 80, 83, 91, 171
Limited Test Ban Treaty, 38, 99–100, 128
Los Alamos Weapons Laboratory, 15

Macmillan, Prime Minister, 11, 34–5, 37, 43–4, 50, 52, 56, 62, 120, 168–9
Manhattan Project, 5–6, 15, 17
Marshall Plan, 7–8, 31
MARV, 40
massive retaliation, 13, 18–20, 22–4; British adoption of, 14, 19–23, 34–6, 120, 125
MAUD Committee, 4–5, 33
McMahon Act, 7, 10, 15, 33, 166
McNamara, US Secretary of Defense, 13, 21–2, 24–6, 63, 139
MIRV, 40, 45, 65, 81, 83, 101–2, 106, 146; first Soviet test, 65
Missile Gap, 21, 169

missiles: Atlas ICBM, 20, 42, 168; Blue Danube, 11; Blue Steel, 43; Blue Streak, 22, 42–3, 120, 167–9; cruise, 40, 75–9, 97, 123, 126, 132; GLCM, 66, 78, 103–4, 126, 129; ICBM, 20, 26, 40, 65, 101, 105–6; US ICBMs, 20, 65, 126; Soviet ICBMs, 21, 31, 102, 125, 169; IRBM, 42, 77; French IRBM force, 142–3, 172; M-1, 143; M-2, 143; M-20, 143; M-4, 143, 146; M-45, 146; M-51, 146; Minuteman, 39; MX, 126; Pershing II, 66, 103–4, 126; S-2, 142; S-3, 142; Skybolt, 22, 43, 78, 120, 168–9; SLBM, 20–1, 65, 68, 76, 79–80, 83, 89, 101, 105–6, 112, 143, 146, 172; SLCM, 76, 78, 83, 105; SRAM, 40; SS-4, 103; SS-5, 103; SS-11, 39; SS-18, 105–6; SS-19, 106–7; SS-20, 65–6, 71–2, 90, 103, 122, 126, 170; SS-24, 107; SS-25, 106; Thor IRBM, 11, 44, 167; Titan II, 39
MLF, 24, 138
Monte Bello test, 10, 119
Moscow criterion, 46, 70, 73
MRV, 40, 45
mutual assured destruction (MAD), 13, 23, 25

Nagasaki, 1, 6
Nassau Meeting, 23, 62, 137–8, 169
National Strategic Target List (US), 21
NATO, 7–8, 23–5, 29, 32, 36, 54, 64–6, 71–3, 90, 98, 103–4, 126, 137, 139–41, 148, 152–4, 156, 160; British contribution to, 55, 64, 71, 89; British influence within, 62–3, 67; candidate states, 154–6; Council Meeting (Lisbon, 1952), 9, 16; formation of, 135; post-Cold War, 157, 175–6
NAVSTAR, 39–40
neutron bomb, 126
New Look Strategy, 17–18, 35
Non-Proliferation Treaty (NPT), 100, 109, 111, 114, 128, 133, 173, 175
North Atlantic Co-operation Council (NACC), 154
NSC-68, 17
NSC-162/2, 18
nuclear: blackmail, 63; club, 14, 108, 120, 136, 168; fission, 3–5, 15, 135; fusion, 15; guarantee/umbrella (US to Europe), 7, 21, 25, 33, 55–6, 64, 67, 104, 158, 170–1; interdependence, 34, 36, 38, 55, 57; parity, 14, 22, 29, 56, 90, 102, 169; proliferation, 72–3, 96, 101, 107–10; stockpile (British), 41; stockpile (US), 7, 15, 18, 126; strategy, 1, 12–13, 15–17, 21–6, 29, 31, 139; tests: Britain's first, 7, 10, 119; Britain's first thermonuclear, 11, 120, 125, 128; China's first, 38; India's first, 65, 108; USA's first, 6; USA's first fusion, 15, 119; USSR's first, 15, 166; USSR's first thermonuclear, 20; triad, 39; triad (French), 141–3; trigger/detonator, 21, 63, 139

Ostpolitik, 38, 65
Outer Space Treaty, 100
overseas commitments, costs, 32, 50, 51

Partnership for Peace (PFP), 154–6
plutonium, 5–6, 108, 117
Poland, post- Cold War, 151, 153–5
Polaris, 1, 14, 20, 23–4, 26, 29, 47, 141, 166;
 costs, 51–2, 54–5, 57, 69, 81; decision, 38, 44,
 52, 122, 168–70; fleet size, 26, 45, 56, 61, 73,
 112, 121; operational capacity, 44–6, 69, 73–4,
 78, 80, 121; replacement, 65–8, 71–4, 79, 81,
 122, 138
Poseidon, 68, 79–80, 121
post-Cold War, 104, 106, 112, 127, 147, 151, 153,
 159, 162
public opinion: American, 159–60; British, 2,
 116, 123, 127–33, 148, 173–5

Quebec Agreement, 5–6,

Reagan, President, 104, 126, 129
research and development (R&D) costs, 49,
 51–2, 79, 89
Reykjavik summit, 104
Roosevelt–Churchill 'Agreement', 6–7
Roosevelt, President, 4–5
Russia, post-Cold War (*see also* Soviet Union,
 former), 106, 107, 154–6

SAC target list, 46
SALT I, 65, 77, 99–102
SALT II, 65, 100–2
Sandys, Duncan, Defence Minister, 23, 29, 34–5,
 37, 50, 53
Schlessinger Doctrine, 65
Sea Bed Arms Control Treaty (1971), 65, 100
SEATO, 32
second centre concept, 71, 139
second strike capability/system, 14, 20–1, 26,
 40–1, 44, 47, 56, 73, 91, 102, 106, 121, 172;
 French, 142–3
secrecy, British political, 45, 51, 116, 119–20
Single Intergrated Operational Plan (SIOP), 20,
 22
Slessor, Sir John, Chief of the Imperial General
 Staff, 16, 35, 46, 138–9
Soviet Union, former (*see also* Russia, post-Cold
 War), 127, 147, 153, 158
special relationship, Anglo-American, 6, 10–1,
 33, 36, 48, 63, 67–8, 92, 109, 114, 136–7,
 146–7, 161, 163, 171, 173
Sputnik 1, 20–1, 31, 125
SSBN, 76–7, 79, 83, 89, 98; French force, 80,
 142–6
SSCN, 76, 83
SSN, 76, 114

START I, 100, 104–7
START II, 100, 106–7, 112, 173
Stimson, US Secretary of War, 6
strategic arms limitations talks, 13, 25–6, 29, 56,
 114, 122, 128, 151, 176
strategic doctrine, 13–14, 17–25
strategic theory, 13, 17–18, 135, 140
Suez crisis, 19, 33, 37, 53, 125, 136, 169, 171
Suez, east of, 32, 37, 50–1, 54
Swinton Committee, 42

tactical nuclear weapons, 25, 32, 112
TERCOM, 75
'The Big Three', 7, 55, 68, 162, 166
thermonuclear bomb/weapons, 15, 34, 41
threshold states, 109–11
Threshold Test Ban Treaty, 65, 100
Tlatelolco, Treaty of, 100
tous azimut, concept of, 140
Treaty on Underground Nuclear Explosions for
 Peaceful Purposes, 65
Trident, 1, 70, 73, 89, 129, 166, 176; C-4 missile,
 80–3, 88, 122; costs, 79, 82–7, 91, 132; D-5
 missile, 80–1, 83, 88, 122; decision, 1, 69–70,
 79–81, 88, 126, 170–1; first operational
 patrol, 123; fleet size, 74, 79–80, 112, 114;
 missile numbers, 78, 91, 106, 112–13, 123;
 sub-strategic role, 113–14, 172
Truman doctrine, 7, 9–10, 31
Truman, President, 6–8, 14

U-235, 4–6
U-238, 4–5
Ukraine, 106–7, 162
UN, 31, 65, 111, 154, 160; Peace Implementation
 Force (IFOR), 154
unilateralism, 124–5, 127–32
uranium, 3–6, 108
USAF, 8, 15, 17–18, 25, 127
USN, 20, 69, 79
US: post-Cold War role, 152–3, 156–61, 172;
 commitment to Europe, 15, 56, 90, 136, 139,
 169–70

verification procedures, 97–8, 102, 105–6,
 109–10

Warsaw Pact, 38; former, 153–5, 162, 175
WE 177 bomb, 112–14
WEU, 152–3
Wilson, Prime Minister, 24, 37, 50, 54, 121

Yeltsin, General Secretary, 106–7
Yugoslavia, former, 154

zero option proposal, 103